Would Your Boomerang Return?

B P Boxholm Press, LLC

Would Your Boomerang Return?

What Birds, Hurdlers, and Boomerangs Can
Teach Us About the Time Value of Money

Brent Pritchard

Published in the United States of America by Boxholm Press, LLC.

Boxholm Press, LLC
PO Box 621
Sanibel, FL 33957

Scripture quotations are taken from *The Living Bible*, copyright © 1971 by Tyndale House Foundation. Used by permission of Tyndale House Foundation, Carol Stream, Illinois 60188. All rights reserved.

This book is available at special discounts for bulk purchases. Boxholm Press, LLC can also bring Brent Pritchard to live events. For more information regarding a bulk order or to book Brent Pritchard to speak at your corporate or academic event, please visit www. BoxholmPress.com.

Publisher's Cataloging-in-Publication data

Names: Pritchard, Brent, author.
Title: Would your boomerang return ? What birds , hurdlers , and boomerangs can teach us about the time value of money / Brent Pritchard.
Description: Iowa City, IA: Boxholm Press, LLC, 2023.
Identifiers: LCCN: 2023934916 | ISBN: 979-8-9859862-1-1 (hardcover) | 979-8-9859862-4-2 (paperback) | 979-8-9859862-7-3 (ebook)
Subjects: LCSH Business mathematics--Handbooks, manuals, etc. | Finance--Study and teaching. | Finance--Mathematical models. | Money--Mathematical models. | Time--Economic aspects. | Financial services industry--Employees--Training of. | Finance, Personal. | BISAC EDUCATION / Finance | BUSINESS & ECONOMICS / Business Mathematics | BUSINESS & ECONOMICS / Finance / General | BUSINESS & ECONOMICS / Personal Finance / General
Classification: LCC HG106 .P75 2023 | DDC 332.4/1--dc23

Printed in the United States of America

Cover design by Foster Covers
Illustrations by Alberts Illustration & Design
Book editing and formatting by Harshman Services

The quotations in this book that are in the public domain have been taken from multiple sources. They and their attributions are assumed to be accurate. In a few instances, minor changes have been made to reflect the usage of "people" or "persons" in place of "men" in modern language.

Since this is a work of nonfiction with true stories, certain names have been changed to protect the "innocent."

This publication and its opinions are designed to provide accurate information with regard to the subject matter covered. It is sold with the understanding that the publisher is not engaged in rendering financial, accounting, or other professional advice, and does not guarantee any specific result or profit. If financial advice or other expert assistance is required, the services of a competent professional person should be sought.

This book is dedicated to my wonderful wife, Sarah, and our daughters, Lydia, Emily, and Chloe:

The precious gift of your lives is a daily reminder that there's more to this life than meets the eye . . . and that you are even more beautiful on the inside.

Without you, I wouldn't have found the inner strength to write and regift this book.

I love you to the moon and back.

"An investment in knowledge pays the best interest."
—Benjamin Franklin

Contents

Preface

"The great aim of education is not knowledge but action."
—Herbert Spencer

The Time Value of Money is foundational to finance, yet my experience in the classroom as a college finance lecturer has provided firsthand evidence that even the most dedicated students can stumble or struggle when confronted with the task of applying the Mathematics of Finance to analyze and evaluate real-world Time Value of Money situations. Based on my direct experience, I believe strongly that this has something—if not everything—to do with how information on the topic has been presented historically. While an age-old concept, the "old" way of learning and teaching the Time Value of Money isn't working.

In addition to clarifying terminology that can be troublesome to some, this book provides a compilation of all the important or essential information you need to apply the Mathematics of Finance—like the 30,000-foot view from a plane seat from which you can see the lay of the land and its sections or parts that look like the squares of a quilt.

Outside the classroom, I found cross-referencing to be the name of the game when it came to finding all the information regarding this all-important topic: it wasn't all in one place or, if it was, it wasn't communicated in clear English. This was a kind of scavenger hunt; however, it wasn't intended to be one—so that got me fired up. I can't imagine how my students felt. But that's not all that is new on this take.

What you have here is the Time Value of Money trifecta. Rounding out this new take on the Time Value of Money is a simple and definitive 3-Step Systematic Approach for applying the Mathematics of Finance, which has benefits as it relates to analyzing and evaluating real-world Time Value of Money situations from the classroom to the boardroom and in between.

Brent, you're saying that finance professionals can also benefit from this content?! That's right! Before I traded in my office in Corporate America for a classroom, I remember one day when the cat had the tongue of not only a very seasoned finance professional but also everyone else in the room. None could find the words to describe Net Present Value!

At the idea stage, the initial purpose of this book was to provide a blank canvas for collecting and organizing in one place my thoughts about the Time Value of Money for the sole benefit of my college finance students. There's nothing more frustrating for a teacher than leaving something out of a lesson due to a time crunch or simple oversight. The Time Value of Money impacts most every decision in finance in one way or another, so if ever there's a place to seek comprehensiveness in a lesson or unit, this is it.

My Time Value of Money lesson has always been the one that packs the biggest punch, both in terms of important information and unfortunately knocking down some students' self-confidence. In addition to being foundational to finance, historically this lesson was also the one that left some of my students with the deer-in-the-headlights look, made some students jittery in their seats, and in some cases put students on the border of becoming fighting mad.

Body language is easy to spot from the view at the front of a classroom regardless of how many pairs of eyes are staring back at you. Body language becomes collective, with students uncomfortable in their seats appearing to move more like an amoeba.

While problematic on a few levels, the issue was made bigger by the fact that many of these students thought they had the Time Value of Money figured out. That is until the rubber met the road and real-world situations were introduced.

Maybe this shouldn't have surprised me after all. Lots of people, when asked about their ability to operate a vehicle, will likely tell you that they consider themselves to be an above-average driver. But that's impossible based on the law of averages! It appeared that overconfidence had started to rear its ugly head regarding the Time Value of Money as well.

It was clear that "the problem" was bigger than any one Time Value of Money problem. I was done being forced to play defense during the days and weeks following this all-important lesson. Problem-solving is in my DNA, so I took to the books looking for a solution.

To my surprise, the research yielded mostly the same old information.

I don't remember exactly what happened next, but I'm sure it likely involved a run. Running is my preferred form of movement and vehicle if you will for experiencing the great outdoors, consuming positive material from podcasts and audiobooks, spending quality time with family and friends, and working out problems on my own.

What I had stumbled upon is what authors refer to as the inciting incident, which is that moment in the story that puts the main character on a journey. Only instead of the main character, I was the soon-to-be author. This was the initial inspiration for the manuscript that would later become this book and all the proof I needed to realize that there was a need for a different approach with respect to learning and teaching the Time Value of Money.

When a problem solver finds himself in a kind of "bear market" as far as pedagogy with respect to the Time Value of Money, what does he do? He takes the bull by the horns and writes the book!

You don't want to be the finance professional who doesn't understand the most important concept in the field. You owe it to yourself to understand the Time Value of Money like the back of your hand. If you're an aspiring finance professional, believe me when I say that you will be presented with real-world Time Value of Money situations day in, day out in industry.

So, terminology. Let's start with a phrase that many aspiring and current finance professionals can recite. "A dollar today is worth more than a dollar tomorrow." But we're not concerned with the Time *Worth* of Money. There's no reference in the Mathematics of Finance to Present *Worth* and Future *Worth*; instead, Present Value and Future Value.

Investors are *indifferent* between values of money *in different* points in time because there are markets for capital. Investors expect to earn an investment yield, which compensates them for delaying consumption, opportunity cost, and for taking on exposure to risk including the risk of inflation. Even if investors don't deploy or invest cash, they must recognize that they could. The presence of investment alternatives keeps investors in the right state of mind which considers that money has time value. If there are markets for capital that consist of equity, debt, and hybrid investments then what's all this talk about compound *interest*? Why not compound yield or compound investment yield? There are more places to invest money than just checking and savings accounts, money market instruments, and bonds that return *interest*.

Finance professionals are well aware of the relationship between price and yield, but nobody is talking about the price that is expected to generate a certain *interest*. There's a difference between return *on* investment and return *of* investment, yet when we get to the point of estimating return *on* investment, are you scratching your head as to why we're not using the investment metric (ROI) that consists of the same words: rather, the Internal Rate *of* Return? That's confusing!

Even in situations where terminology isn't problematic, it's called the Mathematics of Finance for a reason. There are words to understand, and then there are numbers that need to be run. In industry, I found myself taking a self-supported study of the Time Value of Money on more than one occasion. Little did I know that this work, which I really enjoyed, would later turn out to be a prerequisite for this book project. I've had a lot of time over many years to refine the hard skill that is the Mathematics of Finance, but I haven't lost empathy for aspiring and current finance professionals looking to master the concept of the Time Value of Money.

If you're relatively new to the Time Value of Money, it can be hard to make sense of numbers and words using dry textbooks. If you're reading this book, we at least have two things in common. One being a love of numbers and the other an affinity for finance. But we might also have something else in common. Have you ever used a textbook as an unintended bedtime story? Not falling asleep while trying to acquire knowledge from a textbook could be viewed as a victory in and of itself.

Now I love a good textbook. That's the teacher in me. Textbooks obviously have their place. While I've used some great textbooks over the years, I haven't been completely satisfied with the Time Value of Money content.

Prior to this book being published, every publication I had reviewed on the topic fell short of not only what I wanted but what I think aspiring and current finance professionals and teachers need in terms of a resource related to the Time Value of Money. It's not uncommon for finance textbooks to devote only one chapter to the single most important topic related to finance and money. To say that these other publications fall short is an understatement to the nth degree.

Don't get me wrong. There is a lot of great content out there on the topic, but a common theme was starting to develop. In addition to discovering knowledge on the topic to be disjointed, what I found—or better said, failed to find—was eye-opening. The resources attempted to provide a bird's-eye view of the Time Value of Money "forest" (the What) but failed to cover all the important parts of the Mathematics of Finance "trees" (the How) that would allow you to apply the math. And many of the resources didn't even attempt to present a systematic approach. The former is likely a result of certain publishers needing to squeeze the Time Value of Money content into one chapter of a textbook. The latter isn't possible without a solution for the former. Unlike the chicken or the egg thing, it's clear which needs to come first.

My flight path was set from what started out resembling more of a fight scene. These were the two missing pieces that would complete the puzzle and make a resource standalone—providing aspiring and current finance professionals with an effective method for applying the Mathematics of Finance to analyze and evaluate real-world Time Value of Money situations in a repeatable manner while giving college finance instructors and high school teachers an all-in-one resource for teaching the single most important topic related to finance and money.

With gatekeeper publishing houses having developed the blueprint, the content relating to the Time Value of Money in most publications is cookie-cutter. It was in industry literature—papers not books—where I found PhDs or PhD candidates attempting to "enter through the back door." This is where I found attempts to develop systems to provide aspiring and current finance professionals with a method for applying the Mathematics of Finance.

Since my area of expertise is in real estate, that's how I tend to see the world. Traditional textbook publishers had attempted to lay the footings as it relates to the Time Value of Money, but it was as if they had put the house together before the foundation was ready and with missing parts.

Those in academia who had identified part of what I call the "big problem" deserve a pat on the back. It was their work that helped me further see the need for this book. But their attempts at developing a go-to systematic approach left much to be desired. It was as if they were laying the steps by a big hole in the dirt where the foundation should be—instead of building from the ground up. The gaping hole I found in these attempts was that each one lacked definitive steps. Much of what I found consisted of flowcharts with questions that instead of leading to an answer seemed to raise more questions, which is a problem!

Unhappy with the quality of content on the market, I did what an author does. I wrote the book I wanted to find but couldn't because it didn't exist. I took it into my own hands to create an original work on the topic of the Time Value of Money.

And now you're holding in yours the passion project that is a handbook for the Mathematics of Finance.

One of the benefits of creating is that you get a clean slate. Blank space on a white page can be both intimidating and promising. The first thing I wanted to do was clear up confusion with respect to terminology that can confuse some people and create a bad first impression as it relates to the Time Value of Money. This covers letters in the case of the five primary TVM financial calculator keys and the variables in the building block Time Value of Money equations, words that have multiple meanings, and statements relating to rules for the Time Value of Money.

Aiming to create an original 3-Step Systematic Approach that actually works and allows aspiring and current finance professionals to apply the Mathematics of Finance to analyze and evaluate real-world Time Value of Money situations with nothing more than the basic tools of the trade—a pen or pencil, paper, and a financial calculator—I worked backward from the finish line all the way to the start. The endurance event that was the creation of this book essentially started with creating original TVM Rules.

My experience is that while there's some commonality regarding what people call rules for the Time Value of Money, there are some "rules" out there that don't necessarily rise to that prominent position. In this book, I call those the "Need to Knows." The rules of engagement for this project were framed by simplicity, consistency, and connectivity.

As you'll soon find out, the original TVM Rules set is what brings simplicity, consistency, and connectivity to the **TVM Formula**™, the cornerstone of which is the 3-Step Systematic Approach.

I'm with the majority of students who associate with being visual learners. The code was cracked when I realized that the original TVM Rules, which are based on the mnemonic *indifferent*, also provide the blueprint for the 3-Step Systematic Approach that is applied using the visual aid that is the TVM Wallet and which allows you to succinctly step out the process of applying the Mathematics of Finance in such a way that promotes confidence through a repeatable system.

What started as a search for a better resource to help my students master the concept of the Time Value of Money ended with my typing "The End" and this book being published for a bigger audience.

Between these two points in time, I embarked on what people in the real estate industry like to refer to as a "tear down and rebuild" project. People buy houses that are complete and structurally sound. Custom homes are built from the ground up. The main components of a house that I want to zero in on for this illustration are the footings, foundation, frame, walls, roof, picture windows, and steps.

Now let's put this in terms of the Time Value of Money. The footings represent the original TVM Rules based on the mnemonic *indifferent*. The foundation represents the improved building block Time Value of Money equations. Some people reading this will know that foundation walls were once predominately built with cinder blocks, hence the placement of the building block Time Value of Money equations in this illustration. The frame represents the "Need to Knows." The walls represent the "Good to Knows." The roof represents having all the important or essential information on this all-important topic in one place. The picture windows represent the visual aid that is the TVM Wallet. And last but not least, the steps represent the simple and definitive 3-Step Systematic Approach.

Simply put, I put myself in the shoes of someone who had never before been introduced to the Time Value of Money and asked myself the question, "How would I like to have learned about the Mathematics of Finance?" This question served as the

North Star for this project that had me wearing a student's shoes and an architect's hat.

Finance professionals who can't *measure twice* or double-check their work might get *cut once* others are onto them. The age-old fundamentals remain; however, the holistic perspective and 3-Step Systematic Approach will help aspiring and current finance professionals apply the Mathematics of Finance with confidence to analyze and evaluate real-world Time Value of Money situations — in the classroom, in practice, or while sitting for an industry designation examination. This how-to manual for the Time Value of Money will position you such that you can double-check your work using little more than a pen or pencil, paper, and basic calculator functions.

You've likely purchased — and had delivered to your house — one or more products that came with parts to assemble, a user manual, and a simple tool. Have you ever had the unfortunate circumstance of opening a box only to find that one or more pieces are missing? It happens from time to time and crushes your ambition. But presumably every one of the user manuals you've ever handled has provided all the important or essential information needed. Many user manuals include multiple languages. In this case, the first thing you need to do is locate your language. What good are instructions if the words don't make sense? While some are far easier to read than others, there aren't many user manuals out there that require you to go elsewhere because they are incomplete. A company selling a product that repeatedly didn't include in the box all the pieces that would allow the owner to use the item, including a complete manual and the simple tool, would no doubt get bad reviews and wouldn't likely be in business for long.

I wouldn't expect you to think otherwise, yet that's exactly what I'd found in the market with respect to the content related to the Time Value of Money! The product in the box, more precisely the Time Value of Money content within these other books, was missing pieces of information.

Now I'm a pretty practical guy with a good amount of common sense or street smarts. Having worked in industry, I know that quality work product requires adherence to a certain standard of excellence. This is why restaurants have to dish out good food to stay open for business. Word of mouth is still and will always be the best form of marketing or anti-marketing. So it's beyond me how these other providers of content on the topic of the Time Value of Money can continue to dish out a product that leaves people with a bad taste in their mouths.

This handbook that includes the first-of-its-kind user manual for the Mathematics of Finance and the simple tool that is the **TVM Formula**™ will allow you to use the 3-Step Systematic Approach to apply the Mathematics of Finance once you put together all the pieces.

Not everyone reads user manuals from cover to cover. So, in the spirit of the user manual, in Part 2 of this handbook, you'll find chapters named after sections typically found in an actual user manual, which will allow you to quickly access information. Included in the user manual section is a "Quick Start Guide" that describes the original 3-Step Systematic Approach.

Unlike any user manual I've ever held in my hands, this one is fun and engaging. This book is a resource that can be read from cover to cover or referenced as needed. This book appeals to both the user manual readers and the skimmers alike. You know which one you are!

Some people tend to gravitate toward the path of least resistance, but there's no substitute for hard work. Runners know that the hardest step to take is the first one out the door. Once a runner gets a certain level of fitness, the act of running becomes easier. As running gets easier, you like to do it more often. And when you do it more often, you get better at it. It takes training and hard work. That magical moment occurs when you start feeling things get easier. All of the sudden the five-miler feels like a three-mile run.

Gary Whittington (aka Whitt), my mentor both in real estate finance and in running, and someone I'm proud to call one of my best friends and the person who got me into running (and writing), loves to drop all kinds of running wisdom. Everything from "You can't outrun your training or the weather" to "Five miles is the new three." Anyone can toe the line at the start of a marathon, a race covering 26.2 miles, but it takes hard work to achieve the goal of finishing. *Knowledge* of the Mathematics of Finance is to signing up for a race. *Comprehension* of the concept of the Time Value of Money is to toeing the start line. *Application* of the Mathematics of Finance is to running the race. *Analysis, Synthesis, and Evaluation* of real-world Time Value of Money situations is to combining training, nutrition, hydration, and achieving the goal.

The field of finance isn't that much different than the field in a popular marathon. In such races as the Chicago Marathon, where there is more demand than the supply of available bib numbers, certain runners secure entry based on qualifying times or races. In finance, multiple professionals typically compete for one empty seat. Aspiring and current finance professionals need to show their qualifications in part by their ability to apply the hard skill that is the Mathematics of Finance.

If you're looking for a hack, this isn't the book. There's no winging the Time Value of Money. How do I get to the point where I can apply the concept of the Time Value of Money to real-world situations using the Mathematics of Finance? That's where the How section of this book adds value with the first-of-its-kind user manual for the Mathematics of Finance complete with all the pieces, the important or essential information, and the simple tool that is the **TVM Formula**™, which culminates with the definitive 3-Step Systematic Approach. The User Manual is a kind of training plan for success in the field of finance.

What if I'm totally new to the concept of the Time Value of Money or terminology has given me trouble in the past? That's where the What section of this book adds value.

Why does this all matter? An aspiring or current finance professional not only wants to secure but also keep a job in the field—if for nothing else than to develop skills and experiences. That's where the Why section of this book comes in and provides even more practical wisdom to help further position aspiring and current finance professionals for success in the field.

In your hands, you're holding the reframe and new take on this age-old, all-important topic of the Time Value of Money. It's a relatively short and readable handbook about the biggest concept in finance.

I've described when I had the lightbulb moment for this book and where I see problems with how the Time Value of Money has historically been learned and taught and packaged.

This book is my complete unit on the Time Value of Money. It's likely to be unlike any other textbook you've read before. It's fun and engaging, and its content ready to be used. The book can be used to complement—it's the fun cousin—one or more textbook chapters on the topic of the Time Value of Money or as a standalone resource—the information-rich uncle. It's not another textbook that induces sleep. It's not exhaustive in that it is not meant to be an historical account of all things related to the Time Value of Money. It doesn't need to be. To try to compete against the internet would be a fool's errand.

Unlike a traditional academic publication that can be exhausting to read, this is a creative work. It's both original and comprehensive because it needs to be. To say that any book on the topic of the Time Value of Money would be considered a beach read may be a stretch. That said, I challenge you to find one closer than this. It would, however, be disingenuous I do believe for anyone to argue that the **TVM Formula**™, described herein, which encompasses the TVM Rules, the mnemonic and audible aid *indifferent*, the *312* "warm-up" routine, the TVM Wallet that is the visual aid and template, and the 3-Step Systematic Approach, is anything short of original, creative, memorable, and effective.

Whether used as a complementary or standalone resource, this book stands alone in terms of its content and originality. The content of this book includes all the important or essential information on this all-important topic in one place, which will allow you to hit the ground running and apply or use—that's where the user manual comes in—the Mathematics of Finance with confidence using the **TVM Formula**™.

Once I realized that I had a lot to say on this topic, the energy to push this project across the finish line came partly from the belief that I now had a responsibility to share this information with others, not just my students.

Who is the audience for this book? That's easy. The primary audience for this book consists of aspiring and current finance professionals and teachers.

Learning is a lifelong pursuit. Once a student of finance, always a student. Learning is more like a marathon than a sprint. If you're an aspiring finance professional—this includes college finance students as well as high school students—you can use this book to help you wrap your head around this all-important topic. If you're a college finance instructor or high school teacher, you can use this book as required or supplemental material to complement *your*

Time Value of Money lesson or unit or as a standalone resource. As it relates to a unit on the topic, the chapters in the What and the How sections double as individual lessons. If you're a current finance professional, you can use this book to sharpen the hard skill that is the Mathematics of Finance or as a refresher for the Time Value of Money material that will show up on an industry designation examination.

The secondary audience for this book consists of employers in the finance industry and their clients who are also looking to hire, albeit indirectly, finance professionals. Employers in the finance industry might use this book to identify qualified candidates or to train up newly onboarded team members. Individuals looking to hire a finance professional might use this book to gauge one's knowledge base with respect to the Time Value of Money.

I mean it when I tell my students that I wouldn't hire a finance professional who doesn't understand the Time Value of Money like the back of their hand. Trent Farley, who is one of my favorite people and the only person I've ever worked with who could finish my sentences—we were that much on the same wavelength—can attest that my go-to interview question is, "How do you describe the Time Value of Money in your own words?"

This question predated the publication of this book but like this book gets to the heart of the matter: whether a professional is qualified for a position in finance. Now prospective employers and prospective clients have a tool to gauge an aspiring or current finance professional's understanding of this all-important topic. My go-to interview question has been replaced with the "Pop (Open the Back Cover) Quiz." What's more expensive, testing one's comprehension and ability to apply the Mathematics of Finance in service of customers or members by using this book in the vetting process or potentially making the wrong hiring decision?

Regardless of where you are on your educational journey, you will find a fun, new take on the Time Value of Money in the pages that follow. For some, the content of this book might be a refresher. For others, this will be their introduction to the Time Value of Money. The 3-Step Systematic Approach described herein is worth the price of this book and more. In some ways, I view everything else as a bonus. And there's some good "bonus" material as you'll see.

Authors quickly learn that the answer to the question "Who's your audience?" is not "Everyone." But since this book is about challenging the status quo, I do believe that there is a broader tertiary market—there I go again using a real estate term—for this book that consists of anyone who has the ability to earn money. Really: a book for everyone? Okay, so *most* everyone. If you're not picking up what I'm putting down, stay with me for at least as long as it takes to read the rest of this paragraph. Time is your only asset that doesn't include a return *of* investment, and this will be time well spent. You don't have to be a current or aspiring finance professional, college finance instructor or high school teacher, or an employer or client looking to hire a finance professional to benefit from the specialized knowledge in this book that has the potential to get you or someone you care about investing early and often and thereby making time a friend and putting the power of compounding in your corner. Are you *really* trying to tell yourself with a straight face that you'd rather not have millions of dollars to your name: money that could be used to improve your life and the lives of others? Everyone needs money to survive and thrive. It's about time money had a user manual that is readable and will improve financial literacy. Financial literacy starts with knowing TVM. The ABCs of money is spelled TVM. Aspiring and current finance professionals aren't the only ones who need a financial education and who need to take *the time* to know how to determine the *value of money*.

The fact that you're holding this book in your hands is an honor that I don't take lightly. Thanks to the internet—what a former classmate would always refer to as the "information superhighway"—and the publishing industry, my classroom can now come to a classroom near you.

Finance students have found success in my classroom in part because of the focus I place on a practical education. To me, the classroom is a special place and the intersection between specialized knowledge and skills that are in demand in industry.

I also like to refer to any one of my classrooms as an "ultraclassroom." This is a play on the word *ultramarathon*. An ultramarathon is defined as any race beyond a marathon.

There's more to learning than comprehension. Why do you need this book? This book will allow you or someone you're teaching or sponsoring to move from comprehension of the concept of the

Time Value of Money to application of the Mathematics of Finance for the ultimate purpose of analyzing and evaluating real-world Time Value of Money situations in the classroom and beyond.

I hope I'm not giving too much away, but in my classroom, I follow a simple model: it's impossible for people to laugh without smiling, and when people are smiling, they're happy. I truly hope that the content of this book makes you laugh and smile, and happy about a career in finance or simply getting or helping others to obtain a better grasp of the foundational concept of the Time Value of Money.

In writing this book, I researched multiple resources over countless hours—work that could also be measured in terms of days, weeks, or months—to clear up terminology, assemble all the important or essential information on this all-important topic in one place, and develop the **TVM Formula**™ that is an original method for learning and teaching the Time Value of Money. That was both a shame and a blessing! The search for the Holy Grail of the Time Value of Money, which is a simple and definitive systematic approach, had been elusive. That is, until the 3-Step Systematic Approach was created and, along with the first-of-its-kind user manual for the Mathematics of Finance, this groundbreaking new take on the most foundational concept in the field was presented in this book. I consider it a huge blessing to have been given the gift to write this book. My gift is now yours, presented and gift wrapped within the cover of this book. An "anti-textbook" is the antidote!

Introduction

"Never forget where you came from."
—My mom

From the Preface to the Introduction—there's a double meaning there. One is the parts of a kind of letter from the future back to me in 1995. The Preface explains how this book came into existence. The Introduction further explains how I became qualified to write it, which requires a little walk down memory lane.

The year was 1995, and I was a senior in high school in Fort Dodge, Iowa. Things were good in The Hawkeye State. The warm summer air and what seemed to be unlimited free time were helping to offset the uncertainty about the future. In some ways, I was trying to dodge the inevitable knowing full well that time doesn't stand still for anyone. This was the "enlisted" phase of my life as I would later come to think of it. Don't get me wrong; I have great memories from my upbringing. This was just a phase—we all go through it—when I didn't have much say. My life mission wasn't yet clear and as for assigned tasks, well there wasn't much keeping me busy. Unlike some people, I do have regrets about the past. Looking back, I know I should have taken more initiative and gotten after it sooner. But in the same breath, I can say that I do believe that everything happens for a reason.

Some people reading this book may be surprised to find out that my early performance in school was nothing to write home about. I got a rough start when it came to schooling. All these years later, I still remember the grace my fourth-grade teacher extended when she opened my flip-top desk only to find weeks' worth of incomplete work. She knew what was going on. It didn't matter that I'd been sitting in my seat; my mind was not in school.

Fast-forward to junior high school. Poor standardized test scores uprooted me from my circle of friends and relegated me to a classroom of "slow learners."

In high school, one of the things that set me apart from most other people was a non-clique mentality, which was the positive outcome of being part of that "special" class. I liked how I could float around the lunchroom and sit with almost anyone in my class and whomever I felt drawn to on a particular day. And I did. I've always rooted for the underdog, and I liked the positive feeling that came with helping someone who I could feel needed the help. While I struggled with reading and comprehension at a young age, reading people has never been an issue for me. Little did I know that the skills gained from these early experiences would help define my value proposition later in life.

One day in high school, I was sitting across the table from the career counselor. I'll never forget the feelings that came along with being told more or less that I wasn't going to amount to much. Can you believe that happened? In his hands he held a printout based on "small data."

I think I might have even scanned the document looking for someone else's name because it was as if I was looking at a list of possible careers meant for someone else. Deep inside, I knew that I was capable of more than what he was leading me to believe I would become.

Knowing what I know now, I really don't think that it was reverse psychology at work. If he was going for lasting power, he succeeded alright. Although negative in many respects, it ended up being a red-letter day that ushered in the "recruited" era.

Want to see me do something, then genuinely tell me that you don't think I can. Looking back, I think this man's talents could have been better used in another seat, but they weren't asking for my opinion.

Years later, I found a different message from *StrengthsFinder 2.0* by Tom Rath, which didn't exist at the time of the ill-fated "counseling" session. I'm a late bloomer in many respects, and to be fair, I hadn't yet started living with 100% responsibility in all areas of my life. My grades were evidence of this fact. With these events well in the rearview mirror, I'm grateful for each and every one of these experiences, for they remind me where I came from. They help me open my heart to have empathy for my students and others, open my mind to new friendships, and open my eyes to see the potential in each and every person. Hard as it was, I'd do 99% of it all over again if reliving were a thing.

Prior to graduating from high school, I logged more than 100,000 miles on my first car: a two-toned 1977 Pontiac Grand Prix. How I wish I still had that car in my garage. It was a "beaut," complete with a hood ornament that helped keep all of the 18 feet of car in my lane as I drove back and forth to Fort Dodge.

It's one word if you're from there…"Fordodge." Fort Dodge was the town where I attended high school, earned my first dollar, and fell in love with the girl who would later say yes. Since home was thirty miles away, I had my places around town where I could go and hang out.

This was before the advent of the smartphone, a time when most phones were attached to walls. While we didn't have smartphones, the cars were cooler back then. Whether it was the high school parking lot or at random rendezvous points around town as we tried to pull a night together, muscle cars were just as common as foreign imports. A person didn't want to miss the group because it was next to impossible to find his or her friends if that happened. It was high school, and we had our own version of black ops.

During the days, the Trotters' house was one of my homes away from home. It didn't hurt that there was a pool in the backyard. There were lots of reasons to enjoy the Trotters' house. It was a great place to bum around in between school and work or get-togethers. Driving around aimlessly, or worse yet driving all the way home, didn't sound very appealing.

They say certain houses have personality, and that was the case for the Trotters' house in more ways than one. These people were crazy cool. All of them as funny as they were smart. My favorite combination. I had come to enjoy interacting with Mr. and Mrs. Trotter, Mike and Mari, as much as their kids, one of whom was a fellow classmate. I didn't grow up with brothers, so I enjoyed rubbing shoulders with Ann's brothers, Tony and Pat.

Mike was the man of the house and someone I looked up to from the first time I met him. The best words I can use to describe Mike are genius, funny, tough, interesting, and committed. If he had a party stunt, it would have been his ability to slam his fists together at top speed while keeping a smile on his face and acting like nothing happened. Every time I saw him, I asked for the "trick."

I think he liked that I got such a kick out of it. How he didn't hurt himself doing it is beyond me. The loud crack when his fists met made it sound like he broke multiple bones with every connection. Do you know someone who, when they were younger, people probably didn't mess with? I'm pretty sure that was Mike. In fact, I'm quite confident it was because my future father-in-law grew up in town and has told me as much: my father-in-law likes to fish and tell fish tales, which is why I can't provide full confidence.

We've established already that Iowa is The Hawkeye State, but I can't hold anything against Mike for reportedly setting the curve at his alma mater, Iowa State University (ISU). That's saying something given the prestige of ISU's College of Engineering. The story goes that this curve setter flew under the radar. Everyone in class was trying to figure out who this Mike Trotter was, since he was setting the curve so high. His peers might have been looking for a high and tight haircut and khakis in the large lecture halls when they heard that Mike Trotter was present. Instead, they should have been looking for long hair, a sweatshirt with a blast jacket, blue jeans, engineer boots, and pens and pencils in his shirt pocket to boot. Sounds like a then-modern-day Steve Jobs if you ask me. Mike was also an entrepreneur who, along with two others, bought an established company that would provide for his family and others in a meaningful way.

One particular day, I stopped by the Trotters' house, and Mike was the only one home. We were sitting and chatting—I remember it like it was yesterday—and he asked the million-dollar question, "What are you going to do with your life?"

As I look back on my time in Fort Dodge, I realize that more than anything else, I was looking for positive male role models. I was just grateful for his friendship, which put me in the position to have been asked this question in the first place.

An answer to this "What do you want to be when you grow up?" question was going to be like gravy, a bonus. I'll forever be grateful to Mike Trotter, Randy Lohmeier, David Martens, John Nolan, and Bob Riehl, who gave me their most precious resource—time—during those formative years. These men and a few others I would meet later in life have had a profound impact as it relates to nurturing my personality. At any point in time, it's my belief that everyone needs a "High Five." That is, five people they can look up to.

xxx

I told Mike that I was possibly thinking about a career in aviation. He had taken private pilot lessons, and when he told me that I'd likely need to stop the engine mid-flight only to restart it, I suddenly didn't want to be a pilot anymore.

At that point, I said to Mike that I could see myself as a finance professional someday.

While Mike's formal education was in engineering, not much got past this guy. His mind was like a steel trap. Quietly reaching for a nearby Post-it Note and pen, and with a look on his face that told me something big was coming—a big question needs a big answer—he wrote the following equation:

$$FV = PV(1+i)^N$$

A professional engineer, Mike understood well the importance of math in his line of work. Beyond that, he also understood the fact that the finance industry was essentially built on the power of compounding. To this day, he remains one of the smartest people I have ever met. Even though this was the only time Mike held "class," he taught me so much—from the value of marching to the beat of my own drum to being responsible, present, and a provider for my family. I'm proud to say that he's the person who introduced me to the Mathematics of Finance.

Not long after the "Post-it Note event," I found myself at The University of Iowa and in the "volunteer" phase of life. The last words I heard living under my mom's roof were still ringing in my ears.

Maybe I was just hearing my mom for the first time in some time, but it seemed like everything she was saying was profound and worthy of writing down. She made statements from "Make sure you find the library when you get to town" to "Make sure you write home with handwritten letters." In more than one way, I was getting letters that were affirming. Those handwritten from my mom and the "A's" that had lain dormant for some time.

When I look back on my college career, the letters—both types—are what I remember. Things had turned for the better as far as schooling was concerned. Over a period of time that included changing my declared major from art—I've always had a creative side—to business and after years of back row sitting—not that there's anything wrong with that—I had moved up toward the front of class and found my area of interest: finance. For the first time in a long time, school was clicking, and my "letters" reflected that. I was doing something big that I had signed up for, and it felt right. Learning was coming easily, and I was having a lot of fun. I was in the zone. And then it happened.

It was in a classroom at the Tippie College of Business at The University of Iowa in 1999, where I learned I wanted to be a college finance instructor. As I was enjoying my new view from a front row seat, it was as if a little birdie had landed on my shoulder and chirped in my ear, "You'd be good at teaching." That idea stuck, but it would take some time to manifest.

After taking my first job in Corporate America, I spent the next twenty-two years to the day working to gain specialized knowledge and building a reputation for professionalism and quality work product for transactions related to real estate finance and investment opportunities. After graduating with an MBA degree from The University of Iowa in 2011, I determined that my "professional 4-hour marathon goal" was to start teaching within one year of the date on my newest degree. Many first-time marathoners will tell you that they just want to finish the race, and, while this is true, what may be left unspoken or at least not shared with many is the goal of finishing in less than four hours. With LUCK—a backronym for laboring under correct knowledge—I found my way back into a classroom, this time as a teacher. I had found another one of my callings in life.

Toward the tail end of my time in Corporate America, I found myself in Minneapolis at a business dinner and in great company. My recollection is that there were seven or so people in attendance. We were enjoying conversation before ordering dinner. The host was sharing a story about his son who at the time was an intern at a local company.

From the conversation, I gathered that his son, someone who seemed to be very active and at one time had thought about a possible career as a high school PE teacher, was not exactly enamored at the thought of a 40-year "sentence" to the "cubical prison" in business. This guy liked his fresh air, and who can blame him?

The problem, as his dad explained, was that he liked expensive things. That, in and of itself, isn't a crime, but it was clear that some reframing of expectations might be in order should one path be ultimately chosen over the other. From the story, it appeared this young man had taken the time to be introspective and think about what he wanted to get out of both life and work. He seemed to have it narrowed down to two paths: one that seemed to provide money at the expense of work-life balance, and the other that provided passion at the expense of money. Were those the only flight paths?

His dad—someone I wish I could have dinner with once a month because he's that nice—then said something that I will never forget. "Sometimes we need to do the time so that we can later spread our wings and fly into the field and do what we really want to do."

Sometimes I wonder if people understand the gift that they are giving you when they say something like that. It was the runner's equivalent of "time on feet"—that is, doing the work—in the real estate finance industry that allowed me to fly to my ultimate destination: a career in teaching.

Since there's always a cost associated with a benefit, the time you saved from not having to flip to the dedicated part of the book where you learn about your author will come at the expense of what I still think of as one of the strangest analogies I've ever made—even stranger yet because it involves me, so forgive me in advance.

You know when you watch a movie or television show and you associate with one character? For me, as strange as this might sound, the public persona that I could most relate to was that of Dennis Rodman. This one's going to take some explaining, so sit back and get comfortable—maybe grab concessions.

Over my tenure in Corporate America, I met or exceeded all the expectations set for me. For ten of those years—what later I would discover were my last "two quarters" in Corporate America—my night gig was teaching.

As time passed, teaching also took on a mentoring role. I was teaching and mentoring while practicing real estate finance at the highest level. As time passed, I found passion and competency in multiple professional areas. When I sat in my office between 9 AM and 5 PM, I not only thought of myself as a real estate finance professional but also a teacher and mentor. In the evenings when I was in the classroom, I not only thought of myself as a teacher and mentor but also a real estate finance professional. I was somewhat *indifferent* between those two paths because both were satisfying my intellectual curiosity and allowing me to use my talents and skills. And I can't forget about the people. Having great people on both teams made work fun.

Here's the punchline. When I watched Dennis Rodman at the top of his game playing basketball in the NBA, he appeared—at least to me, an onlooker—as if to be *indifferent* between sharing a court with the best basketball players in the world or giving it all up and riding a bike and being a free bird. That feeling—I'm not talking about basketball, motorcycles, or shenanigans—spoke directly to my soul.

From time to time, in Corporate America I would hear people say that some of the things they were doing—work to me that seemed very emotionally draining at times—didn't feel like work. It wasn't until I found teaching—or teaching found me—that I could relate to work not feeling like work. This is the best way I know how to describe the feeling of being on the right path. The real estate finance industry and practice of teaching are similar in that one can learn something new every day and create something of value from scratch. I describe both as "right brain and left brain" fields. As a creative, that's extremely satisfying to me. Ultimately teaching and a desire to expand my influence outside of Corporate America won the day.

This book is written in the unique style in which I teach that draws on professional and personal experiences—real-life stories that you may be able to relate to. As a result, this book may be unlike any other "textbook" you've ever read. Just like I approach the classroom and learning environment somewhat differently than many instructors. If you were in my class, you won't catch me lecturing 100% from a textbook. I'm constantly looking for opportunities to facilitate student engagement, establish relevance, and make connections—both interpersonally and emotionally in part by using analogies. It's the only way I know how to do it, it's my modus operandi, it's fun, and it's effective.

People learn in multiple ways, but I've found that a common denominator is familiarity. And the best delivery system? Stories. One of my specialties is simplifying and relating complex topics, and students enjoy when I weave into my lessons everyday objects, situations, and stories. You'll find this approach at work in this book. While memorization has its place in education, you may catch me saying, "It's for the birds." The "Why" is the name of the game.

Early in my teaching career—in fact when I didn't even realize I was being interviewed for my first teaching gig—I learned the value placed on a practical education. I'm consistently blessed with great students who find value in my teaching style that emphasizes a practical education and leverages professional and personal experiences. As the saying goes, "If it ain't broke, don't fix it." So this book, written in the style in which I teach, is an authentic extension of my classroom.

Without boring you with the details of my teaching philosophy, let's just say that I'm constantly looking for opportunities to help students of finance further refine and develop the skills that "pay the bills." The lightbulb moment as it relates to general pedagogy followed learning about Bloom's Taxonomy, which is essentially a pyramid with six hierarchical levels of learning: from the bottom to the top are Knowledge, Comprehension, Application, Analysis, Synthesis, and Evaluation. Since I'm a visual learner, I started mapping out switchbacks—think of these as waypoints—up Bloom's "mountain." What I saw popped off the page. The soft (marketable) skills I keep emphasizing to my students as being key to a finance professional's success seemed to naturally coincide with the switchbacks up the top half of the mountain. Analytical thinking skills, as the name implies, are required to move past application to gather and *analyze* information for the ultimate purpose of interpreting information and supporting eventual positions or decisions. Problem-solving skills are needed to *synthesize* and make sense of large amounts of information and—along with creative thinking skills—to develop value-added solutions. Critical and independent thinking skills are needed to do one's own "homework" to *evaluate* information analyzed and synthesized which is necessary to form one's own position. Effective communication skills are needed to work with others to develop and then to pitch a recommendation.

On paper this looks great, but ascending from comprehension of the knowledge of the concept of the Time Value of Money to application of the Mathematics of Finance and ultimately to analysis and evaluation of real-world Time Value of Money situations trips some aspiring and current finance professionals up like tree roots do a mountain trail ultramarathon runner. Climbing the mountain isn't supposed to be easy. Your educational journey can be likened to the sport of running, which can have both a team and individual aspect depending on the situation. Three out of six—Knowledge, Comprehension, and Application—might get you an "A" in school, but Corporate America is a playground for decision makers. Reaching the point at which a decision can be made requires that you progress up the higher switchbacks that are singletrack trails. There are no shortcuts. This book prepares you for this eventuality as it relates to applying the Mathematics of Finance to analyze and evaluate real-world Time Value of Money situations.

Good teachers or mentors always want to see their students or the people they're mentoring succeed. I believe that one of the best gifts I can give people is a way of thinking about things. It's been said that practice doesn't make perfect, and the same is true when we think of practice in the context of the finance industry.

Unfortunately, not all finance professionals completely understand the concept of the Time Value of Money. Unlike Texas pitmasters who use the "Texas Crutch"—aluminum foil wrapped around barbecue toward the end of cooking—to make the meat potentially worthy of high praise, some finance professionals use financial calculators like a crutch to help them limp along in industry.

If you're an aspiring finance professional, rest assured knowing that there is such thing as perfect practice as it relates to the Mathematics of Finance. In a perfect situation, that perfect practice comes before ever setting foot in the field. But it doesn't always work out that way. This will be time well spent, since there's not a competent finance professional who doesn't completely understand the Time Value of Money like the back of their hand. This is why it makes me nervous when I hear a finance student tell me that they don't like math: the name that's used for the most foundational concept in the field has "Mathematics" in the title.

If this is you, don't fret. This book was also written for you. Before you consider repurposing your timeline drawing skills for a career in the arts, give this book a try. At the very least, it will be a kind of "TVM Crutch" or your version of my "Post-it Note event" at best.

Whether you're looking to sharpen the hard skill that is the Mathematics of Finance or for a refresher on the topic of the Time Value of Money, you'll find that and more in this book—it's the only place you'll find the first-of-its-kind user manual for the Mathematics of Finance and the simple tool that is the **TVM Formula**™, which will allow you to use the 3-Step Systematic Approach to apply the Mathematics of Finance to analyze and evaluate real-world Time Value of Money situations.

This book that you hold in your hands will in a way hold your hand as you work on comprehension and application of this specialized knowledge related to the topic of the Time Value of Money—Part 1 of this book—before acquiring certain resources—in Part 2 of this book—as it is at base camp for the mostly solo trek to the peak of the mountain. As a mountaineer needs to pack necessities that are light, this small handbook is perfect for your backpack and journey in the classroom or in Corporate America. The **TVM Formula**™, which includes both a mnemonic (audible aid) and visual aid (template), provides a kind of map to assist you on your solo journey of applying the Mathematics of Finance on the singletrack trails over Analysis Pass, around Synthesis Lake, and culminating at the peak at Evaluation Point (aka the Decision Point). Whether you find yourself in your own enlisted, recruited, or volunteer phase, thanks for allowing me to share half of the path with you.

When I was in the enlisted phase of life, I was a night owl. It was not uncommon for me to stay up until 2 AM. This was partly due to the fact that I worked many nights until 11 PM. If you're like me, you need downtime at the end of a hard day's work. One night after the long drive home, I remember finding my mom in tears. She was watching a tribute show that spotlighted some of Stevie Ray Vaughan's recorded performances. His untimely death in a tragic helicopter crash was still reverberating through the music world. My mom and I couldn't get enough of watching these past performances, watching late into the night TV shows about the life and music of this incredible man—someone who turned his life around against all odds. Supposedly, the great Texan and guitarslinger had a limited knowledge of musical theory, couldn't read music, and never played a song the same way twice. While that's an incredible gift if you're a musician and virtuoso, aspiring and current finance professionals need to have a sound grasp of the concept of the Time Value of Money, should be able to read the numbers, and ultimately find confidence through repetition. The hallmark of the **TVM Formula**™, which is the 3-Step Systematic Approach, provides just that, so you can get about sharing your unique skills and experiences with the world in your current or future capacity as a finance professional.

Mike Trotter (L) and yours truly (R) (1995).

Abbreviations

"You can't spend money while you're working."
—Bob Riehl

In my past career, I figured out that I have a knack for reviewing complex legal documents as a finance professional—not an attorney. I wouldn't wish being a lawyer on my worst enemy, but I'm glad that I had some of the best and brightest on speed dial to help me figure out whether my interpretations of provisions in legal documents were right on. If you've ever reviewed a legal document, you are likely familiar with the "Definitions" section. This is my version of that: abbreviations style. Rather than having to redefine common Time Value of Money abbreviations over and over again in the paragraph in which one of these terms first shows up in a chapter, to clean up the text here are a few common terms and abbreviations that will keep showing up throughout this book:

Time Value of Money (TVM)

Future Value (FV)

Present Value (PV)

From time to time, I'll bounce back and forth between the abbreviation and the long-form depending on the context.

I hope you enjoy this book as much as I enjoyed writing it.

With gratitude,

Brent Pritchard

Part 1: The What

New Take, Take One: The Time Value of Money

Chapter 1: Birds

"A bird in the hand is worth two in the bush."
—Ecclesiastes 6:9

I'd be on a beach somewhere if I had a dollar for every time I've watched someone stumble or struggle trying to apply the Mathematics of Finance to analyze and evaluate a real-world Time Value of Money situation. Having made a living *practicing* what I *teach*, I've come to believe through firsthand experience that some of the confusion surrounding this all-important topic in finance has to do with how the Time Value of Money has been traditionally presented. Here I want to focus on wording or terminology:

"A dollar in the present is worth more than a dollar in the future."

The above statement or some variation can be recited by many aspiring and current finance professionals. While correct and theoretically sound because inflation erodes a future dollar's purchasing power, where I think it misses the mark is no reference to markets for capital and the associated issues of perceived risk, return *on* investment, delaying consumption, and opportunity cost. To expand on the last two points, have you ever thought that *no* not only comes before *yes* in the dictionary but in real-life situations? Opportunity cost speaks to all the instances of no—those investments that were forgone by saying yes to an investment opportunity and ultimately delaying consumption. Can you think of a situation for which there is only one alternative? It takes saying no to one or more opportunities before one can ultimately say yes and pursue a certain investment opportunity. Speaking of the dictionary, *The Britannica Dictionary* defines *worth* as follows:

: an amount of something that has a specified *value*, that lasts for a specified length of *time*, etc.

: the amount *of money* that something is worth

: usefulness or importance

No wonder why the word *worth* was chosen in the above statement. The definition coincidently includes the words *Time, Value, of,* and *Money*. Whoever wrote this definition deserves a raise! While this is quite impressive, I'd like to propose another statement for you to think about as you wrap your head around this concept:

"I would rather have a dollar today than a dollar in the future."

I hope you'd say the same, because a dollar in the hand today—or any day for that matter—can be invested. Notice that in the new statement, there's still reference to money and time; however, value is implied. This brings us to the two words I'd like to focus on at this time.

Some of the confusion with respect to the concept of the Time Value of Money appears to stem from the words *worth* and *value*. The two words have similar meanings, but the nuance is important, especially in the context of the Time Value of Money. Whoever coined the term the Time Value of Money chose the word *Value* over *Worth*.

As we'll discuss later in this chapter and throughout this book, money has time value. In other words, we can estimate the Future Value or Present Value of money at a certain point in time. Notice I didn't say Future *Worth* or Present *Worth*. Money has time value, not *time worth*. It's worth something to have the ability to invest (money) today. Why? Because you want the value of your investment to be—see how easy it is to want to use the word *worth* here—more in the future.

While both "worth" and "value" rightfully imply monetary value, in the context of the Time Value of Money, it seems more useful to think of "worth" as describing something conceptual and "value" as referring to monetary value. It's *worth* something to have the ability to invest money at any point in time. Notice how *value* isn't a substitute for *worth* in that context. This is how you should be using *worth* when it comes to the Time Value of Money.

The Time Value of Money is also known as the Mathematics of Finance. Because math is a kind of language, and languages have rules, we first need to discuss the Time Value of Money rules. These are the footings on which I was able to develop the original 3-Step Systematic Approach, which is the cornerstone of this creative work.

Notice I didn't say "textbook." Textbooks can get a bad rap, and I get it. The word can carry a negative connotation when it comes to the traditional variety. While this book can be used as a textbook, I prefer to think of it more like the handbook that it is.

A fundamental concept of the Time Value of Money is compounding: discounting is just the opposite of compounding. Compounding is also referred to by some as compound interest. The streets are lined with people who have heard of compound interest. For some, the Time Value of Money may not be a household term. Money has time value because of the concept of compounding or return *on* return *on* investment. Investors wouldn't make investments and take on exposure to risk without the expectation for a given return *on* investment. Because one wouldn't exist without the other, this is the closest thing we have to the chicken or the egg dilemma in finance. Which came first: return *on* investment or markets for capital?

When you understand the TVM Rules, you'll be talking my language in more than one way, since the TVM Rules form the basis for the original 3-Step Systematic Approach—the most effective method I know of for how to apply the Mathematics of Finance to analyze and evaluate real-world Time Value of Money situations time after time.

The Time Value of Money is commonly abbreviated TVM. It's *worth* noting the Time Value of Money shorthand because it consists of three letters. Just like there are three letters in TVM, there are three TVM Rules. As you'll see later, the dialing in of these original TVM Rules extends beyond being minimalistic. Spoiler alert: the first relates to *Time*, the second to *Value*, and the third to *Money*. Now isn't that a novel idea? It actually is, which means it was long overdue. Doing any of these is a Time Value of Money no-no:

1. Add or subtract or compare money *in different* points in time.
2. Fail to correspond the time span *in* between periods or payments (on the timeline) and the time span of the true investment yield.
3. Neglect to consider *different* payment types and signs.

We'll be discussing the TVM Rules multiple times throughout this book, so don't worry if one or more are not clear at this point. That's my job and one of the purposes of this book. In fact, the first-of-its-kind user manual for the Mathematics of Finance, Part 2 of this book, wouldn't be possible without the original TVM Rules. Those, along with the 3-Step Systematic Approach and other creative works, form the simple tool that is the **TVM Formula**™. In addition to appearing multiple times throughout this book, the TVM Rules will be presented in different ways marked only by minor or nonsubstantive changes in the language. For example, a switch from the negative to affirmative, etc. The **TVM Formula**™ is the glue that holds the 3-Step Systematic Approach together, and the most active ingredient is the TVM Rules!

My Grandma Schlieman loved to say, "Never say never." Most of the time, I stick to her guidance. When I use the word *never*, it's usually to emphasize something very important.

TVM Rule #1 is *never* add or subtract or compare money *in different* points in time. Why? Because there are markets for capital. Those who have money to invest and those who need or want money and are willing to pay for it in the form of an expected investment yield, which could but doesn't have to take the form of interest. As a result, there is a value—not *worth*—that makes an investor *indifferent* between money *in different* points in time for a given investment yield and certain investment period.

Take another look at the opening quotation—which possibly could be the first known saying from a time long past that sums up the concept of the Time Value of Money—with a critical and literal eye. And now the opening statement. Here is the opening statement to save you from needing to look back: "A dollar in the present is worth more than a dollar in the future."

Have you picked up on the other issue and potential point of confusion? This statement could be interpreted to say it's somehow acceptable to compare money *in different* points in time, and nothing could be further from the (Time Value of Money) truth.

Even though I'm always reminding my students to *never* add or subtract or compare money *in different* points in time, it seems like there is always someone who breaks *TVM Rule #1*.

The TVM Rules aren't to be confused with guidelines, which open the door to exceptions. Rules aren't meant to be broken; rather, it's about dotting i's and crossing t's. It just so happens that *time* has both a *t* and an *i*! If we were having a discussion about the price of a dozen eggs back in 1922 compared to today, you'd likely quickly and rightfully articulate that one can't compare these two values: the "egg values" are *in different* points in time.

I'm going to go out on a limb and say that most people if asked about the rules for the Time Value of Money would say something to the effect of *TVM Rule #1* and stop there. This is another reason why *TVM Rule #1* holds the top spot, but there's more.

TVM Rule #2 is *never* fail to correspond the time span *in* between periods or payments (on the timeline) and the time span of the true investment yield. Stay tuned for more about the true investment yield later in this book: a whole chapter has been devoted to the topic. The short answer is you need to first focus on how you're "telling time" *in* between periods or payments (on the timeline) and then make sure that that time span corresponds with the time span of the true investment yield.

Your birthday provides an example of what I mean by the concept of time span. You likely celebrate a birthday every year, but you could also celebrate your birthday semiannually (children love to celebrate half-birthdays), every quarter, every month, every week, every day, or in the case of a leap year, in four-year increments if your birthday falls on February 29. Here's a "rule" you may not like if your birthday falls on February 29. Did you know that leap year is skipped when the year is divisible by 100 but not 400? In fact, there's nothing stopping you from celebrating your birthday in any increment. For example, every five years, etc. But this would raise the question, "Why don't you want cake or pie and nice cards, some of which are lined with money?" And being alive is something to celebrate every day.

The time span *in* between birthday celebrations is the "n" of the "in" of *in* between periods (or payments if you're lucky) on the timeline, for this example. The time span of the true investment yield is the "i" of the "in." Going back to the egg example, if we're "telling time" on the timeline with annual periods, then only a true—other people might call this an effective or equivalent—annual investment yield would fly. Solving for the true annual investment yield in the egg example is the same thing as solving for the true annual rate of inflation.

Before we move on, you need to know that there's a difference between the true investment yield and the real investment yield, the latter of which considers inflation and what's left—the real return *on* investment—after the inflation "dust" settles. Think of the real return *on* investment as what's left from the birthday loot if a sibling were to come a-knocking with an IOU in hand and seeking a payday from some of your newfound money.

TVM Rule #3 is *never* neglect to consider *different* payment types and signs. As the name implies, every Time Value of Money question that you encounter will have a *Time* component, a *Value* component, and a *Money* component. With respect to money, there are two *different* payment types or classifications. The first is a lump-sum payment, which is also known as a single payment. The second is a series of payments, which falls into one of four *different* subclassifications: an even annuity, even perpetuity, uneven annuity, or uneven perpetuity. Regardless of which one you're dealing with, the *different* signs matter.

To build on the birthday example and keep it real, let's wind back the clock to my early childhood in small-town Iowa. Every year when my sister and I were younger, my Grandma and Grandpa P. would send us birthday cards in the mail—from their home six miles away. Go figure. Every year, inside the card I found a crisp $2 bill. (At Christmastime, they always wrapped our presents in similar wrapping paper and would switch the presents on purpose. They always got a laugh out of watching me hold up the gift that was meant for my sister! I guess some things *never* get old.) For me and my sister, this was an example of an even annuity, since the frequency of the payment was more than once and the amount and timing of the payment were level. This wasn't a perpetuity because, well, kids grow up and unfortunately grandparents pass on. If we were to plot on a timeline Grandma and Grandpa P.'s birthday cash, we could figure out from whose perspective the timeline was being drawn based on the signs associated with the $2 payments. Positive (no sign) values associated with the $2 payments would denote (birthday) money inflows—this is why it's called cash flow—to the birthday boy or girl: the Birthday Boy's or Birthday Girl's Timeline. A timeline with negative signs and values associated with the $2 payments would represent cash outflows or money given, not received: the Grandparents' Timeline. Outside of this specific birthday example, negative signs and values denote money invested or deposited, and positive (no sign) values represent money received or withdrawn.

So there you have it. These are the TVM Rules as I see them. Leaner and meaner—because they're packing a bigger punch—than ever before. For one, these TVM Rules were developed from the mnemonic *indifferent*. In my mind, the Time Value of Money can be summed up in this one word, which speaks to the fact there is a value—not *worth*—that makes an investor *indifferent* between money *in different* points in time for a given investment yield and certain investment period.

Now do you see how the TVM Rules can be remembered with just one word? This *one* word, with its *two* main components, will help you remember the *three* TVM Rules. This handbook provides *my two cents* on the Time Value of Money, which can be fully realized using *your two senses* of hearing and seeing.

In addition to remembering the TVM Rules, when you get to the **TVM Formula**™ in Part 2, the mnemonic and audible aid *indifferent* will serve as a blueprint to also guide you through the steps of the visual aid and template for the 3-Step Systematic Approach that is the original TVM Wallet. The TVM Wallet has "windows" for each of the TVM Rules—the three components of *Time (in different)*, *Value (in)*, and *Money (different)*. This is where the "as I see them" comes in!

Not everything has to be new and shiny to be worth its weight in gold. The original—and in this case I don't mean new—visual aid is the trusty timeline. "When in doubt, draw a timeline" are words I heard all throughout my college career, and they have stood the test of time.

The Time Value of Money provides you with the opportunity to find your inner artist. Okay, not really, but there is drawing involved. I've yet to meet a person who can't draw stick people, and the timeline is even more basic than that. It really does help to draw a timeline, which is a visual representation of when you expect certain amounts of money to be invested or received.

In the original—and brand-spanking-new as of this publication—TVM Rules I chose to include words between parentheses because a timeline isn't what makes the *Rule*; instead, it's the *Rule* that makes the timeline relevant. You shouldn't, however, think of money moving along the timeline. I like to think of the action, compounding or discounting, happening below the timeline by way of what I call *"indifferent* lines." At both ends of the *"indifferent* lines," you find the values—not *worth* or the plural form, which isn't a word—for which an investor is *indifferent* based on a given investment yield and certain investment period.

Part of why I started calling them *"indifferent lines"* is because each dash looks like the uppercase of the letter *"i."* Do the *"indifferent* lines" remind you of anything else? What about the lines down the middle of a highway? Here's a question that the above-average drivers will nail. Can drivers pass when there's a solid line down the middle of the road? No, they can't. This should remind you that you can't move money along the solid timeline. It's a Time Value of Money no-no to add or subtract or compare money *in different* points in time (on the timeline). Compounding or discounting by way of *"indifferent* lines" allows you to add or subtract or compare money at a certain point in time (*below the timeline*). Think about *"indifferent* lines" as facilitating time travel.

To illustrate this point of time travel as it relates to the Time Value of Money, we can look to the Hollywood blockbuster *Back to the Future* starring the fictional character Marty McFly. In the movie, Marty McFly is able to travel back in time using a car that had been converted to a time machine thanks to a core component: the flux capacitor. He travels back in time to his parents' younger years. At first, he's misunderstood. Then he starts to fit in with his newfound friends — including *his parents* — as he wears clothing and listens to the music of the time period before stealing the show and teaching the generation a few new guitar licks.

In real life, we have Marty McFly to thank for inspiring John Mayer — my second favorite guitarist behind the late, great Stevie Ray Vaughan — to pick up the guitar. Well done, McFly!

At the end of the movie, with the help of a good friend, "Doc" Brown, Marty is able to harness the power of lightning to get back to the future.

The first time I watched this classic, little did I know that in adulthood I would write a book about a different kind of time travel — the kind made possible by the Time Value of Money. Because fictional time travel in *Back to the Future* was accomplished using a Delorean outfitted with a flux capacitor, we can really drive home this point of moving money values through time using *"indifferent* lines" that look like the lines down the middle of a highway.

When it comes to the Mathematics of Finance, we don't have a time-traveling Delorean, but aspiring and current finance professionals do have a handful of building block Time Value of Money equations permitting time travel for money by way of (1 +

i)^N. This is why I refer to $(1 + i)^N$ as the *Flux Capacitor of Finance*. (In the building block Time Value of Money equations for a perpetuity, it takes the form of "i̱" or $(1 + i)$; however, as described later, you could plug "9999" for the variable "N" in the building block Time Value of Money equations for an annuity and get the same answer you would when using the building block Time Value of Money equations for a perpetuity. And since the building block Time Value of Money equations for an annuity rely on $(1 + i)^N$, this mathematical expression really is the *Flux Capacitor of Finance*.)

Now get this. It took plutonium for "Doc" Brown to take Marty McFly back in time. Aspiring and current finance professionals use the building block Time Value of Money Present Value equations—plutonium and Present Value both start with *P*—to estimate the value—not *worth*—of money at a certain earlier or present point in time.

It took a flash of lightning to get Marty McFly back to the future. Aspiring and current finance professionals use the building block Time Value of Money Future Value equations—flash of lightning and Future Value both start with *F*—to estimate the value—not *worth*—of money at a certain later or future point in time.

Now I hope you can see how Marty McFly traveling through time with money in his pants pocket would have been a kind of violation of *TVM Rule #1*. It would have been better for him to recognize that there are markets for capital and to have invested the money before his rendezvous at the clock tower!

In *Back to the Future*, Marty McFly travels back in time to what then became the present time. This is another important concept as it relates to the Time Value of Money, because there's nothing in the building block Present Value equation, for example, that says the present is today. Similarly, a whole bunch of present points in time get you to a future point in time. Said another way, sooner or later, the future becomes the present.

In thinking about this, it occurred to me that the film company got the *Back to the Future* title right from a Time Value of Money perspective without probably even meaning to do so. Forward time travel and the title *Back to the Present* wouldn't jibe with the Mathematics of Finance. Estimating Present Value under the timeline by way of *"indifferent* lines" directly or indirectly using one of the building block Time Value of Money Present Value equations requires discounting, which involves moving from one point in time to an earlier point in time: from right to left in terms of the timeline. Estimating Future Value under the timeline by way of *"indifferent* lines" directly or indirectly using one of the building block Time Value of Money Future Value equations requires compounding, which involves moving from one point in time to a later point in time: from left to right in terms of the timeline.

When it comes to keeping time in real life, I prefer an automatic or mechanical wristwatch. In case you're not familiar, this is a watch that is powered by a movement not a battery. The movement is what makes telling time possible: power or energy is stored in the mainspring and is slowly released through wheels and pinions that compose the gear train, which ultimately move the hands on the dial.

If there's one thing that makes the Time Value of Money a thing, it's this idea of being *indifferent* between values of money *in different* points in time, which is a result of there being markets for capital. There are people who have money to invest, and then there are those who need or want money and are willing to pay "financial rent" for the use of other people's money over a certain investment period.

The real estate professional in me is excited to have found the opportunity to use the word *rent* when discussing the Time Value of Money; however, it needs to be stated that the term "financial rent" doesn't need to represent fixed payments any more than return *on* investment needs to come in the form of *interest*. Here, "financial rent" or return *on* investment refers to the true investment yield, which is ultimately a product of cash flow.

Just like the Mathematics of Finance isn't about the Time *Worth* of Money, it also isn't really about the Time Value of *Dollars*. Of course we'd rather have a dollar today because that dollar can be invested and earn a return over time, but the same would be true for any currency—physical or virtual—in the world. I've seen lots of change on my watch and virtual currency is one of them.

In closing this chapter, let's revisit the opening quotation, but let's revise it such that birds become dollar bills:

"A *dollar bill* in the hand is worth two *one-dollar bills* in the bush."

The opening statement included the word *more*, and since an investor expects an investment to have a future value that is more than the value of an initial investment, it's also fitting that two one-dollar bills are in the bush.

Really think about this revised quotation for a moment. Why might this be?

Before I pose the next question, imagine it's a windy day: we need to replicate the tendency for two one-dollar bills to potentially fly away. If you had a dollar bill in the hand this very moment, and off in the distance you saw two one-dollar bills in the bush, given windy conditions, what would you physically have to do to potentially put both hands on the two one-dollar bills in the bush? You'd have to open your hand and let go of the one you have. This not only illustrates that you expect the Future Value to be more than the Present Value but also provides a visual of the direction of cash flow, outflow or inflow, and the risk–return tradeoff or relationship.

There are no guarantees when it comes to an investment. You could lose it all. In this illustration, the wind symbolizes (perceived) risk, which includes the risk of inflation. Nobody can anticipate with certainty when and where the wind will blow. Risk by its very definition is uncertainty. The actual outcome—think Future Value and true investment yield—could fall short of your expectations based on internal performance or because of externalities—think risk—such as inflation that reduces purchasing power, or both.

Either one or both of these conditions would be likened to dropping the dollar bill in the hand only to get one or none of the two one-dollar bills previously in the bush. Now you can see why you'd rather have a dollar in the hand than a dollar in the bush. It's windy out there!

But wind also allowed Benjamin Franklin to fly his kite outfitted with a key to prove that lightning was electricity. This later earned him the distinction of having invented the lightning rod. Can't think of a better real-life example than this one, from a person who had an understanding of the Time Value of Money, to describe the risk–return tradeoff or relationship. And since birds have *bills*, this revised quote really isn't that much of a deviation from the ancient proverb…

The one thing that is missing in this ancient proverb is reference to time. Without knowledge of time, it's impossible to estimate the true investment yield. For example, expecting to give one bird to get two birds over the next year offers a different "true investment yield" than expecting to give one bird today for the chance to get two birds, say, tomorrow.

We'll be covering the topic of the true investment yield in the next chapter. Having one value in the present and a greater value in the future—even if they are birds—speaks to this fundamental concept of being *indifferent* between money *in different* points in time for a given investment yield and certain investment period. We know of at least one person who was *indifferent* between one bird in the hand and two in the bush. Money—or *Birds*? Check. Time? Don't know: it's unknown. Value then, as denoted by the true investment yield, can't be determined since there's a break in the chain of information. With an unknown time span *in* between money—or "birds"—it's not possible to know the time span of the true investment yield.

Time is something you want on your side. That's one of the best ways I've come to summarize the Time Value of Money. In the Preface, I said that I have a few regrets. One of those is not executing on this idea I had when our daughters were born, which was to save $1,000 on each date of birth and each annual celebration thereafter through and including their 18th birthdays. Assuming a true annual investment yield of 10%, each of these annual investments would have been expected to grow to $1,739,611 by the time each of our daughters turns fifty-five and $4,512,103 at the age of sixty-five. (I guess I have some books to sell…)

Like these numbers? Then keep on reading! Don't worry if you don't know how to calculate Future Value at this point. This book, in particular Part 2, will help you with that. These numbers obviously don't consider ups and downs in the markets; here our focus is simply on the Mathematics of Finance. Did you pick up on the fact that we're only talking about nineteen annual deposits of $1,000! In the absence of this investment strategy and assuming the same true annual investment yield of 10%, if one were to invest $1,000 annually starting on their twenty-third birthday and continuing through and including their fifty-fifth birthday, they would expect to have an investment with a balance of $222,252. Adding ten more years of annual deposits of $1,000 the savings would be expected to grow to $592,401 by their sixty-fifth birthday. That's a far cry from $1,739,611 and $4,512,103, respectively. It is estimated to take thirty-three annual deposits of $7,827.22 from one's twenty-third birthday to fifty-fifth birthday or forty-three annual deposits of

$7,616.64 from one's twenty-third birthday to sixty-fifth birthday to expect to accumulate $1,739,611 or $4,512,103, respectively. Again, this is assuming a true annual investment yield of 10%. Move over birthday gifts that collect dust and take up room in a corner...show me the birthday money! See what I mean by wanting time on your side?

By delaying consumption and investing in the future, you have the potential to change your family tree and provide a legacy for not only your children but their children's children and beyond. Let's go back to the example that contemplates nineteen annual deposits of $1,000. You'll want to know how much that would be expected to grow to over a total investment period that includes seventy-five years. That number would be $11,703,233. Still not enough? Are you sitting down? After a total investment period that includes eighty-five years, this investment strategy would be expected to have a future value of $30,355,174. Now that's a nice nest egg!

Chapter 2: Hurdlers

"Compound interest is the Eighth Wonder of the World."
— Albert Einstein

Mattresses come in different shapes and sizes. Some people prefer the softness of feather mattress toppers while others want the stiffness similar to that of a wood table. Regardless of one's preference, one thing that people should be able to agree on is that we shouldn't store money under a mattress. Why is this?

Well, it's because money, when invested, can earn a return. Said another way, investors—providers of capital—require a return *on* investment. Now, I'm careful with the wording here because every investment has an expected return, but not every expected return comes in the form of interest. Institutional investments fall along a spectrum, from equity to debt—fixed income—with hybrid assets in between. This doesn't include other assets such as fine art and anything else that one might consider an investment, such as baseball cards, etc.

So there are markets for capital, which are a thing because of investors with money to invest and those who need or want money to finance an investment. There are investors who have and investors who have not and want or need what other investors have and are willing to pay for temporary use of other people's funds.

Early in my life, my mom taught me the difference between needs and wants. You may have learned a similar life lesson, which has relevance in finance. For example, an investor may have enough capital on hand to finance an expansion but may want to go to the market to secure funds from others to allow for diversification of assets, the potential for financial leverage, and possible tax advantages. Providers of capital are banking on an *expected* return *on* investment from cash flow, which ultimately comes from income or appreciation—or both. Some say that investing is a two-way street, but I prefer the roundabout visual.

At the time of the initial investment, one investor is *giving* and the other is *getting*. But then *in* one or more *different* points in time over the investment period, the tables are turned. Those who *give* money expect to *get* or earn a return *on* investment: this is what brings it full circle, and why a roundabout is a better visual than a two-way street. In Time Value of Money verbiage, we refer to this true investment yield as "i."

Investors require a true investment yield for delaying consumption, opportunity cost, and for taking on exposure to risk including the risk of inflation. Risk covers a whole host of unknowns from business risk to inflation risk: the sky's the limit in terms of risk identification. Risk and return. Risk requires return. This is a fundamental concept in finance and usually one of the first things out of the gate the first day in most introductory finance classes.

In the first chapter, you were introduced to what constitutes a Time Value of Money "no-no." It just so happens that the mirror image of "no-no" is "on-on," which speaks to compound "interest" and the primary reason why money shouldn't be stored under a mattress. During the period of time that money is invested, the investment period, investors can potentially earn return *on* return *on* investment.

Just as farmers plant a field for potential yield, so too do investors invest for the potential for true investment yield or compound investment yield. Those are one and the same, since the "true" of true investment yield tells us that it considers the effects of compounding. The notation for the true investment yield, "i," somewhat resembles crops you might find growing in a field in Iowa and beyond. And in the words of the late and legendary Iowa football head coach Hayden Fry, "America Needs Farmers."

Since this book is all about a new take on the Time Value of Money, it's worth mentioning how ludicrous it sounds to even say "interest *on* interest *on* the outstanding principal balance of a loan" since most loan documents require simple accrued interest and amortization over their respective loan terms.

Having worked in a lending capacity for a global asset management company for twenty-two years to the day, I'm trustworthy when I say that compound accrued interest and negative amortization aren't very common in the market. Either or both would contribute to return *on* return *on* investment.

Enough with this "compound interest" language already. The "banker's year," also known as the 30/360 day-count convention, is a thing because it's simple, which is why the product of this simple calculation is simple accrued interest. The value investors see in investing should be thought of as the true investment yield because it works in every situation regardless of where an asset falls along the investments spectrum.

Let's bring our attention for a moment to two brilliant people. There's no question that both Albert Einstein and Warren Buffet both were blessed with major smarts. Albert Einstein is known for developing the theory of relativity, which fundamentally changed our understanding of space, time, gravity, and the universe. Warren Buffett is known as the "Oracle of Omaha" and one of the greatest investors to have ever lived. Warren obviously knows all about the Time Value of Money.

The opening quotation tells us that these men had at least one thing in common that might have served as a talking point: compound interest. Warren Buffett has been known to make statements to the effect that "Compound interest is your best friend." In the last chapter, it was established that time is something you want on your side. But time alone doesn't benefit an investor any more than storing money under a mattress has the potential to get you anything more than $2 from the Tooth Fairy. Albert Einstein reportedly also said that "Compound interest is the most powerful force in the universe." Remember the word *powerful*, which we'll be coming back to in a bit. There have been a lot of technological advancements since Albert Einstein was walking around on planet Earth, one of which is the smartphone.

Imagine for a moment that Albert Einstein is still alive and having a conversation with Warren Buffett. Next, imagine Warren reaches for his phone, accesses his camera app, and then hears Albert say something like, "Make sure you tape this."

To that, Warren responds, "You mean 'record this?'"

Videography was a thing during Albert's life, but you can see how this terminology could lead to a person scratching their head. Both of these men have been quoted using the term "compound interest." I realize why: because this is a term that has meaning in the finance industry. But "compound interest" is so back then. While no industry is free from terminology, it can cause one's head to spin, and it creates space for potential confusion to set in.

We've already stated that math is a kind of language. Language, in addition to having rules, changes over time. Every year, new words are added to the dictionary. Growing up, I was told, "*Ain't* ain't a word." Well now it is. Compound interest is just another way of referring to the true investment yield or yield for short.

The risk–return tradeoff no doubt takes the cake as far as relationships in finance are concerned. Not far behind is the price–yield relationship. Price influences yield, and yield influences price. Others and I have been known to shortcut it and say, "price to yield," which speaks to this relationship. Notice nobody is saying "price to interest." This further supports my theory that terminology can muddy the waters.

As a young real estate finance professional, I was always surprised by the variance in market prices, in particular, the seller's asking prices and the price buyers were willing to bid.

Then I realized that it all boils down to two things: cash flow projections and *expected* return *on* investment for the level of perceived risk. Each investor or prospective investor will have their own view with respect to cash flow projections. In addition, each investor has a *required* return *on* investment. These two are related.

You'll hear others refer to a "minimum" *required* return *on* investment. I think this is somewhat oxymoronic. When a line is drawn in the sand, you know what's required—no *minimum* about it when you separate *required* return *on* investment from *expected* return *on* investment, a point of which isn't lost with the hurdle rate (singular). Have you ever heard someone refer to a minimum hurdle rate? In the case of a loan asset with a fixed interest rate, the *required* return *on* investment is the same as the *expected* return *on* investment, which goes to show that the risk-adjusted spread that goes into building up the interest rate considers profit.

From firsthand experience, I can tell you that one upright of the hurdle (rate) considers pricing premiums for such things as overhead, illiquidity, and the like. In the case of a commercial mortgage loan, the illiquidity premium accounts for the fact that the whole loan asset will be held on the books, which isn't as marketable as a marketable security, hence the name. The other upright factors in market yields for *external* assets.

Once an investor feels that they've made a realistic forecast with respect to the cash flow projection, and barring any new material information that would lead to a change in one or more assumptions, the only two other moving parts are price and yield. In the game of "This or That," I would view cash flow projections as being more static and price more dynamic.

Think about love birds who are tying the knot outside of the arranged marriage tradition. Months or years are taken to form a commitment, then a wedding date is circled on the calendar. I'm a big believer in working backward from a problem to find a solution, but a solution in search of a problem would be circling a wedding date only to then go in search of a better half. This isn't how it typically works.

You also have to be sold on the cash flow projections before the commitment to invest funds. So it's not a surprise that cash flow projections tend to be stickier than the bid price. Price influences yield, and yield influences price. For a given cash flow projection, if you all of the sudden *required* more for a return *on* investment or true investment yield, the bid price would need to be reduced all else equal. Why? Because something's got to give.

Alternatively, if you found yourself in a bidding war and needed to increase your bid price, the more static nature of the cash flow projection would mean that you probably just lowered your *expected* return *on* investment or true investment yield. You might be wondering why we can use the term true investment yield to refer to both the *expected* return *on* investment and *required* return *on* investment? That's because return *on* investment is synonymous with the true investment yield: the words *expected* and *required* just further describe the return *on* investment.

One of the smartest people I've had the fortune of rubbing shoulders with in business was Douglas Fairchild. In my mind, he's the epitome of a businessperson, and I mean that as a sincere compliment. In my office, I have a handwritten note that he gave me. Strange as it sounds, I treasure that note and consider the fact that it came from his desk to be one of my greatest accomplishments in business.

Watching this guy think was a sight to behold. He once told me that finance professionals are paid to be "crystal balls." The comment was made in the context of cash flow projections and investment analysis or decision-making. Having an understanding of how *cash flows* is the first step in analyzing any real-world Time Value of Money situation.

For the finance professional, projecting cash flows is about making realistic assumptions. As far as I'm concerned, the only place we should assume anything is when we're working with math. Outside of math—in our professional or personal lives—"to assume can make an 'ass' of 'u' and 'me.'" (Thanks for that lesson, Kate Arnett. I'll never forget it.)

Since computers are used to model cash flows, we can't forget about the "Garbage in, garbage out" principle. But here's the crazy thing about projections: you know you're going to be wrong as soon as the forecast is finalized. Being wrong while being as close to right by making a realistic cash flow projection is what a good cash flow forecast is all about. It's about minimizing the variance or error. Estimating cash flows is about good inputs and solid assumptions.

Be cautious of a cash flow projection that changes in the absence of material new information. I'm from the school of thought that the cash flow projection should model how cash is expected to flow. Padding the numbers doesn't jibe with this philosophy. In my opinion, that's what alternative or stressed analysis is for: to see how an asset will weather "storms" or unfavorable conditions. Weatherpersons actually get their forecasts right more than finance professionals. Don't believe me? Over more than two decades in business not once have I made a 100% accurate forecast or projection of cash flows. And if you go into the profession, neither will you.

It's not uncommon for some cash flow forecasts to include multiple numbers, some into the millions, over multiple line items and over multiple years. Nobody is that good. You just want to feel good about your cash flow forecast. It's a lot easier to predict the temperature within a reasonable degree range for a typical day in a certain location or whether it's going to snow—it's going to snow or it isn't.

We'll stay in winter to illustrate the concept of the true investment yield with snowballs one would roll for the ultimate purpose of making a snowman. Snowperson doesn't quite roll off the tongue the same way as weatherperson, so I've taken the liberty of writing this like it's 1885 before people were wound so tight and PC referred to neither politically correct nor the personal computer. Ironically, Albert Einstein, who later in life would famously say, "If you can't explain it to a six-year-old, you don't understand it yourself," was six years old in 1885. No doubt that a young Einstein would have understood the meaning of the snowball illustrations that follow if they would have been published back then. Today, this is likely the closest thing we have to the "six-year-old test" for the Time Value of Money. Imagine that you had the benefit of gravity and a mountain to form snowballs for your snowman. Further assume that as a snowball is rolled from the peak and travels the distance of the mountain slope, it picks up snow evenly until it reaches its resting place at the bottom. The size of the snowball is a function of the height of the mountain and the linear horizontal distance that the snowball will travel from the peak to the base. Below the concept of compounding is illustrated with snowballs, complete with "*indifferent* lines":

In theory, an "*indifferent* line" is scalable and a graphical representation of "i" and "N" on the Y-axis and X-axis, respectively—although we're not actually concerned with scale when we draw a timeline. In other words, "i" represents the true investment yield—in this illustration the height of the mountain—and "N" represents the investment period—the linear horizontal distance that the snowball will travel from the peak to the base in this example. Remember the word that we were going to revisit: *powerful*. Compound investment yield is a thing because "$(1+i)$" is raised to the *power* of "N."

Since this is an illustration about the Time Value of Money, the snowballs represent amounts of money: the smaller snowball represents the Present Value, and the larger snowball represents the Future Value. The timeline brings in the elements of "Time" and "Money," while the "*indifferent* lines" bring in the elements of "Time" and "Value" and "Money."

Remember, the value investors see in investing is the potential for true investment yield or compound investment yield, which affects the value of money over time. Just as the timeline is two-dimensional, so too is value. Value can be expressed using both a

23

% sign for the true investment yield or $ sign for Present Value and Future Value.

We know that "What goes up must come down." The last example illustrated a snowball rolling down the mountain slope. With just a minor adjustment and a slight change to the storyline, we can also illustrate the concept of discounting with snowballs. Instead of starting with a snowball that will get rolled down the mountain, the snowball at the top of this mountain represents the end result of a snowball getting rolled up the mountain slope. Seems like a lot of work—I know—but this is the only other storyline that works given the parameters.

Now the X-axis "*indifferent* line" is on the left because we're operating on the left side of the mountain and the Y-axis "*indifferent* line" is associated with the Future Value, not Present Value. Below the concept of discounting is illustrated with snowballs, complete with "*indifferent* lines":

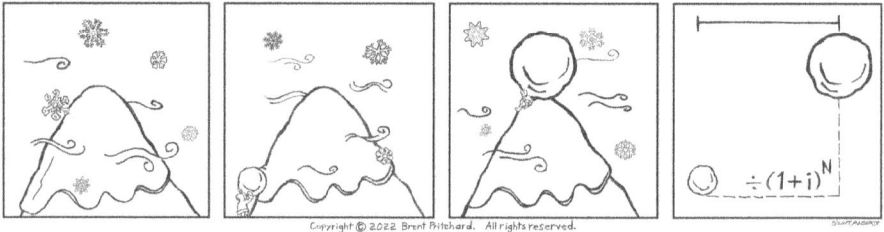

Both illustrations show the Before and After pictures of the snowball. The Before picture of the snowball represents the Present Value, and the After picture of the snowball represents the Future Value.

We can think of compounding as involving a multiplication sign and discounting as involving a division sign, but it's really a matter of which direction you're "time traveling." If you're starting with a Present Value and looking to determine the Future Value, then a multiplication sign is needed and vice versa.

But I want you to see that there's also a discounting perspective in the first comic strip as well as a compounding perspective in the second comic strip. In other words, in each of the last frames, the opposite mathematical operation will get you from one snowball to the other—or from a Future Value to a Present Value and vice versa. In other words, it's not a one-way street.

If compound investment yield is an investor's best friend, time is a close second. In the Time Value of Money nomenclature, the *expected* return *on* investment or true investment yield is denoted with an "i." It's the exponent "N" that makes return *on* return *on* investment or compound investment yield possible. It's because of the *power* of "N" that Albert Einstein reportedly thought that "Compound interest is the most powerful force in the universe." Implicit in this statement is that he thought it was even more powerful than gravity, which ironically helped the smaller snowball roll down the mountain in the comic strip illustration!

The true investment yield or *expected* return *on* investment as denoted by "i" is not to be confused with Return on Investment (ROI). ROI doesn't consider that money has time value. To illustrate this point, let's reconnect with our "investor" from the last chapter who had a bird in the hand and was staring at two in the bush.

The ROI on a successful "bird investment" would have been 100%: two birds for one. But there was no mention of time. Was this ~~investor~~ hunter thinking that delaying consumption—this takes on a new meaning—of the bird in the hand was worth two in the bush…in twelve months? In other words, should 100% have been thought of as a true annual investment yield? Time is an important consideration when it comes to determining the true investment yield. See how ROI ignores time. ROI has application in practice, and there's a time and a place for using this and other metrics to measure and evaluate potential investments. But it's not in the context of the Time Value of Money.

Since ROI doesn't consider that money has time value, it's incompatible with the Mathematics of Finance. ROI is a simple measure of return. When we dive deep into the discussion regarding the true investment yield, you'll discover that the word *simple* or *nominal* is used to describe an investment yield that doesn't consider the effects of compounding.

So if the investment metric ROI isn't "i," then what is? That would be the Internal Rate of Return (IRR or as I like to write it, i(RR)). *The i(RR) is the discount rate that sets the Present Value of the future expected cash flows over the investment period equal to the investment.* Unlike ROI, i(RR) is Time Value of Money approved! The time span of the i(RR) must correspond with the time span *in* between the periods or payments (on the timeline). For example, if the time span *in* between period markers on the timeline represents annual periods, then the i(RR) is a true annual investment yield. A product of the finance industry, of course i(RR) is going to consider time.

Finance professionals use i(RR) in conjunction with other measures to evaluate a potential investment opportunity. The i(RR) measure is typically used ex ante—just a fancy way of saying based on cash flow forecasts—to evaluate potential investment opportunities.

It's not a stretch to say that ROI is more of an ex post—after the fact—measure. A brief history lesson sheds some light on why this is.

We have accountants to thank for ROI. People say we shouldn't dwell on the past. Don't tell that to accountants, who make a living by looking backward. ROI is one of the first equations I remember learning in my undergraduate studies. I wish I could remember if it was introduced in a finance or accounting class. Even though some of the memory is vague, I remember it like it was yesterday when the instructor wrote the ROI equation on the board: "(End − Beg.)/Beg." ROI can also be expressed "(Final Value − Initial Value)/Initial Value." Both equations drive home the point of ROI being ex post with the use of the word *End* or *Final*.

Finance professionals use Discounted Cash Flow (DCF) Analysis to determine the Present Value of an investment opportunity by discounting forecasted cash flows. There's a reason it's not called "Discounted *Income* Analysis." Finance professionals are focused on cash flows whereas accountants tend to focus on income or earnings.

We can think about i(RR) and ROI being as different as finance and accounting professionals. Sure, there's some overlap, but there are some major differences. Don't believe me? I have an accounting class to thank for helping me realize that I wanted to be a finance professional.

Whitt—my wingman in those special servicing asset manager meetings, a former big city attorney by way of Houston, Texas, and the only person I know of who started a day in a corporate conference room only to later that same day, thanks to planes and trains and automobiles, have the runner's chance of a lifetime as he had a chance encounter and night run with the Tarahumara Indians after having learned about their scheduled run as he checked into the hotel in Mexico's Copper Canyon—has a running mantra:

"Relaxation and gratitude." He also likes to say, "There's no such thing as bad weather, just bad wardrobe choices." True and true.

If you've ever participated in a race, then you know that there's a total race time also called the chip time, and your average pace per mile. ROI is the equivalent of the total race time, that is the time from when your foot crossed the start line to when you cross the finish line. Do you see the problem with only providing someone with your total race time? When you sign up for a race you sign up for a distance, not a time. The time comes later. In this example, the only information this other person has is your chip time but no idea what distance you ran. For example, 5K, 10K, etc. Just as chip time is dependent upon distance, more information is needed to help someone make sense of the result.

On the other hand, i(RR) is like the runner's average pace per mile. The average pace per mile provides information that can be interpreted and analyzed, regardless of the distance of the race. If the only race distance in the world was a one-miler, then the total race time and average pace per mile would be the same. But we know that foot races cover a wide variety of distances. Some are super short, such as a kids' fun run, where participants are rewarded with cookies on the other side of the finish line. Race length goes all the way to ultramarathon endurance events covering 100 miles or more. Runners in these endurance events don't usually have to wait until crossing the finish line to find treats, which are typically stocked at aid stations along the route.

Similarly, investment or holding periods are not cookie-cutter. Instead of i(RR), some people like to refer to the Holding Period Return (HPR), which is typically annualized. As it relates to the Time Value of Money, our focus will be on the true investment yield or i(RR), which considers that money has time value, can take any time span, and is the most commonly used measure to evaluate potential investments in practice.

Running has taught me a lot about myself over the years. Here the running example continues to teach us about the relationship between i(RR) and the discount rate. In other words, the difference between the *expected* return *on* investment and the *required* return *on* investment.

During one class, recognizing a teachable moment was at hand, I set my coffee on the floor, backed up to the wall on the other side of the classroom, and with smiling onlookers ran across the front of the class in business attire pretending to be a hurdler. In this short "running event," my one hurdle was a piping hot cup of coffee.

No coffee spilled.

I cleared the hurdle.

That was good because that night class was fueled by coffee! This is why the *required* return *on* investment is often referred to as a hurdle rate. At a track-and-field event, hurdlers are required to clear the hurdles if they are to run a successful race. Not clearing one or more hurdles would lead to disqualification.

Unlike back in the day, today's hurdles can be adjusted by the race director or volunteers to meet the requirements for a certain race. Just as hurdlers encounter hurdles with different heights, so too does an investor have a different *required* return *on* investment or hurdle rate based on perceived risk, including the risk of inflation, and opportunity cost.

Remember that the *expected* return *on* investment or true investment yield as denoted by i(RR) is ex ante, which means that it's based on a projection. Just as hurdlers don't know how a race will turn out until it's over, so too do investors face uncertainty over the total investment period. Hurdlers approach races in a kind of ex ante way that is influenced by a lot of factors including the height of the hurdles.

Now let's think about how this relates to the Time Value of Money variable "i." When you input a value using the "i" key on your financial calculator, it's like setting the height of the hurdle. That's the *required* return *on* investment or the hurdle rate. When you need to run the numbers to solve for "i," that value is the *expected* return *on* investment or true investment yield.

Do you see why I prefer to write it "i(RR)"? It's because at times you can solve for the true investment yield using the "i" key—one of the five primary TVM financial calculator keys—rather than having to use the IRR function of the financial calculator which applies when there are uneven cash flows.

My Grandpa P. was an identical twin. Most people couldn't tell my Grandpa P., Harold, apart from his brother Howard. In fact, at Howard's funeral, the celebrant referred to the deceased as "Harold." That got a few odd looks, one from my Grandpa P. who was sitting in the front row as the casket—that at least one person thought he was in—was getting ready to be lowered into the ground. Not even their girlfriends could tell them apart. As the story goes, on at least one double date at the movie theatre, they did "the old switcheroo."

When I was younger, I used to love going over to my Grandma and Grandpa P.'s house, where we spent most of our time around the kitchen table while my Grandpa P. would tell stories from his childhood. They lived in Pilot Mound, Iowa, which in the 1980s had a population around 200. Not much has changed.

One of my favorite stories he told had to do with changing basketball uniforms at halftime when the better free throw shooter was in foul trouble. It seemed like every story he told involved his twin brother, who lived across town (more like a nine iron away).

My Grandpa P. lived within a couple of miles of his twin brother his whole life—sometimes within a couple of blocks. He and his twin brother used to travel the state of Iowa doing an original tap-dancing routine that involved their legs being tied together with a chain.

Would you be surprised if I told you that i(RR) has a closely related investment metric? I'm referring to Net Present Value (NPV). You can think of ROI as the third wheel as far as investment measures are concerned. Like anyone who found themselves in a room with my Grandpa P. and his identical twin, who were best friends, ROI is great company, but it's not in the same league as i(RR) and NPV.

Just as hurdlers can't run a race without hurdles, you can't analyze i(RR) or NPV without a hurdle rate. In other words, the *required* return *on* investment. NPV need not be a confusing concept. It's simply the Present Value of the future *expected* cash flows over the investment period *net of* the investment. *The i(RR) is the discount rate that makes the NPV of an investment equal to $0.*

Before we go too far, pay special attention to "i(RR)" and "discount rate" in this definition. The word *is* tells us that i(RR) and the discount rate are one and the same when—*when* is another key word—you want to know what Present Value of the future *expected* cash flows when added to the initial investment produces an NPV that is equal to $0.

Here's where we need to pause and take a breather, because *words matter*. It's because of this definition that when calculating

NPV we intentionally need to think about comparing i(RR) to the hurdle rate or *required* return *on* investment and not think so much about the discount rate. Why not the discount rate, which is expressly stated in the above definition? Because one of the objectives of this book is to clear up issues with terminology as it relates to the Time Value of Money.

The discount rate is the hurdle rate or *required* return *on* investment. Can it be exactly equal to the i(RR) or the true investment yield or *expected* return *on* investment? Sure it can, but that's a unicorn.

Don't lose sight of the purpose of the above definition, which is to explain how an investment can have an NPV equal to $0: when i(RR) or the true investment yield and the discount rate or hurdle rate are one and the same. When an investment is *expected* to produce a true investment yield that is greater than the hurdle rate, *then i(RR) is not equal to the discount rate*, and the project is said to have a positive NPV.

Think about it. That's because the *required* return *on* investment is lower than the *expected* return *on* investment: the investment is expected to clear the hurdle. When an investment is *expected* to produce a true investment yield that is less than the hurdle rate, *then i(RR) is not equal to the discount rate*, and the project is said to have a negative NPV.

The *required* return *on* investment is not exactly another way of referring to the WACC (Weighted Average Cost of Capital). What I refer to as the hurdle rate implicitly considers not only how capital is financed but also the *required* return *on* investment for the level of perceived risk and opportunity cost. These are the considerations as it relates to the *required* return *on* investment. This explains why an investment opportunity with an NPV as low as $0 might be considered accretive to value. Don't believe me? Try telling a (for-profit) lender their math that includes discounting future expected cash flows at the coupon rate is wrong. Math that would result in an NPV of $0. To say that a $0 NPV doesn't add value is to discredit the entire fixed-income sector. In the real estate industry, there's an adage that, "All liens are encumbrances, but not all encumbrances are liens." Well, in finance, "Every WACC is a hurdle rate, but not every hurdle rate is a WACC." But as described above, there is a WACC component to every hurdle rate.

I've read and listened to other people who say that you should pursue an investment opportunity with a positive NPV and reject an investment opportunity with a negative NPV. But this leaves out the investment opportunity with an NPV equal to $0. We can look to baseball for guidance: a tie goes to the runner. As it relates to an investment opportunity, it's really a point of there not being much difference between $0 and $1 of positive NPV. If we wanted to get really specific, it actually comes down to the difference between $0 and $0.01. NPV is a statistic that finance professionals can use to answer the question, "Does it fly?" For the finance professional, the answer to that question is "yes" or "no" just like the umpire at first base will call the runner safe or out. There's no "maybe." That and the i(RR) definition are why I think that an NPV of $0 should be viewed as a positive. When I was a loan officer, countless times I heard colleagues say that an investment wasn't going to go off the tracks because of one additional dollar lent or invested. While an additional dollar invested would change the math in the above example from $0 to $1 of negative NPV, I hope you can see that there are lots of moving parts. That said, we need NPV and similar measures to guide decision-making, which give finance professionals the ability to draw a line in the sand.

Actually, the four forces of flight relate to the topic of the Time Value of Money. "Does it fly?" in the context of flight comes down to drag, thrust, weight, and lift. Drag refers to the force that pulls things backward. Thrust refers to the force that pushes things forward. Weight refers to the force that pulls things down. Lift refers to the force that pushes things up. In the context of the Time Value of Money, we can think about discounting as drag, compounding as thrust, the hurdle rate as weight, and NPV as lift. While there are four forces of flight, lift is the outward sign of flight. In the context of the Time Value of Money, a positive NPV is the signal that an investment opportunity will "fly." A pilot's preflight check can be likened to a finance professional needing to double-check his or her math.

The risk profile of the investment, which includes a projected future cash flow stream, is picked up in the discount rate or hurdle rate.

Risk is not always easily quantified. For a certain i(RR) or true investment yield, the *expected* return *on* investment, you have to know the discount rate or hurdle rate, the *required* return *on* investment, to know whether NPV is positive, negative, or equal to $0. The i(RR) is the discount(ing) rate, "i," that gives you a big fat goose egg for NPV. That is, an NPV that is equal to $0. First comes the cash flow projection, next the estimation of i(RR), then the hurdle rate, and last the estimation of NPV. NPV tells you whether a deal will potentially fly. Peanut butter goes with jelly. Harold went with Howard. And i(RR) and NPV are close relatives.

A great teacher and person I look up to once gave me some wisdom about presenting that I later learned is credited to Aristotle. He said, "Tell them what you are going to tell them, tell them, and then tell them what you told them." Man, was he right. Since i(RR) has been defined and the definition restated, in the spirit of this great wisdom, here's take three. While it's mostly a repeat, a few words have been changed, and the five primary TVM financial calculator keys, which are also the variables in the building block Time Value of Money equations, have been added to get you thinking differently about the concept. *The i(RR) is the discount(ing) rate that sets the future expected cash flows (PMT or FV) over the investment period (N) equal to the investment (PV).*

I've never seen i(RR) defined in terms of these inputs or variables, and this is just one of many examples of the new take on the Time Value of Money you'll find in this book.

We'll be working with the financial calculator and building block Time Value of Money equations in the next section.

When you start working with the Mathematics of Finance in the How section of this book, you'll learn that you could find the PV for a series of uneven cash flows using just the five primary TVM finance calculator keys and an iterative process. While it would take longer, such a "scenic route" can be avoided by using the IRR function: since there would be no investment to *net* out, you'd really be calculating a PV when you press the NPV key. You really need a financial calculator or spreadsheet software to estimate i(RR). Fortunately, your financial calculator can perform in a split second all the mathematical iterations necessary to determine the *one* discount rate that sets the Present Value of the future *expected* cash flows over the investment period equal to the investment.

No investment metric is perfect. Half the battle is knowing a metric's limitations or shortfalls and then proceeding with caution. The same can be said for "quick math." We know that we can't add or subtract or compare money *in different* points in time: *TVM*

Rule #1. Yet one *quick* way to tell if an investment is expected to produce a positive true investment yield is by eyeballing the future expected cash flows to see if the undiscounted sum is greater than the investment.

This isn't the kind of analysis that you'll want to use to reach a decision about an investment opportunity. First and foremost, it's a violation of *TVM Rule #1.* Also, the "Eyeball Analysis" doesn't tell you the i(RR). As a result, you're not able to determine how the true investment yield compares to the hurdle rate, so NPV is not able to be estimated.

Don't confuse a positive true investment yield with a positive NPV. There's no relationship between a positive true investment yield and positive NPV: as discussed, it's a matter of how the true investment yield compares to the hurdle rate. There's nothing wrong with some "quick math" so long as you know not to hang your hat on such analysis. There's a reason why it's called IRR Analysis and NPV Analysis, and why eyeballing numbers will *never* be formally referred to as "Eyeball Analysis." Since IRR Analysis and NPV Analysis are closely related, it goes without saying that both have the Time Value of Money stamp of approval. Just like there's a time and place for everything, so too is there an appropriate situation for the ROI metric and "quick math."

The two most popular return metrics are ROI and i(RR). Think of them as the two most popular in school—they are in business colleges. Have you had the experience of hearing someone's name and thinking to yourself, *With a name like that, so-and-so is destined for stardom*? That's the way I first felt about ROI. The one thing that ROI has going for it is a great name that includes the word *on*. Three words, none wasted for this investment metric. Investors invest for "return *on* investment."

Aside from the cool name, we've already discussed how ROI doesn't consider time. I'm sure you know someone who has no regard for time. It's annoying. You want dependability and not to be left hanging.

On the other hand, if i(RR) were a person, it would be the one you would want to bring home to meet the parents. Nobody living today is perfect. The same is true for measures to evaluate a potential investment. The shortcomings—yes, you read the plural correctly—for i(RR) will be discussed in the next chapter. But I still love "i(RR)," and so should you. Don't let the name fool you. ROI has nothing to do with return *on* investment as we think about true investment yield or "i" in the context of the Time Value of Money.

It's worth noting that an investor's position might lead to different interpretations as it relates to the true investment yield. For example, a lender's *expected* return *on* investment is a borrower's effective cost of capital. Regardless of one's position, the one-size-fits-all variable is "i."

Bob Feller was playing baseball in Van Meter, Iowa, when my Grandpa P. was a young man. For those of you who don't know, Bob Feller was known as "The Heater from Van Meter." He pitched for the Cleveland Indians and has been credited with throwing a baseball 107.9 miles per hour. That's fast! In baseball, they teach you to keep your eye on the ball. In the context of the Time Value of Money, you need to keep your eye on "i."

There's a difference between the true investment yield, which is represented by "i," and the simple investment yield, which doesn't consider the effects of compounding. One is Time Value of Money friendly. The other isn't. Remind you of something else we've talked about in this chapter?

Let's revisit the example that ended the last chapter and build on the storyline. Now, we're going to assume a true annual investment yield of 10% with monthly compounding. In other words, monthly compounding is what produced the true annual investment yield of 10%. The simple annual investment yield without considering the effects of (monthly) compounding is 9.5690%.

In the How section of this book, you'll learn how to calculate both the true investment yield and the simple investment yield and how with one, you can solve for the other.

That said, you *never* want to use the simple investment yield when analyzing a Time Value of Money question. The true investment yield is where it's at and where your focus will be. If I had told you in the example that closed the last chapter to assume a simple monthly investment yield of 0.7974%, it would have been incorrect to simply multiply by 12 and determine the Future Value at the end of the investment period that covered eighty-five years.

Why?

Because you'd be working with a simple annual investment yield of 9.5690%. Remember what Albert Einstein reportedly said about the power of compound [investment yield]. You'd need to raise 1.007974 to the power of 12 to calculate the true annual investment yield. Why twelve? Because we're "telling time" on the timeline with annual periods and we know from *TVM Rule #2* that it's a Time Value of Money no-no to fail to correspond the time span *in* between periods or payments (on the timeline) and the time span of the true investment yield. Since 0.7974% is the simple monthly investment yield and there are twelve compounding periods within the time span *in* between periods (on the timeline), you would need to raise 1.007974 to the power of 12 to calculate the true annual investment yield. Using the simple annual investment yield of 9.5690% would violate *TVM Rule #2* because it's not a *true* investment yield.

Don't get me wrong. The amount of $22,289,623 is *still* a lot of money. But it would have been the wrong number because the Future Value was estimated using the simple annual investment yield not the true annual investment yield that considers the effects of compounding as represented by "i."

As this chapter comes to an end, here's one of my favorite running stories that you probably haven't heard.

One day, I found myself looking over Whitt's shoulder in his office as we both stared with jaws on the floor at the course map for his upcoming ultramarathon. He was preparing to run a stage race that covered approximately 150 miles over six days. Little did he know that the story that he would bring home was even more epic.

The hot stretch from the first two days extended into Stage 3, which covered approximately nine miles. With three stages in the books, day four was a scheduled rest day to help runners recover for Stage 4 and Stage 5, which would cover fifty-three miles and twenty miles, respectively.

Around the finish line for Stage 3, he noticed people jumping off a high bridge into the cool Colorado River water below.

What he later came to realize was that these were younger race volunteers. They hadn't run any of the more than seventy miles that made up the first three stages. I guess sometimes in life, people really do need to answer the question, "If everyone else jumped off a bridge, would you?"

Unfortunately, Whitt didn't enter the water as gracefully as the other jumpers. Right before entry, his torso angled just enough to liken the impact to that of hitting a concrete wall.

When he was back in the office, he showed me a picture of a bruise that extended from his armpit to below his hip. He ended up breaking two ribs that day. A couple days after the jump, the race doctor said that he would not have let him run and would have taken him to the hospital to check for a ruptured spleen. But there was no reason for the MRI anymore, he said, because Whitt survived.

Whitt's ribcage had begun to contract overnight. In order to breathe, Whitt had to expand his chest against the tightening scar tissue. But gradually, by taking on a little more pain, his chest opened up and he could breathe better.

In indescribable pain, he went on to finish Stage 4 and Stage 5. Oh, and I should add that the routes the last two race days included crazy elevation changes. Needless to say, he was one of the slowest runners on the course those last two days. Ultra-endurance events like this one have what they call sweepers—people on bikes—who ensure that back-of-the-pack runners don't get left on the course. When he got back to the office and shared the story with me, he got very emotional as he relived the event. The course sweeper had told him something to the effect of, "I've been around all kinds of world-class athletes, and I've never seen anything like this before." Those two days, that sweeper had a front row saddle seat to two of the most epic and unreported endurance "events" to ever have taken place.

While Whitt finished each of the stages, he technically did not finish Stage 5 under the cutoff time, which earned him what in the ultra community is referred to as a DNF (did not finish). At the celebration event that was put on for runners at the conclusion of Stage 5, fellow runners rallied around Whitt to recognize this incredible feat of endurance.

Over the years, our family has tracked many of Whitt's adventures from afar. One particular day, we were at the dinner table as Whitt—miles away—was preparing to run over desert dunes at night with little more than a headlamp and a few other runners who shared the same passion. Just as they did at the dinner table that night, still to this day, our daughters can finish the sentence that starts with, "If Gary can run fifty-three miles with broken ribs," with "you can do anything you put your mind to." If that doesn't inspire you in some way, I don't know what will.

The new take on the Time Value of Money introduced in this section will position you for success as you take a deep dive into practical application of the Mathematics of Finance in the How section. Well rested and comfortable, if you spend the same amount of time studying as Whitt did running in pain (1,596 minutes to be exact), you can learn the Time Value of Money like the back of your hand. Sound like too much work? Want to know what Whitt would say? "Suck it up whiny babies!"

Chapter 3: Boomerangs

"No matter how thin you slice it, there will always
be two sides."
—Baruch Spinoza

One day, Whitt and I were having a conference call. His office was both a place for work and a place to gather before heading down to the locker room and ultimately out for our routine midday runs. That particular day, it served both those purposes.

His corner office was different from most. As unique as its occupant, the wall was adorned with race medals, and anywhere there wasn't a stack of paper on his desk, there were many objects from a life well lived and traveled—including teapots for the afternoon tea ritual, tea canisters from his most recent trip to New York City, rubber stamps, fountain pens, and the latest books he was reading. By the windows that would bring in a chill when the winds started swirling during the winter months, a fake frog kept warm with a knitted sweater.

He was a true Renaissance man if ever there was one.

We needed to talk with a borrower who was complaining about our loan documents. The call was short. Probably would have been even shorter if the person on the other end had the same view I had of this man's workspace, which was a kind of "Exhibit A" to the audible and faceless voice on the phone that would have provided anyone who was still undecided with a further glimpse into his complexity and smarts.

As Whitt was placing the phone's handset on the receiver, I knew something special was coming. I never saw this guy lose in any negotiation. As he slowly leaned back in his chair and twisted around with feet off the ground for the debriefing, I prepared for the lesson.

He wasn't going to listen to some borrower complain about the fact that we were preparing to wire multiple millions of dollars to their bank account in exchange for a lien on real property. As he grabbed a stack of papers from his desk, shaking them in his hand, he said, "You better believe that this heap of paper is worth as much or more than the money that we are preparing to lend them."

This is why that conversation was so short. Whitt told it like it is: "Don't be surprised that this document includes language that is very lender friendly." I'm not telling you anything that should surprise a finance professional. To ignore this point is to ignore the fiduciary responsibility, which is the furthest thing from professional and will get a person shown the door.

Having cut my teeth in underwriting and credit analysis, I'm well aware that "It's easy to lend, but hard to get paid back." That's why it's been said that "Lenders wear belts and suspenders." If you don't like the visual of what those accessories are trying to keep from exposing, "Surprises are for birthdays" gets the same point across.

For reasons you'll soon understand, our tour of the continued discussion regarding i(RR) will be guided by topics related to the commercial real estate (CRE) finance industry. In addition to the way it provides a great backdrop for this discussion about i(RR), it's important to recognize that there was a day when I didn't know one thing about commercial real estate finance. The hard skills required of real estate finance professionals to provide investors with good risk-adjusted returns and a real asset can be acquired.

Before too long, words will inevitably fall short and be replaced with numbers to effectively communicate thoughts about this investment metric, so it's a good thing this is the last chapter of the part of the book that is more focused on words than numbers.

Midday runs can be a great way to burn off stress, find more productivity, and flat-out have fun. Whitt was the organizer of the midday running club that was full of personalities and was credited with getting lots of people—including me—into running. Around the time he was getting ready to retire, our company was preparing for a move to another location across town.

We were spoiled because over lunch we had access to some great running: upward of twenty running routes that covered anywhere from two to eight miles. They were runs that had affectionately been named for something that happened on the route: Taming Bestick's Dog (yes that one involved a dog nipping someone on the leg); Myer's Bain, because the namesake never liked the hill that was more than a half a mile long at the out-and-back point; Medium Miguel, named after a mysterious and recently arrived Spaniard—Whitt gathered this much from the conversation that was taking place well above a conversational pace—who came running out of nowhere and tried to give Whitt a run for his money, which didn't work; Spider Woman, named after the sunbather who was pleading for a superhero to save the day and get her mail that was sharing space with a spider just moments after Marty Morrison and all the other guys in the group started to run a little taller and higher on their feet with a running form that would impress Olympic coaches as the one woman in the running group, Dawn Leviska, shook her head; The Ostrich Run, named after the birds which had a home along a gravel road that was north of town and which Leviska didn't see while she was running past them. Who misses ostriches?

As the moving date neared, we made sure to do as many of these runs as possible. I remember being taken by emotion during a couple of our farewell runs—one that was more than a run and involved bushwhacking and unexpected wading through a shallow stream—as I recalled all the memories, people who had come and gone, and time that passed too fast.

Over almost two decades, I had learned about running from running with Whitt and others and rekindled my love for the great outdoors. There were countless times when Whitt, Morrison, Leviska, and I were stopped dead in our tracks because we were laughing so hard. I couldn't have picked better people with whom to share some fresh air, the road, and countless miles and hours.

One day Morrison and I were running the numbers. A conservative estimate is that we probably logged at least 17,000 miles together over the years from 2001 to 2018. On one run during this span of time, I told the group about one of my recent purchases: a boomerang. To say that I provided the material for that run's comic relief is an understatement.

Sometimes knowledge of the wrong way is what leads to the right path. That's as true for commercial mortgage loan (CML) underwriting and credit (risk) analysis as it is for throwing a boomerang.

Within moments of unboxing my new toy—or was it a tool—I realized that there's great skill involved in getting a boomerang to return. My experience with boomerangs started and ended on the same day. I was just glad our daughters and dog didn't take chase. That's right: the boomerang left my hand never to return. It doesn't take being a boomerang extraordinaire to realize that there's both an art and science to throwing those curved objects.

The same is true with many skills, including projecting cash flows, estimating value, structuring real estate deals and the like. Clearly my technique wasn't where it needed to be. Had I stuck with it, I would have looked for guidance from those who had mastered the craft and worked to refine my technique through perfect practice. Some refer to this kind of practice as mirroring. Even as an inexperienced boomeranger, I can tell you that elbow action plays a big part in determining whether you experience the return of the boomerang.

In writing this book, I studied up on the history of the boomerang. What I found out was not only interesting but fitting. Get this! Did you know that back in the day boomerangs were used to hunt birds? From what I've read, apparently, boomerangs were thrown just above tall grass to imitate prey birds so that people could catch them by other means. To complete the picture, visualize Aborigines with nets in hand hurdling over objects on the landscape in fast pursuit of birds.

With this complete picture of birds, hurdlers, and boomerangs in your mind's eye, it's pretty easy to differentiate between what the Aborigines might have referred to as return *of* investment and return *on* investment. The latter represents the hunted bird in the hand. The former represents the boomerang. A run never got named after my boomerang story, but after more time, something would.

As it relates to a CML, a good investment or loan is generally defined as one that stays current or performing. In other words, a loan that doesn't default and one for which the credit metrics remain "above water" even in trying times or when conditions have deteriorated compared to when the loan was made.

The primary credit metrics in the commercial real estate finance industry are the Debt Service Coverage Ratio (DSCR), Loan-to-Value (LTV) ratio, Debt Yield (DY), and the Loan Constant (LC). The DSCR compares a property's annual Net Operating Income (NOI) to the annualized required monthly debt service payments and is the primary measure of *cash flow or capacity*: the 1st "C" of Credit. The LTV ratio compares the outstanding principal balance of the loan to the value of the property. Since real estate *collateral* is a secondary form of repayment and because the LTV fails to consider the direct or implied Cap Rate (CR) used to estimate value for the underlying collateral, the better measure of the 2nd "C" of Credit is the DY.

Here is something that is not openly acknowledged or talked about that often: LTV is overrated. The LTV metric doesn't consider the CR. Unfortunately, we can't combine these two acronyms to form a word that will help you remember to avoid this pitfall without "buying" a few vowels. By adding "Y" and "E" and "O" to the mix, we can spell "covertly," which speaks to how deceptive LTV has been for so many people over the years. Let's not repeat this history. Be a yeoman and remember that DY is a better metric from the lender's perspective, since it considers the amount of mortgage capital and thus is the approximate cap rate that would lead to the return *of* investment.

The CR is a market fundamental statistic related to sales transactions that is expressed in decimal form and which, when divided into pro forma NOI, converts income to a direct capitalization valuation. This assumes a constant delta between the discount rate and the growth rate of NOI. I informally refer to this as the "quick math" method of estimating value by "capping" NOI, but formally it's known as the Direct Capitalization Method.

When the property value is estimated using the Discounted Cash Flow (DCF) Method, the implied CR is found by dividing Year 1 NOI from the cash flow projection by the DCF value estimate.

The real moment of truth for a CML comes on the maturity date. Maturity risk is measured primarily by the going-in DY or exit DY. The going-in DY is measured by dividing underwritten NOI by the outstanding principal balance of the loan. The exit DY is calculated by dividing NOI one year beyond the maturity date by the balloon loan amount.

This is why people in the industry talk so much about exit strategy. Prior to a loan being made, lenders want to know the borrower's plan for paying them back, which could take the form of a refinance or sale.

Over the term of the loan, there are mini moments of truth each month marked by the payment due date. Term risk is measured primarily by DSCR. Some loan documents require interest-only payments, but more often than not, the required monthly loan payment includes a principal (P) component and an interest (I) component: this is where we get the term "P&I" payment.

The former refers to a scheduled partial return *of* investment based on a certain amortization schedule. The latter refers to return *on* investment as determined mostly, if not exclusively, by the interest or contract rate.

Finance professionals use the Mathematics of Finance to calculate the required debt service payments, which are probably made in monthly installments and based on an amortization schedule, as well as the balloon amount, if applicable. Amortization is synonymous with pay down, so the amortization schedule shows how a CML is expected to pay down over the life of the loan. Some loan documents require full amortization over the loan term, while others require partial amortization or no amortization in the case of interest-only payments. The LC expresses the annualized debt service payment in terms of the percentage of the outstanding principal balance of the loan.

When a loan doesn't fully amortize over its term, a balloon amount is due at the maturity date. Even though loan documents reference an "interest rate," the lender investor thinks in terms of the true investment yield. Regardless of whether an investor is a debt investor or an equity investor, the true investment yield will be influenced not only by return *on* investment but also return *of* investment.

As a real estate finance professional, I can tell you that while no investor wants to earn less than what was expected or bargained for in terms of return *on* investment, it's a bad day when principal is believed to be at risk or is lost. Here I'm referring to the return *of* investment. It's one thing not to get all or some of the expected return *on* investment, but to not get a full return *of* investment, that's bad. Like "What were you thinking?" bad. Like "looking up to see a security guard accompanying an HR (Human Resources) representative carrying an empty box for you" bad.

The DY is the "Cap Rate on the Debt" since it considers how a property is financed and is the CR that is expected to provide a lender with return *of* investment.

Let's revisit a quote from earlier: "It's easy to lend, but hard to get paid back." To recognize the full spectrum of institutional investments and take a holistic perspective, it would be better worded, "It's easy to invest, but hard to get the expected return *on* investment."

Considering the two quotes together, we can see that return *on* investment is influenced in part by return *of* investment—the latter refers to an investment returning to the investor's hand from which it left. This is why I refer to an investment opportunity as the *Boomerang of Finance*. Whether a boomerang is going to fly and return to the thrower's hand depends in large part on elbow action.

So, whether an investment opportunity is going to fly in the eyes of an investor has to do with the *expected* return *on* investment or the i(RR) that's found in the elbow of the "*indifferent* lines" under the timeline, where the perpendicular "*indifferent* line" meets up with the parallel "*indifferent* line" and how that compares to the *required* return *on* investment.

This isn't the first time, and it won't be the last time that we discuss "*indifferent* lines." But it is the first time we've drawn attention to the "elbow" of the "*indifferent* lines." The use of the notation i(RR) recognizes that the discount rate in the elbow of the "*indifferent* lines" will be an *expected* return *on* investment or *required* return *on* investment. Similarly, the notation i(RR) recognizes that the key on your financial calculator for the true investment yield can be viewed as the *expected* return *on* investment when solving for i(RR) for a series of even cash flows, or it's the *required* return *on* investment when the (d)i(scount rate) is known and the value keyed into the financial calculator.

In the below illustration, you're solving for the *expected* return *on* investment or i(RR) for a series of cash flows for either an equity or debt investment:

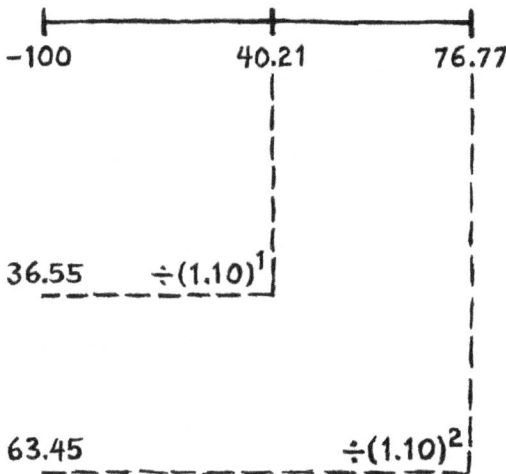

Remember that *i(RR) is the (d)i(scount rate) that sets the Present Value of the future expected cash flows over the investment period equal to the investment.* In other words, i(RR) *is the (d)i(scount rate) that makes the NPV of an investment equal to $0.* It's no surprise that the sum of each Present Value in the above illustration *net of* the investment is equal to $0.

Most loans require regular debt service payments. In such situations, i(RR) is bargained for and can be interpreted as both the *required* and *expected* return *on* investment. The best we can say is that it's *"expected"* because sometimes a borrower doesn't keep the *promises* that are described in the Promissory Note. When considered with the initial loan balance (PV), the amortization schedule (N), and the future loan balance (FV), you can calculate the required monthly debt service payment (PMT): FV is inputted as "$0", which recognizes that the loan would fully pay down over a loan term that was equal to the amortization schedule.

For this example, let's assume a three-year amortization schedule. If the above illustration considered a two-year loan term, a balloon amount would be due at maturity since it would take three annual debt service payments to fully amortize the loan, and the loan documents would only require two debt service payments.

I should also note that most loans require monthly debt service payments. Here we're assuming annual debt service payments to keep things simple and the timeline consistent with most of the timelines you'll likely be working with. Also, in practice, i(RR) may be stated in annual terms.

Below, you'll find a three-year amortization schedule that assumes an annual fixed P&I payment and a true annual investment yield of 10% with simple accrued interest:

N	Beginning Balance	Interest	Principal Paydown	Ending Balance
1	$100	$10	$30.21	$69.79
2	$69.79	$6.98	$33.23	$36.56
3	$36.56	$3.65	$36.56	$0

In the amortization schedule, notice how the portion of the fixed P&I payment that goes to interest reduces over time to the extent of the increased partial principal pay down or repayment. Since this is a fixed payment, something has to give. The interest component of the P&I payment reduces over time as the principal balance of the loan pays down or amortizes, which influences the amount of the simple accrued interest between the two payment dates.

It's worth noting the relationship between the amortization schedule and the timeline. For example, the 1 for "N" in the amortization schedule relates to the first period on the timeline. In other words, the time span *in* between period marker 0 and period marker 1. Since period marker 1 represents both the end of the first period and the beginning of the second period, this explains why the ending balance for the first period matches the beginning balance for the second period in the amortization schedule and so on and so forth.

To get a different perspective, the below timeline incorporates simple accrued interest, most of the information from the amortization schedule, and how cash is expected to flow:

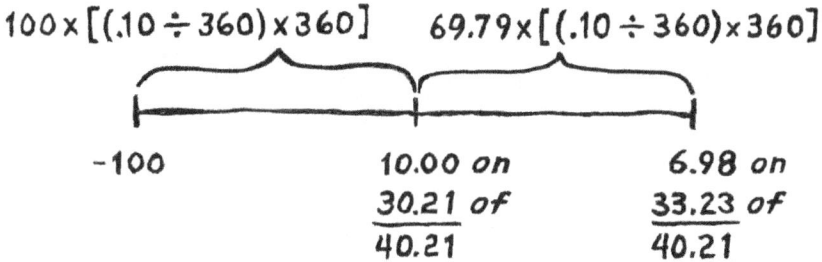

$$100 \times [(.10 \div 360) \times 360] \qquad 69.79 \times [(.10 \div 360) \times 360]$$

-100	10.00 *on*	6.98 *on*
	30.21 *of*	33.23 *of*
	40.21	40.21

You can find the principal pay down component of the P&I payment by subtracting the simple accrued interest from the P&I payment.

My experience is that some students struggle to wrap their heads around the difference between return *on* investment and return *of* investment as it relates to the i(RR) discussion.

If you find yourself in this camp, it might be helpful to stay with the debt example since loans that require regular debt service payments can drive home this point. Unlike debt assets, an equity investment isn't subject to an amortization schedule. But here's the kicker. The math is the same regardless of whether you're analyzing an equity or debt investment. In other words, it's as if there's an amortization schedule even if there isn't.

Do you see any similarities between the last two illustrations and the first one presented in this chapter? The summation of the *on* and *of* cash flows and the ending balance at the end of the second period line up exactly with the cash flows from the first illustration that related to an equity or debt investment. The most recent example relates to a debt investment and includes more information, including simple accrued interest which is the return *on* investment. This example doesn't consider additional financing charges such as a loan origination fee.

As a coin has two sides, there are only two types of cash flows regardless of the type of asset. There's return *on* investment and then there's return *of* investment. The i(RR) math considers both return *on* investment and return *of* investment—the two sides to the i(RR) coin.

You are going to work alongside some interesting people in your career. Another one of those interesting people for me was Dennis Bakley. This guy was as cool as he was smart. He was a great leader and public speaker. I learned a lot from Dennis. He was one of the top dogs in the company, but he was also a model to many. One, this guy never took himself too seriously. Two, he was a rare breed in that he had more inspiration in his pinky than most people have in their whole being. He loved to hunt in his free time, and I mean hunt. This guy traveled all over the world in search of his next adventure. I remember hearing that one trip involved Russia and a satellite phone. This guy didn't mess around.

One day, I found myself in the locker room for a late-in-the-day run. Dennis was also getting ready for a workout. He was always laughing and poking fun at things, and that particular day, he shared some wisdom with me in his signature way. We were still on the clock, and if memory serves me correctly, I think it was a Friday. The Investments Committee had its regularly scheduled meeting every Monday at 1 PM, and packages were distributed on Thursdays or Fridays, which gave committee members—of which Dennis was one—time to review the proposals. The packages must have been distributed, because somehow our conversation got to underwriting.

Dennis said something I've never forgotten. He said something along the lines of, "A loan officer's [insert the word "investor's" if you'd like] underwriting skills lie in his or her ability to make good investments, and if one makes too many bad investments, they won't be around that long." In other words, one can tell how good a loan officer is by the number of originated loans that go bad. He had to have been thinking about a specific deal, and I was happy I didn't have a deal in committee the following Monday!

All finance professionals should consider themselves managers of risk. Underwriting is about getting comfortably uncomfortable. I liken this to a tempo run where a runner is pushing the pace yet holding back just a little something. In finance, we operate with incomplete information. It's about getting enough information to feel comfortable with making a decision or recommendation. Risk by its definition is uncertainty. It's not called the "no risk–return tradeoff"; rather, the risk–return tradeoff.

One of the best ways of managing risk in the global commercial mortgage loan industry can be traced back to the small town of Bernard, Iowa. Everyone there has a nickname that is given to them by hometowners. Squeak, as I would later learn was his nickname, in the spirit of the rich tradition of nicknaming that is a Bernard thing would give a name to one of the best ways to mitigate risk in a commercial real estate transaction. He coined the term "pre-amortization," which simply means lending fewer dollars.

At the most basic level, determining whether an investment has lived up to the expectation or hype is pretty simple. Has the recipient of capital — the borrower in the case of a CML — done what they said they were going to do? In the context of CML assets, that involves paying the debt back as agreed and compliance with the loan documents. Return *on* investment and return *of* investment.

Unfortunately, sometimes things don't go as planned, and circumstances throw a wrench into the process. Wrenches don't fly and return like boomerangs! I'm referring to times when cash flow projections for an investment need to be modified because some or all *of* the investment isn't *expected* to be returned as planned. This point is illustrated with the loan example. If some or all of the required debt service — annual and balloon — payments end up being less than what's projected, that is going to impact the investment's return *on* investment. For example, if the lender only expects to collect $32.90 of the $36.56 balloon payment, the forecasted i(RR) would be revised to 7.9413% from 10.00% as a result of subperformance. The interest rate might be 10.00%, but that's only consistent with a measure of the true annual investment yield when there are no additional financing costs and there are no surprises.

Investment yield is what matters. Forget about the interest rate already.

In this example, the expectation that the borrower might fail to perform would have implications for the overall investment yield…and the underwriter's track record! This example shows you the relationship between the return *of* investment and return *on* investment:

$$
\begin{array}{lll}
\vdash\!\!\!-\!\!\!-\!\!\!-\!\!\!-\!\!\!-\!\!\!+\!\!\!-\!\!\!-\!\!\!-\!\!\!-\!\!\!-\!\!\!-\!\!\!\dashv \\
-100 & 40.21 & 40.21 \\
& & +\,32.90 \\
& & \overline{73.11} \\
& & \\
37.25 \div (1.079413)^1 & & \\
& & \\
62.75 \qquad\qquad \div (1.079413)^2 &
\end{array}
$$

You've seen already how the *expected* return *on* investment will impact the split between return *on* investment and return *of* investment over the investment period. If this cash flow projection were for an equity investment, each payment is now going to have a different split between the return *on* investment and return *of* investment based on the *expected* i(RR) of 7.9413%. In other words, if this timeline were associated with an equity investment, the as if debt "amortization schedule" would no longer apply. Remember, it's only an as if debt "amortization schedule" for an equity investment since a real amortization schedule doesn't exist. Numbers that move around would impact i(RR), and as a result, the split between return *on* investment and return *of* investment. But for a debt investment there's a difference between the two sides to the i(RR) coin and the extent of actual *coins* or money the borrower is required to remit with each debt service payment, which depends on the actual amortization schedule. It's like the difference between theory and practice.

With this example, you see how the *anticipated* return *of* investment influences the *expected* return *on* investment or i(RR). If this risk were anticipated prior to the investment being made, the underwriter would have considered whether such a downside return *on* investment of 7.9413% would fly. In practice, this is referred to as alternative or stressed analysis based on certain *conditions*: the 3rd "C" of Credit.

The best way I've found to do a conditions analysis is not to pile on more assumptions on top of assumptions; instead, look at what you have and how bad it could get before the loan might be at risk of default or return *on* investment or return *of* investment being compromised.

In other words, if market analysis suggests a CR of 5.50% and the going-in DY is 9.13%, then the property could absorb a 363 basis points (bps) increase in the CR before the first loan dollar is at risk, etc. (A basis point is equal to one one-hundredth of a percent.) All else equal, that's a better risk profile than a loan that could only absorb a 75 bps increase in the CR.

Similarly, you could look at how much of the property's NOI at maturity is expected to be available for debt service upon refinance given a certain DSCR. This is where the LC comes in. If you were to assume that upon refinance the new lender would require a minimum DSCR of 1.35x, then based on an exit DY of 12.18%, pro forma NOI at maturity would be able to support a 9.02% LC: 12.18% ÷ 1.35.

Again, part of underwriting is realizing when to make assumptions. Avoid pulling numbers out of thin air. Assuming that a refinance lender is going to be willing to write new loans sized to a DSCR of 1.35x is a good assumption if it can be supported based on current market conditions. The thinking is, this is reasonable and since the market is sizing deals to a DSCR of 1.35x today, why wouldn't such terms be available five years from now?

Trying to guess where the conditions in the capital markets will be five years from now is pointless. About as pointless as jumping on a trampoline and trying to mark how high you jump with only the air you reach out to "grab" with your hands. The LC tells you what you need to know in terms of what the property can be expected to support as it relates to a P&I or interest-only payment upon refinance. For example, if the existing interest rate is 4.25%, based on the above numbers, the refinance interest rate could increase by 477 bps and still be able to support interest-only debt service payments to a DSCR of 1.35x: 9.02% – 4.25%.

As with any statistic, you use credit metrics to make sense of how an investment opportunity compares to others with similar perceived risk. In the real estate finance industry, people talk about taking a deep dive into the numbers. A diving platform is a better visual than the aforementioned trampoline for how to use such credit metrics. When you know the height of the diving platform, you know the distance to the water. And more importantly, at what level the deal is "underwater" as they say in this industry. A loan that is underwater is a loan for which the market value of the collateral is less than that of the outstanding principal balance of the loan. In the context of real estate finance, "water" isn't only symbolic of the outstanding principal balance of the loan, but is also a larger metaphor of whether you're on the right side of whatever number is of interest. It's this kind of analysis that separates loan originations from one CML platform to the next. You can see that the DY and LC tell you a lot about the risk profile of a CML investment. Breakeven Analysis also provides statistics that are crucial to determining an investment's level of term risk and maturity risk.

Without leaving you hanging, there are two other "C's" of Credit, but in my opinion, *capital* and *character* are lower ranking. Don't believe me? Has anyone ever let you down? Unfortunately, not all people do what they say they're going to do.

In the most recent i(RR) example, the required interest rate was unchanged. The lender and borrower didn't enter into a loan modification agreement to reduce the interest rate from 10.00% to 7.9413% or to discount the balloon payment from $36.56 to $32.90. The borrower, however, entered into "self-help," as it's known in the industry, and chose not to comply with the loan documents as promised. The note is also called a Promissory Note for a reason. The true investment yield will be affected by the amount, timing, and frequency of the investment's future *expected* cash flows.

In the example, the lender has a "Hope Certificate" in the Promissory Note that requires a certain amortization or payment schedule, including the balloon payment of $36.56 at maturity. If the forecast improves and the borrower is expected to pay more than $32.90 for the balloon payment at maturity, the lender will expect to get closer to the bargained-for return *on* investment. This is why lenders are generally against modifying loan documents. One possible counterargument to a borrower's request for a loan modification is that the borrower wasn't calling the lender to renegotiate the interest rate higher when rates ran after the true investment yield was circled and the loan made.

In life, as in business, if we waited for conditions to be perfect, there are so many things we wouldn't get around to doing. Going to college, buying a house, and starting a family are just a few examples. One doesn't need to have a life or career plan set in stone before stepping onto a college campus. In fact, one of the biggest value propositions I see in a college education is that it's a kind of practice field for a field of practice, a place where hard and soft (marketable) skills are refined and developed, and where ways of thinking can be acquired.

Few people wait to purchase homes until they have 100% of the purchase price saved; real estate is expensive.

Waiting to have children until you feel financially ready is a fool's errand. As a father of three wonderful daughters, I can tell you that having a family is expensive and that you could always have more resources to support your lifestyle and hopes and dreams. But family is also priceless.

Looking back, I wish Sarah and I would have started a family even earlier—when we had less money to our name than we did the day we welcomed our oldest daughter into the world.

To bring this back to the Time Value of Money, let's just say that the Mathematics of Finance wouldn't have fully developed if we were waiting for a perfect metric to estimate the true investment yield.

That's right, i(RR) is far from perfect. But it doesn't have to be perfect so long as it's the closest thing we have to perfect. With knowledge of the underlying assumptions, you can use this investment metric while exercising caution.

It took me years to figure out what the "Internal" of "Internal Rate of Return" was all about. Here's how I describe it. You could substitute "Isolated" for "Internal," and it may be even clearer.

An "Isolated" … Return creates the kind of vibe that is consistent with the assumptions. The problem is that isolated investments aren't made in laboratory-type environments; instead, in real-world markets. The i(RR) is only a true representation of the true investment yield in one situation. That situation is one that does not involve incremental cash flows. Why is this? What does an investor do with cash flows? Invests them.

Have I mentioned how I don't like the word *Internal* in Internal Rate of Return? Earlier, I also told you why I don't like the word *of* in Internal Rate of Return. The slight changeup from "Internal" to "Isolated," even if fleeting, helps communicate the point. It's true that the opposite of "Internal" is "External," and that there is such a thing as the External Rate of Return that represents what investors can earn on their own should they put their money to work in an (external) investment with like-kind risk to that of the level of the perceived risk profile of the internal investment opportunity. There's always a question of whether finance professionals should recommend that money be invested in an *internal* investment opportunity or returned to shareholders, for example, if they have better uses for the capital. The External Rate of Return recognizes the opportunity cost of capital. But here opposites don't attract. Unlike i(RR) that is the *expected* return *on* investment, the External Rate of Return is a *required* return *on* investment from the finance professional's perspective. The interplay between the External Rate of Return and the discount rate or *required* return *on* investment for a particular opportunity, the latter of which considers internal numbers such as the WACC and a risk-adjusted spread that is unique or isolated to a specific project, is what determines the hurdle rate and ultimately NPV. Modern-day hurdles consist of two uprights that can be adjusted to raise or lower the hurdle. That's how I think about the interplay between the discount rate for a specific investment opportunity and the External Rate of Return, the latter of which is a kind of discount rate in the context of NPV Analysis. The higher of the two establishes the height of the hurdle or the hurdle rate. It's worth repeating that there is only one hurdle rate. And it's also interesting to point out that in a race, hurdlers don't get disqualified for hitting the hurdle. While I understand that zero is not a positive number, this is food for thought as to why an NPV equal to $0 might be viewed as a positive.

So the first primary issue with i(RR) relates to cash flows. We'll start by examining intermediate incremental cash flows. An underlying assumption of i(RR) is that incremental cash flows are reinvested at the true investment yield that is i(RR). This may not be realistic. But where there's a problem, there's a solution.

Enter the Modified Internal Rate of Return. With the Modified Internal Rate of Return, there's an intermediate step that addresses the issue of the reinvestment yield. All the positive intermediate incremental cash flows are compounded to the end of the investment period using the reinvestment yield, which may be lower than the i(RR). At that point, you have one Future Value that needs to be discounted back to the time of the investment. So *the Modified Internal Rate of Return* is the (d)i(scount rate) that sets the *Future Value at the end of the investment period* of *all* the future expected cash flows *compounded at the reinvestment yield* equal to the investment.

The words in italics show how the original i(RR) definition is *modified* to fit that of the Modified Internal Rate of Return. The issue of the reinvestment yield and its impact on i(RR) needs to be considered and further supports why i(RR) is used to analyze and evaluate potential investment opportunities based on forecasts rather than actual performance. As it relates to the four forces of flight in the context of the Time Value of Money, compounding or the "force of thrust" pushes things forward and is what separates the Modified Internal Rate of Return math from i(RR) before discounting or the "force of drag" pulls things backward. And as with other i(RR) calculations, together with the other "forces of the Time Value of Money," the NPV shows us whether an investment opportunity will "fly."

We've described and illustrated how i(RR) is defined as *the* — that means singular — (d)i(scount rate) that sets the Present Value of the future *expected* cash flows over the investment period equal to the investment. This takes us to the issue of unconventional cash flows.

In a perfect world, your initial investment is enough and then you plan on just sitting back and receiving cash inflows. This is referred to as a conventional or "normal" cash flow forecast, which isn't always the case. Some investments require additional capital infusion during the investment period. Having negative future expected cash flows during the investment period is in effect the same thing as an additional capital infusion. In situations where there is negative cash flow, money sourced from some place other than the investment will be needed to keep it afloat. In other words, to cover expenses, whatever those might be. Sources and uses is a very important concept in finance. Unconventional cash flows refers to more than one negative sign or investment over an investment period, which can lead to a situation where there are multiple i(RR)s. In fact, there could be as many i(RR)s as sign changes in the cash flow stream. And that's an issue because the i(RR) definition tells us that this TVM variable flies solo.

Again we can use the Modified Internal Rate of Return to solve for this problem. Regardless of whether you choose to compound all the positive intermediate cash flows to the end of the investment period using the reinvestment yield, the one thing you will be doing is discounting negative intermediate cash flows to the beginning of the investment period using the financing rate. If you choose to compound all the positive intermediate cash flows to account for a reinvestment yield that is less than i(RR), then you could simply use the five primary TVM financial calculator keys to solve for (the Modified) i(RR).

For an investment that doesn't have any negative cash flows beyond the initial investment, there is only one sign change. In other words, from the negative cash flow to the first positive cash flow whenever that is expected to occur.

This brings us to the next issue with cash flows which is that signs matter. This is because it's a matter of perspective. The lens through which you view a financial situation is important. If you're a borrower subject to a commercial mortgage loan agreement, you prefer a commercial mortgage loan with a 5% contract rate of interest, an *expected* annualized i(RR) from the lender's perspective, more than one with a 6% contract rate of interest, all else equal. In this example, if you're the borrower, you're on the right side of 6%.

Another issue is to make sure you consider all the cash flows related directly or indirectly to a project. Seems like common sense when we're talking about directly related cash flows. But if an investment opportunity is dependent upon a "sister" project, for example, then such a related project and its indirect cash flows also need to be considered. The costs of an opportunity forgone would be another example of indirect cash flows, since that's what could have been.

The second primary issue with i(RR) has to do with timing. If you're thinking that there may be multiple dimensions to the issue of time as with the other primary issues with i(RR), we're on the same wavelength. Front-loaded cash flows will lead to a higher i(RR) all else equal. Think this one through. The earlier cash flows don't benefit as much from compounding. In other words, time is not doing as much as it could.

Obviously, i(RR) is just one number among many that finance professionals will analyze and evaluate when considering an investment opportunity. But I've got to be honest. This issue of cash flow timing makes me scratch my head a little because what investor doesn't want to get paid back sooner rather than later, especially in light of the fact that there are no guarantees with respect to investments?

This issue is related to that of intermediate incremental cash flows. There will be a magnified effect when the cash flow projection is front-loaded and includes bigger cash flows earlier, and the fewer the compounding periods the greater i(RR), all else equal.

The other issue of timing relates to the investment period. This is really a reinvestment yield issue in disguise. Even if an investment opportunity doesn't contemplate intermediate incremental cash flows, a "unicorn" in the commercial real estate universe, i(RR) doesn't consider the markets for capital in the intervening time between the end of one project and another. This is another example of where the Modified Internal Rate of Return saves the day turning lemons into lemonade and helping us make sense of "apples" and "oranges."

We have two down and two to go. As we've seen and will continue to see, commercial real estate investments provide a great backdrop for this study of i(RR) since real estate investments are expected to generate intermediate cash flows. (Let this serve as "recruiting" material if you haven't already entered your "recruited" era.) The third primary issue with i(RR) relates to multiple discount rates.

With respect to commercial real estate investments, cash flow from operations is generally thought to be more durable than the cash flow that would be generated from the sale of the asset. Real estate finance professionals model a resale specific discount rate indirectly through the terminal CR, which is essentially the denominator of the Constant Growth Model. The "Constant Delta Between the Discount Rate and Growth Rate (of Inflation) Model" would have been kind of wordy, but that's really more fitting since it's the delta between the two that drives value. The discount rate is what we know to be the true investment yield. Before someone accidentally burns themself with smoldering pipe tobacco, let me say that I know why the phrase "Constant Growth" was chosen for that model. Because a constant growth rate (of inflation) is a key assumption.

In the commercial real estate industry, real estate finance professionals use the Gordon Growth Model to determine the

Resale or Terminal (Future) Value by "capping" or dividing NOI in the year following the last year of the cash flow projection or investment period by the terminal CR. This should sound familiar. Here the next expected payment is represented by the acronym NOI, which is technically the variable PMT in the building block Present Value of an Ordinary Perpetuity equation.

In theory, the terminal CR is the discount rate minus the constant growth rate (of inflation) of NOI. In practice, a hybrid multiple discount rate approach is used since there's an implied discount rate in the calculation used to determine the Resale or Terminal (Future) Value by way of the terminal CR and a stated discount rate that is used to determine the (Present) Value of both the cash flow from operations and the cash flow from the would-be sale of the asset.

In other words, real estate finance professionals already recognize the need for multiple discount rates: one, albeit implied, and one that is the discount(ing) rate used to determine the Present Value of the future expected cash flows over the investment period.

In theory, another expressly stated discount rate could be used for the Resale (Future) Value assumption, but in practice, I haven't seen this happen with much frequency. However it's modeled, it makes sense to recognize for investments that different cash flow streams have different risk characteristics. Since i(RR) is the [one] (d)i(count rate) that sets the Present Value of the future expected cash flows over the investment period equal to the investment, you can see the shortcoming.

Last but not least is the fourth primary issue with i(RR) which has to do with value maximization. Given consideration to all the issues with i(RR) described above, let's recognize the obvious, which is that percentages aren't deposited in banks or invested; instead, money is the currency of investments. As a result, we can't ignore the magnitude to which an investment is accretive to value. NPV is needed to make "dollars and *sense*" of i(RR), which is why it's number-one in the eyes of finance professionals.

I learn best from extreme examples, so let's use an extreme example to communicate this point. Would you rather make an investment that is *expected* to generate an i(RR) of 77% or one with an i(RR) of 44%? Let's assume that each investment contemplates a three-year investment period. What if I told you the investment opportunity that is *expected* to yield a true annual investment yield of 77% requires an investment of $100 and that the alternative with an *expected* true annual investment yield of 44% requires an investment of $1,000,000?

It's a question of whether you think stakeholders want to potentially capture a return *on* investment in dollar terms of $454.52 at the end of the three-year investment period, which is over and above the return *of* investment of $100, or potentially capture a return *on* investment in dollar terms of $1,985,984 at the end of the three-year investment period, which is over and above the return *of* investment of $1,000,000.

Some people's take on this issue takes the form of "unequal investments," which is a "what" that relates to the "why" of the objective of value maximization.

Before we move on, there is one honorable mention. First I must say that in no way, shape, or form am I trying to dilute the concern regarding mutually exclusive projects in the context of i(RR). It's just that when I hear teachers mention this issue of mutually exclusive projects, many of them stop short by simply telling you to use NPV instead of i(RR). If you've considered all cash flows, direct or indirect, associated with the investment opportunities, then I guess it is that simple. Once again, the stage is set with a real estate example. If you were choosing between two mutually exclusive investment opportunities that occupy different locations, then the idea of using NPV to reach an investment decision is straightforward. But say the investment decision is whether to sell an unimproved parcel of land or develop that parcel with an income-producing property. This analysis looks a little different, since both investment opportunities occupy the same place in space. With the first example of mutually exclusive investment opportunities all we know is that both can't occur at the same time. Maybe this is because of constraints with respect to capital. In the second example, it's pretty clear why the investment opportunities are mutually exclusive: you can't have your cake and eat it too. When confronted with mutually exclusive projects, you should use the NPV metric instead of i(RR) for reaching an investment decision. But in the same breath, we must recognize that there would be no NPV without i(RR) and the hurdle rate. Indirect cash flows or opportunity costs associated with the forgone investment opportunity would impact both i(RR) and NPV. Failing to consider such opportunity costs would create an upward bias in NPV, and i(RR) all else equal. The "issue" of mutually exclusive projects connects the dimension of needing to consider all cash flows and the dimension that considers the objective of value maximization. In this way, mutually exclusive projects is the finance version of a rip or tear in the space-time continuum. The word *omnipresent* is a good one for describing mutually exclusive projects in the context of i(RR). Saying there are four primary issues with i(RR) is a lot better than needing two hands to count all the primary and related issues.

As mentioned, we can't ignore the issue of accretion to value, or the scale of economics of an investment opportunity, which is one of the benefits of the NPV metric. This illustrates why IRR Analysis and NPV Analysis go hand in hand. The left hand needs to know what the right hand is doing.

Finance professionals have different metrics at the ready to analyze and evaluate finance and investment decisions. The primary focus of this chapter is how cash flow influences return *on* investment or i(RR), but any discussion regarding i(RR) should also consider NPV. Some people like to unnecessarily overcomplicate things, and in the field of finance, I see lots of people doing this with NPV. It is simply the Present Value of the future *expected* cash flows minus or *net of* the Present Value of the investment. Remember that i(RR) is the (d)i(scount rate) that makes the Net Present Value of an investment equal to $0.

When NPV is greater than $0, i(RR) is greater than what an investor *requires* for return *on* investment for a given level of risk. When NPV is less than $0, i(RR) is less than what an investor *requires* for return *on* investment. NPV will be exactly equal to $0 when i(RR) is equal to the *required* return *on* investment. In two of these three situations, an investor may reach the conclusion that the investment opportunity, the *Boomerang of Finance*, could potentially fly.

NPV also allows an investor to figure out how much, if any, cushion there is in a deal. In other words, how much more the prospective buyer could offer or how much less the seller could accept.

In the above example, if the investor with the $1,000,000 investment opportunity could settle for a 35% i(RR) based on the risk profile of the investment, the *price* could be increased by $213,629.63 *to yield* 35%. The IRR function of your financial calculator will display a positive NPV of $213,629.63 based on the future *expected* cash flow stream over the three-year investment period assuming an investment of $1,000,000 based on a (d)i(scount rate) or a *required* return *on* investment of 35%.

The way this should be interpreted is that your bottom-line bid to produce at least an i(RR) of 35% is $1,213,629.63. An investment amount between $1,000,000 and $1,213,629.63 would be *expected* to produce an i(RR) between 35% and 44%. It works the other way as well. The NPV metric tells an investor how much they would "leave on the table" if they made an investment with an *expected* return *on* investment that was estimated to be lower than the *required* return *on* investment.

In other words, assume that the investor's *required* return *on* investment for the $1,000,000 investment opportunity were revised to 45%. The NPV for this investment opportunity would be estimated at negative $20,547 (rounded). The *price to yield* 45% would be $979,453 (rounded): $1,000,000 − $20,547.

All investors are focused on yield, whether or not investment yield takes the form of interest. For proof of this, we need look no further than loan documents and a provision that is commonly included and titled "Yield Maintenance." It's not called "Interest Maintenance," even though interest is the form most, if not all, of the yield takes for the loan.

A mortgage lender may require that a borrower pay yield maintenance (aka a prepayment premium) if the loan is prepaid early to compensate the lender for the loss of the bargained-for yield. Again, not "bargained-for interest."

And for the record, it's not a "prepayment *penalty*." One of many lessons real estate attorneys have taught me is that one can only get what another has to give. A lender gives a borrower the right to prepay the mortgage loan, and as a result, the borrower gets the flexibility that comes with holding an option.

Investors pay a *premium* for an option. In the case of a CML, the borrower controls whether to exercise the option and thereby prepay the loan. The agreement is governed by the loan documents that describe this right, among others, and create the bargained-for deal. Some people like to refer to the lender–borrower relationship as a "two-way street," but I prefer the roundabout visual. It's not the initial give and get that defines the relationship as much as it is the agreement that the getter will give and the giver will get. That's what makes it come full circle. In the example, the getter received a right or option—but don't stop short, there's more—based on what was bargained-for. If the option is exercised, the only thing the getter can give is what was received, which is the bargained-for right to pay the required prepayment premium.

Still not convinced the correct term is prepayment *premium*? Are you a borrower?! If you still insist on calling it a "penalty" then know that it's a penalty from the lender's perspective. I know the argument: "But our profit from the sale of the real estate will be reduced to the extent of the prepayment premium." That's right, it will. And that's why a holder of a traditional put option is willing to pay a premium that just might cut into their profit. Given the zero-sum nature of options, when the right is exercised one investor's premium will result in another's penalty. While a topic for another day, real options theory suggests that an investor will take the deal on the table and exercise the option if it's believed that a better profit in present value terms won't come around in the future.

It takes a lot of resources and time to originate a mortgage loan, which is mutually beneficial to both borrower and lender. And because mortgage lenders and other investors may match assets to liabilities (aka asset-liability management or asset-liability matching), it would be an unfortunate event if a mortgage loan were repaid early in any interest rate environment, especially when yields are low. If you want to know more about the topic of prepayment premium, Megan W. Murray has a great paper titled "Prepayment Premiums: Contracting for Future Financial Stability in the Commercial Lending Market" which is published by the *Iowa Law Review*. In her paper, she references the court case *Santa Rosa KM Associates, Ltd. v. Principal Life Insurance Co.* in which the court referred to the absence of a prepayment premium for a fixed interest rate commercial mortgage loan as a "heads I win, tails you lose" proposition because "the election to prepay the loan is entirely in the borrower's hands." When market investment yields or interest rates rise above the note rate, borrowers "win" because of the fixed contract rate of interest. And when market investment yields or interest rates fall below the note rate, lenders "lose" absent a prepayment premium should the loan be prepaid. Considering I came up with the mental image of the two sides of the i(RR) coin before reading this paper, you can imagine how happy I was to find that the court, in the public record, was also using a coin to illustrate a point about yield maintenance or, more precisely, the absence thereof. This is why yield maintenance is a thing.

The yield maintenance or prepayment premium is a kind of fee that compensates the mortgage lender for the loss of bargained-for yield. Calculating yield maintenance or the prepayment premium is an example of the NPV calculation used in practice. The investment that the PV math is *net of* is the outstanding principal balance of the loan. The loan documents will specify the (d)i(scount rate) or the true investment yield that is to be used to determine the Present Value of the remaining cash flow stream, but it's typically calculated using the on-the-run investment yield—not the coupon rate—for a treasury note or bond with a term approximate to the remaining loan term.

It shouldn't be this way, but there is a subset of borrowers that always complain that they don't want to pay the agreed-upon or bargained-for prepayment premium to the mortgage lender. A promise is a promise. Some borrowers are worse than kids in a checkout line at a store asking a grown-up for anything within arm's length. Loan documents are "arm's-length" negotiated agreements. When the "cow" finally comes home—which in this case represents the prepayment of the loan made with many zeros and which is subject to loan documents that were agreed upon oh so long ago—some borrowers aren't happy unless they milk it for all it's worth. I'm being a little dramatic here. Over my time in industry, I worked with some amazing borrowers. I'd be remiss if I didn't point this out. And when I say great, I'm talking about the cream of the crop. Like any industry participant, as a lender, we believed the industry mantra that relationships matter. The reason certain experiences are burned on my mind more than others likely relates to something I learned in retail when I was in high school. One of the first things I was told was that it took ten happy customers to make up for one bad experience. Whether it was in retail or selling money, there's some truth in this saying. Over time, you get somewhere when, as Jim Sellers says, you "work hard to develop relationships, and do what you say you are going to do."

Are you up for a little conspiracy theorizing? Since this book is about a fun, new take on the Time Value of Money, let's speculate for a moment. When you think of a one-dollar bill, what's one of the first images to pop into your mind? For many people, it's the image of the eye in the pyramid: the Eye of Providence.

While we may never know the real meaning behind this iconic and somewhat eerie image, the finance professional in me would like to think it's a reminder of the "Eighth Wonder of the World."

The Great Pyramid of Giza is one of the original Seven Wonders of the World and could very well have inspired the image of the pyramid on the back of the one-dollar bill.

What if the symbol of the eye in the top of the pyramid is a hint to the power of the compound investment yield? Maybe it's not too far-fetched after all. Clearly a raised "i" wouldn't have had such a dramatic effect. It's worth revisiting that Albert Einstein reportedly referred to "compound interest"—we know this as compound investment yield or compound yield, but who am I to correct such a genius—"as the most powerful force in the universe."

The Mathematics of Finance tells us that the variable "i" or more precisely the mathematical expression "$(1 + i)$" needs to be— get this—*raised* by the power of "N" for compounding to work its magic. What is that saying so many aspiring and current finance professionals can recite? "A dollar in the present is worth more than a dollar in the future." Funny how this symbol only shows up on the back of the one-dollar bill. I'm just saying. Still think this conspiracy theorizing is a stretch? Do we know how the pyramids were built?!

By now you know that the true investment yield is my preferred term when talking about return *on* investment. There are lots of words that show up in each of the three chapters that make up the What section of this book. However, the one I want to draw your attention to is "yield." Yield is what it's all about. Investment yield or compound investment yield is why investors invest. You don't hear people referring to the "return curve." It's the "yield curve." A good metric like i(RR) considers that money has time value, that there are two sides with respect to return, and that return *of* investment impacts return *on* investment. It takes parting with something—whether a bird or boomerang or money in the hand—to potentially earn a return *on* investment.

So i(RR) that can be shortened to "yield" or simply "i" is—get ready for this—a catch-all term. This section was all about the concept of the Time Value of Money. In the How section, you'll be putting it all together using the Mathematics of Finance.

Part 2: The How

New Take, Take Two: User Manual for the Mathematics of Finance

Chapter 4: Contents: TVM Formula™ "Tool" and Pieces

"Tool" (aka "the glue")

TVM Formula™

INGREDIENTS:
TVM Rules, *indifferent* (mnemonic and audible aid), *312* "warm-up" routine, TVM Wallet (visual aid and template), 3-Step Systematic Approach.

Pieces

Chapter 5: Disclaimer: First Things First

"If you want to make enemies, try to change something."
—Woodrow Wilson

In no way, shape, or form is it my intention with any of the content of this book to try to rouse even the slightest idea that there is something wrong with the principle of the Time Value of Money. The Time Value of Money is foundational to finance, and it's a very strong foundation at that. The principle has stood the test of time. Even as the idea of money is changing from paper to digital currency, the Time Value of Money is ready for anything the future throws at it: investors will always require return *on* investment for delaying consumption, opportunity cost, and for taking on exposure to risk including the risk of inflation.

Nor am I trying to make any kind of academic argument. That's for the PhDs in academia—some of whom are my colleagues and friends. Instead, this book is about *agreement*. But just because it "ain't broken" doesn't mean that it can't be improved. The new take on the Time Value of Money continues into this section, only this time the new information is something you can use, hence the user manual.

In the What section, we discussed the potential issue of terminology, which I believe has its roots in ambiguity. You might be in the camp for which terminology isn't a problem. If that's you, then consider yourself lucky. For others, terminology is proof that the little things can, and do at times, stand in the way as obstacles in pursuit of a big goal.

Sometimes people learn best by examples that consider extremes. In the context of problems with words, international marketing blunders due to meaning being lost in translation take the cake.

The year was 1987, and Braniff Airways was excited to tell customers and the world about their new leather seats. The slogan,

"Fly in leather," however, had one major drawback—or benefit depending on how you look at it. The ad was translated into Spanish to target people living in Latin America. But customers in Mexico may have interpreted this advertisement to say don't pack as much in terms of clothes because there it meant "Fly naked."

Unfortunately, words that have multiple meanings can be problematic because of similar yet subtle differences in terminology. Let's just hope nobody showed up to the airport ready to test out just how formfitting those leather seats were. If this were a nightmare, that's when you want to wake up! As you'll see, terminology issues aren't always isolated to words.

In the How section of this book, our attention turns to numbers, words, and letters. By making slight changes or improvements to how we think about and write certain variables relating to the building block Time Value of Money equations and financial calculator inputs, ambiguity is out in favor of agreement.

Change is nothing new when it comes to mathematical variables. The word *variable* comes from a Latin word meaning "changeable," which explains why variables are placeholders for values, whether numbers or the decimal form of percentages, that change based on the situation.

This user manual is made possible because of the simplicity related to the TVM Rules, consistency among the improved building block Time Value of Money equations, and connectivity throughout the **TVM Formula**™ that culminates in the 3-Step Systematic Approach. You won't find any superfluous information or terminology in this handbook. Every component or piece has a purpose right down to the letter, literally.

One example of such change is the use of "N" instead of "n" in the building block Time Value of Money equations. The variable "N" represents the number of consecutive periods, or payments for an even annuity, that are subject to the same true investment yield and the same time span *in* between periods or payments (on the timeline). The investment period may or may not equal the total investment period.

Think back to *TVM Rule #2*: it's a Time Value of Money no-no to fail to correspond the time span *in* between periods or payments (on the timeline) and the time span of the true investment yield.

Thus, "N" is not to be confused with "n" that represents the time span *in* between periods or payments (on the timeline). It's "n" that allows you to "tell time" (on the timeline) for a given situation and to ultimately determine the true investment yield for a certain time span. In other words, "n" is *in* between the period markers on the timeline. The timeline is the visual representation of the total investment period, which will consist of one or more "N's."

It's beyond me why so many other people have failed to recognize this important distinction and—as far as I'm concerned— incorrectly use "n" as a variable in *their* building block Time Value of Money equations. This shows me they're loosey-goosey on the whole thing and may have fallen victim to the whole "We do it this way because we've always done it this way" line of thought.

I'm not complaining, because it's improvements like this—not fixes, because nothing is broken—that led me to write this book. My goal is to clear things up and ultimately create the first-of-its-kind user manual for the Mathematics of Finance and the simple "tool" that is the **TVM Formula**™. The formula includes, among other original works, the 3-Step Systematic Approach for applying the Mathematics of Finance to analyze and evaluate real-world Time Value of Money situations.

If considered in isolation, it might not appear that the use of "N" in the building block Time Value of Money equations is a change worthy of being called an improvement; however, the value of the user manual is in the whole rather than the sum of its parts.

In traditional textbooks, the use of the notation "n" in one or more of the building block Time Value of Money equations is widespread. In all fairness, I can kind of see why other people might choose to use "n" in *their* building block Time Value of Money equations. This may be too forgiving, but I would like to think that these other people are thinking that using the variable "n" instead of "N" makes sense because there are going to be times when there is only one "n" in an investment period or because the summation of multiple "n's"—the number of periods (on the timeline)—won't always equal the total investment period. I get it, but the improved definition of "N" recognizes this.

Recall that the variable "N" represents the number of consecutive periods, or payments for an even annuity, that are subject to the same true investment yield and the same time span *in* between periods or payments (on the timeline). There's not even a direct reference to an investment period let alone the total investment period. Sometimes "N" will equal the total investment period. Sometimes it won't. Sometimes "n" will equal "N," but those instances will be few and far between. The definition of "N" has both these potential arguments covered.

Frankly, other people's use of "n" in *their* building block Time Value of Money equations is probably more a result of there not having been a definitive systematic approach in print. But that's changed with the publication of this handbook!

Another benefit that can't be overstated is how separating "n" from "N" gets people focused on making sure to correspond the time span *in* between periods or payments (on the timeline) (n) and the time span of the true investment yield (i).

By now you know that I don't agree that "n" is the right variable to be used in the building block Time Value of Money equations. But get this. Sometimes you'll find that "n" has a partner in crime in some other people's building block Time Value of Money equations. This related notation might take the form of "m" or "t."

Now this is one that has me scratching my head. The purpose of "m" or "t" or whatever other letter might be used is to introduce the number of compounding periods. Tell me this: where do you find the letter "m" or "t" in that? At least there's an *n* in the definition of "N": the number of consecutive periods, or payments for an even annuity…

And oh, by the way, there's no math in the alphabet. I can't help but wonder if the person who is trying to represent synergies with mathematical equations like "1 + 1 = 3" is the same yahoo who thinks this nonsense that "n" and "m" or "n" and "t" when taken together is equal to "N." And where are the keys on your financial calculator that represent the "m" and "t" variables? I don't see them on my trusty HP-12C. Simpler is better, and "n" and "N" are the only two choices for representing that letter in the alphabet.

As far as I'm concerned, the absolute worst offender is when "n" shows up in the building block Time Value of Money equations for an annuity. In the building block Future Value equation, Present Value can be thought of as a single or lump-sum payment. The same is true for Future Value in the building block Present Value equation. The payment is not frequent. In the building block Time Value of Money equations for an annuity, PMT doesn't need to be interpreted because it's aptly abbreviated for the even payment stream it is: unlike a single payment, an even annuity is made up of frequent payments that are level in terms of amount and timing. In the building block Time Value of Money equations for an annuity, "N" represents the number of consecutive payments for an even annuity that are subject to the same true investment yield and the same time span *in* between payments (on the timeline).

At the very least, "N" is equal or closer to the total investment period than "n" will ever be. In fact, it was the building block Time Value of Money equations for an annuity that made me realize that improvements could be made to how we think about and write certain variables relating to these building block equations and the five primary TVM financial calculator inputs.

Another variable that you have likely encountered for building block Time Value of Money equations and the primary TVM financial calculator inputs in many traditional textbooks is "r" or "i" for the true investment yield. At first, one might think that this is not that big of a deal. But it's a really big deal when one of the objectives is to eliminate ambiguity and create agreement by making all the pieces fit together.

For reasons that will become clear as you flip the pages of this book, I landed on the letter "i" to represent the true investment yield for more than the fact that *i* is the first letter of "investment" or "investment yield." I took the liberty of eliminating the "r" variable.

In the building block True Investment Yield equation, the simple investment yield is denoted by "s." The "s" variable remains. But since the true investment yield *is*—get it, "i" and "s"—what it's all about when it comes to the Time Value of Money, your focus will be on the "i" variable.

From time to time, you'll need to work with the real investment yield. You might think that "r" would be the way to express "i – g" since the "real investment yield" starts with the letter *r*. But not so fast. Since the true investment yield will be equal to the real investment yield when the growth rate of inflation or "g" is equal to zero, the **TVM Formula**™ calls for simply underlining "i" when referring to the real investment yield in the building block Time Value of Money equations for a perpetuity. I don't know about you, but it's hard enough for me to read my own handwriting, let alone trying to add italics into the mix. That is why the underline is the way to go. Makes sense, right?

You may find yourself rewriting other authors' variables related to the building block Time Value of Money equations or primary TVM financial calculator inputs to make them jibe with the **TVM Formula**™ and the original 3-Step Systematic Approach, which are presented in this book. That's OK, but the other way around won't fly.

If you think I'm blowing this out of proportion, I've seen authors define "n" in *their* building block Time Value of Money equations as, "the number of years" and, "m" as "the number of compounding periods within a year." See what's wrong with this?

It is misguided to think that periods or payments (on the timeline) will always be annual. Again, I think the main culprit for why other people choose to settle for using a variable other than "N" is that they are lacking a definitive systematic approach. But just using "N" doesn't solve the bigger problem! There's more to it than that, which is where simplicity, consistency, and connectivity come in, and why a formula, the **TVM Formula**™, needed to be developed. In the 3-Step Systematic Approach presented herein, you'll be calculating the true investment yield as your "warm up" before "working out" the math. The **TVM Formula**™, which allows you to apply the Mathematics of Finance to analyze and evaluate real-world Time Value of Money situations using the 3-Step Systematic Approach, is a one-size-fits-all tool.

What I'm about to say next is the stuff arguments are made of. That said, I doubt many PhDs are going to take the bait, which is part of the bigger problem. This is because these super smart PhDs are of the mindset that there are bigger fish to fry in the finance field as evidenced by the number of new papers published on the topic of the Time Value of Money in a given year. Some might say that the ship has sailed as it relates to the Mathematics of Finance. Others might say the Time Value of Money is old hat.

An old hat can become "garbage" that turns into someone else's "treasure." I'm happy to have found a new way to learn and teach how to apply the Mathematics of Finance building on this age-old and time-tested principle of the Time Value of Money. What I have to say about a potential argument is short because, well, this book and the **TVM Formula**™ are about agreement, remember.

Scratching someone's back is better than the alternative, which is to ruffle someone's feathers.

To develop the 3-Step Systematic Approach that is the cornerstone of the **TVM Formula**™, the user manual, and this book, great care was taken to ensure that no piece of the puzzle was missing. With the knowledge that a 3-Step Systematic Approach would be the Holy Grail of the Time Value of Money, the goal was set. Working backward from the objective, it became clear what needed to happen. First of all, the rules of the Time Value of Money needed to be completely reframed and boiled down to their purest elements—*Time*, *Value*, and *Money*—while also being memorable and linking directly to the 3-Step Systematic Approach. Simplicity is not the absence of complexity. While the TVM Rules are minimalistic, they are also quite complex in that they are constructed around the core concept of investors being *indifferent* between values of money *in different* points in time.

In addition to helping you remember the TVM Rules, the mnemonic *indifferent* also provides the blueprint and audible aid for the 3-Step Systematic Approach.

This user manual will help you use the 3-Step Systematic Approach using the simple "tool" that is the **TVM Formula**™. The full scale of the **TVM Formula**™ can be illustrated with an accordion, which provides a perfect visual to show you how there is connectivity between the five components of the **TVM Formula**™. On one hand of this accordion, you've got the TVM Rules, and on the other hand is the 3-Step Systematic Approach. As you expand the instrument, the bellows housed between the two ends are revealed:

- the mnemonic and audible aid *indifferent*
- the *312* warm-up routine
- the visual aid and template that is the TVM Wallet

In addition to allowing you to use the 3-Step Systematic Approach, this user manual is complete with all the important information you'll need to develop the hard skill that is the Mathematics of Finance and put it to use in the classroom or practice. It's about time money had a user manual.

With images of birds, hurdlers, and boomerangs still flying around in your mind's eye, now we'll get about the business of application.

Unlike some traditional textbooks that "under pack" the Time Value of Money information, here you'll find what you need. In business, people love to say that "Change is good." What you'll find herein is a good change in how to learn and teach the Time Value of Money, including the 3-Step Systematic Approach that is built on common sense. This is the Time Value of Money version of packing light but with all the essentials in your carry-on. Consider this your upgrade! I'd be surprised if every person reading this book is going to understand all the points made in this "disclaimer." That's what the user manual is for.

It's with great excitement that I present to you the first-of-its-kind user manual for the Mathematics of Finance and the simple tool that is the **TVM Formula**™. This is a user manual that you can't afford not to read: it's the solution for analysis paralysis as it relates to applying the Mathematics of Finance and knowledge that has the power to change your future!

Chapter 6: Safety Instructions: TVM Rules

"Labor disgraces no person; unfortunately, you
occasionally find people who disgrace labor."
—Ulysses S. Grant

At the most basic level, there are three requirements to play a game of baseball. Here I'm referring to a schoolyard game, not one under bright lights in some big city. The three requirements are a baseball, bat, and ball field. Some people might think a glove or other things are required to play baseball, but that's simply not the case. I've seen plenty of fans catch foul balls with their hands in the stands. In the major league, one of the best plays I've ever seen in baseball was when outfielder Kevin Mitchell of the San Francisco Giants made an amazing barehanded snag of a ball hit by Ozzie Smith of the St. Louis Cardinals. Ironically, Ozzie Smith was known as "The Wizard of Oz" and won multiple Golden Glove awards, but that day Kevin Mitchell had a trick up his sleeve and didn't need a glove. The content in this book will help you "barehand" the Time Value of Money using nothing more than a pen or pencil, paper, and basic calculator functions—should such a course of action be deemed the best play.

Beyond the three requirements, there are things that one would classify as need-to-know and good-to-know information. These are examples of need-to-know information:

- Three strikes and you're out.
- Runners must touch the bases.
- A tie at first goes to the runner.

This need-to-know information is pretty important in the game of baseball. If one were to start rounding the bases at third, that could lead to not getting asked back to be part of the schoolyard baseball team.

Then there are things that would be considered good-to-know information:

- Helmets are a thing.
- See the first strike.
- Be a good sport.

As a kind of tip of the hat to America's National Pastime, this chapter describes the Time Value of Money equivalent of a baseball, bat, and ball field to the game of baseball—the three TVM Rules.

From what I can tell, there isn't a set list of rules for the Time Value of Money in the finance industry. It's not like there's a TVM governing body like there is in the MLB (Major League Baseball).

There are some similarities between the original TVM Rules as defined in this book and what other people might call rules for the Time Value of Money. But I've seen others liberally give out rule status to what I would call need-to-know information. This is a close relative to the discussion regarding terminology. Some of the confusion with respect to the Time Value of Money comes from inconsistency with respect to what constitutes a rule.

A rule rises to the level of being put in stone. Just look at the Ten Commandments that were written into stone, reproductions of which are displayed in public and private spaces. While the list of possible transgressions in life is endless, each relates back to one or more of the Ten Commandments that Moses brought down from Mount Sinai back in the day. And for fans of the movie *A League of Their Own*, you can rest more comfortably since it doesn't appear that crying in baseball would constitute a sin. This frame of mind is what got me focused on creating concrete TVM Rules that were all-encompassing.

These rules were first introduced in chapter one. It's a Time Value of Money no-no to:

1. add or subtract or compare money *in different* points in time;
2. fail to correspond the time span *in* between periods or payments (on the timeline) and the time span of the true investment yield; and
3. neglect to consider *different* payment types and signs.

In addition to being original and bare-bones, the TVM Rules that are based on the mnemonic *indifferent* also provide the blueprint and audible aid for the 3-Step Systematic Approach. One word, with its two main components, will not only help you remember the three TVM Rules but also the three simple steps needed to apply the Mathematics of Finance using the visual aid and template or "insurance policy" that is the TVM Wallet. The TVM Rules are the source for all the parts of the user manual and provide the source code for the 3-Step Systematic Approach.

Don't let the simplicity of the TVM Rules fool you. There's a lot going on here. Every one of what I call the "Need to Knows" relates back to one or more of the TVM Rules. But wait, there's more! Now this is starting to sound like an infomercial. But that's okay because you'll want to pick up what I'm putting down. Each of the TVM Rules relates to one of the key words of *Time*, *Value*, and *Money*.

Last but not least, each of the TVM Rules relates to one or more of the five primary TVM financial calculator keys and the variables in the building block Time Value of Money equations. A lot of thought went into creating simplicity as it relates to the TVM Rules. Needless to say, these weren't just slapped together overnight.

This is just one example of how simplicity and consistency and connectivity are at work in the **TVM Formula**™, which is bookended by the TVM Rules and the 3-Step Systematic Approach. It's almost too good to be true, which has me believing that more than just my hand was at work.

Unlike some things that aren't worth the paper they're printed on, the marriage of simplicity and complexity of the TVM Rules makes them a candidate for being carved into stone. Come to think of it, putting these TVM Rules in stone not only sounds like a nice addition to my office but would certainly help get the point across that these TVM Rules carry weight. Breaking any one of these TVM Rules would be considered the equivalent of a cardinal sin "go, Cubs, go" of the Mathematics of Finance.

Visit a baseball field on game day, and you'll see a lot more than balls and bats. If you saw someone with only a ball and bat walking to a ball field, you might think they're ill-prepared. If you saw someone with all the baseball getup walking to a football field to practice, you'd be right to think they're getting ready to practice in the wrong field.

Similarly—and this one really hits home—you wouldn't want someone to tell you that you're not well suited for practicing as a finance professional, or worse yet, that you're practicing in the wrong professional field.

Learning a sport starts with learning the fundamentals. The most fundamental part of the Time Value of Money is comprehension of the TVM Rules. One of the first ways that you can prove to yourself—not yet others at this point—that the finance field is right for you is comprehension of the TVM Rules.

I'm a big believer in dressing for success in business, but you can't buy skills related to the Mathematics of Finance any more than you can buy your baseball game by dressing the part. You can't "fake it" and "make it" as a finance professional.

Once you've learned the fundamentals of the Time Value of Money in the TVM Rules and feel comfortable with the simple tool that is the **TVM Formula**™ and the "Need to Knows" found within the user manual, then you'll be in a position to put it all together using the 3-Step Systematic Approach. Knowledge of the "Good to Knows" will make it even easier for whatever the profession throws at you. I liken this to a batter being able to read the seams of a pitch. It isn't required but doesn't hurt and makes a batter better.

Finance professionals give or receive pitches for investment opportunities day in, day out in industry. One of the first ways that you can prove not only to yourself but also to others that the finance field is right for you is comprehension of the concept of the Time Value of Money through application of the Mathematics of Finance.

The sweet spot of the How section is the original 3-Step Systematic Approach for applying the Mathematics of Finance to analyze and evaluate real-world Time Value of Money situations. But just as the sweet spot of a bat won't do anything for a major leaguer unless they keep their eye on the ball, this section starts by winding up the pitch to prepare you for the "big show."

In other words, it's the point where you will have earned your stripes and can show off the hard skill that is the Mathematics of Finance. It's been said that people are rewarded in public for all the hours of hard work they did in private. There's no such thing as an overnight success. It takes hard work for the baseball player to arrive at The Big Show, the major league.

Think of this section as preparing you to make the jump from the minors to the major league as far as the Time Value of Money is concerned. Regardless of whether you are an aspiring or current finance professional, this user manual will help you in your major line of work.

Chapter 7: Setup Instructions: Money Has Time Value

"Time is money."
—Benjamin Franklin

Who doesn't love their first-grade teacher? Of all the elementary teachers who have left a lasting impression, first-grade teachers seem to commonly be number-one in the eyes of so many of their former students. There are likely a few reasons for this. First, to be a first-grade teacher requires a ton of patience and a big heart. Being held in such high esteem may also have something to do with educational experiences and how much people learn from their first-grade teacher. My wife, Sarah, started her teaching career teaching first grade. Having attended countless graduation parties and experienced chance meetings around town over the years, I've heard firsthand how her former students feel about their first-grade teacher.

My first-grade teacher wasn't the only first-grade teacher who has taught me a lot. As I was getting into teaching college courses, one of my best lessons came, albeit indirectly, from another first-grade teacher. My first teaching gig involved teaching five-week, four-hour accelerated courses in business at a smaller university. It was also a crash course for me.

I went into my first classroom thinking that time could be a potential issue—four hours is a long time. What if I ran out of material midway through class? What I quickly learned was that classroom management is the real McCoy. Without it, time management doesn't matter. One night when we were sitting around the dinner table with our oldest daughter, I asked my wife— who I affectionately refer to as the real teacher in our family—for advice about how to deal with a behavioral issue in my classroom, which I didn't have a handle on. She went to school for school, whereas I had worked my way into a classroom from industry.

After a long pause, and expecting advice from my wife, our then-seven-year-old daughter said, "Dad, why don't you tell them what Mr. Vollstedt says?"

I guess you could say I was desperate since I was ready to enlist the help of a first grader.

She had my attention, and what she said next not only helped me get things back on track but proved to be an instant classic. "Dad," she said, "Mr. V. says, 'If you take my time, I'll take yours.'"

10–4!

So excited about my new find, I was quick to thank Lydia's first-grade teacher for his words of wisdom. Mr. V. wasn't looking for proof of concept outside of his classroom, but I franchised it!

While this makes for a funny story for my current and future college finance students, and one that allows me to poke fun at my start and first year in teaching, the message is a serious one that speaks to the truth that time is money. It's good to know that the "time is money" lesson is being taught and learned at an early age.

In first grade, students are pretty much introduced to every topic. Topics such as how to tell time, read and write, and count money.

Having transitioned out of the "forest" that is the "What" of the Time Value of Money, we ease into our journey through the "trees" that are the "How" of the Mathematics of Finance. This chapter provides an introduction to what comes later, similar to first grade.

Before you can apply the Mathematics of Finance, first you need to learn how to *count money, tell time, and read and write* as it relates to the Time Value of Money. As you'll soon learn, each relates to one of the TVM Rules. While introductory, the information presented in this chapter is meaningful.

Since first grade, have you kept counting money, telling time, and reading and writing? Exactly! This chapter provides important information that you'll be using every time you apply the Mathematics of Finance to analyze and evaluate real-world Time Value of Money situations. The information below could be enough to help you get a good first grade related to an easier Time Value of Money question, but that's not the point since luck might also play a part.

There's a difference between luck and LUCK—Laboring Under Correct Knowledge. With a sound understanding of how the TVM

Rules apply to real-world Time Value of Money situations, you want to be laboring under correct knowledge. The simple tool that is the **TVM Formula**™ and came with this user manual and all the important pieces related to the Mathematics of Finance will allow you to use the 3-Step Systematic Approach to analyze and evaluate real-world Time Value of Money situations once you put all the pieces together.

Just as the first-grade experience is not easily forgotten and the topics remain relevant, you'd do well to absorb the information in this elementary yet important Time Value of Money lesson.

Now that my wife and I are both teachers, someday we hope to take advantage of having summers off by traveling America. One of the things my wife and I would like to do is tour the backcountry on our bicycles from a moving base camp that is an Airstream trailer. Not a one-and-done bucket list item, it's something that we want to start doing someday.

Another thing I haven't told you is that we love Chicago and dream of it being our future home (sweet home) someday from where we'll depart on our travels. In the rest of this chapter, you'll find the major first-grade topics married to the TVM Rules and expressed by way of Chicago's area code, *312*.

In the previous chapter, the TVM Rules were listed. The order is on purpose and by design, because it gives us the mnemonic *indifferent* that helps us easily remember the three TVM Rules. Below, instead of finding the "no-no" language, you'll find a few minor and inert changes, including the words *Time* and *Value* and *Money*, to get you thinking about how the TVM Rules can also be remembered by recalling "Time," "Value," and "Money," in that order:

1. Time: Consider money *in different* points in time.
2. Value: Correspond the time span *in* between periods or payments (on the timeline) and the time span of the true investment yield.
3. Money: Consider *different* payment types and signs.

Have you had one or more moments in life when you just knew you were on the right track? When I was writing this book, one of a few of those moments happened when I substituted the words *Time* and *Value* and *Money* for the "no-no" language in the TVM Rules. It's clear that "Time" is the major point of *TVM Rule #1*, that "Value" is the major point of *TVM Rule #2*, and that "Money" is the major point of *TVM Rule #3*. We don't call it "the Time Money of Value" or "the Money Value of Time." You get the point. It's *the Time Value of Money: 1,2,3*. The order of the TVM Rules matters. As you'll see later in this book when the 3-Step Systematic Approach is introduced, this isn't the last time you'll be counting to 3.

You might be thinking, *If the TVM Rules can be remembered with 'TVM' or 'Time' and 'Value' and 'Money,' why do we need the mnemonic indifferent?* The answer is as easy as the mnemonic is to remember. The mnemonic *indifferent* provides an audible aid that makes the TVM Rules easy to remember to the word while also providing a blueprint for applying the 3-Step Systematic Approach using the visual aid and template that is the TVM Wallet.

You'll be applying the Mathematics of Finance using the 3-Step Systematic Approach to work out real-world Time Value of Money situations by progressing through the TVM Rules in the order listed (1, 2, 3), that is after the warm-up.

It was during elementary school that I realized that counting doesn't just go two ways: up and down. Our elementary school PE teacher, Mr. Schomberg, had this special way of counting out repetitions during our warm-up routine so that we knew where we were at any point in time. It went like this: "One, two, three; two, two, three; three, one, two, and halt." You need to warm up after you're dressed and ready to go but before you start to work out; so too is there a kind of warm-up routine with respect to the Mathematics of Finance, in particular the 3-Step Systematic Approach.

Before we can get to the fun stuff—that is application—the warm-up routine ensures that we're ready to work out the math. We knew it was time to work out when we heard Mr. Schomberg count, "3, 1, 2," and you'll know you're ready to exercise your skill related to the Mathematics of Finance when your thinking and warm-up routine progresses from *Money* to *Time* and concludes with *Value*. It's 312 because *Money* (*TVM Rule #3*) has *Time* (*TVM Rule #1*) *Value* (*TVM Rule #2*). Now 312 is more than Chicago's area code!

It's worth mentioning that there's some cross-pollination with respect to the TVM Rules. This makes sense because we're working with a one-word mnemonic with two main components, and there is a total of three TVM Rules.

TVM Rule #1 references "money *in different* points in time"; however, the reference to "money" is a minor point. The major point of *TVM Rule #1* is *time*.

TVM Rule #2 references "time span *in* between periods or payments (on the timeline)," but the major point of *TVM Rule #2* isn't time; rather, it's *value*. The minor point of *TVM Rule #2* is time. It's expected that money when invested over time will increase in value, which stems from the true investment yield. The true investment yield when considered with time, $(1 + i)^N$ or what I like to call the *Flux Capacitor of Finance*, is the value activator since time alone doesn't bring about more value for money.

TVM Rule #3 references "*different* payment types" and, as you'll learn, a payment is classified based on frequency, amount, and timing. The major point of *TVM Rule #3* is *money* while the minor point is time. Once you know the timing of the payment(s) you know how to "tell time" as it relates to the situation and you can draw a timeline. And once you know how to "tell time," you can also correspond the time span *in* between periods or payments (on the timeline) with the time span of the true investment yield.

See how time permeates the TVM Rules. This makes sense because time is the major point of *TVM Rule #1* that includes both the "in" and "different" of *indifferent*, so of course the "in" and "different" when considered separately are going to have a time consideration, albeit minor.

In addition to being the one thing that everyone reading this book has in common, it's also the one thing each of the TVM Rules has in common: You can't compare money *in different* points in time because value is created *in* due time as a result of the true investment yield.

Here are the TVM Rules that have been slightly modified to consider the topics taught in first grade and reordered for the *312* warm-up routine—this one being mental, not physical—for applying the Mathematics of Finance using the 3-Step Systematic Approach, which will be presented later in this user manual:

3. "Counting Money": considering *different* payment types and signs;

1. "Telling Time": looking at money *in different* points in time; and

2. "Reading and Writing": corresponding the time span *in* between periods or payments (on the timeline) and the time span of the true investment yield.

Money (*TVM Rule #3*)

When it comes to money in the context of the Mathematics of Finance, it would be good for you to start thinking or hearing "payment" every time you hear "money." All payments have three characteristics, which are frequency, amount, and timing.

This is pretty easy to remember with the acronym "FAT." I know, this isn't very PC. But we're talking about payments, people! I'd take a big fat payment over a skinny one every day of the week. How about you?

At a high level, there are two *different* payment types or classifications and four *different* subclassifications. The two classifications of payments are lump-sum or single payments and annuities. Payment frequency will allow you to figure out whether you're dealing with a lump-sum payment or a series of payments. The four payment subclassifications relate to the *different* types of annuities. Amount and timing of each annuity payment will allow you to understand what you're dealing with as far as the annuity subclassification. An even annuity is a series (frequency) of payments with level amount and timing. An even perpetuity is a series (frequency) of even payments (amount) that continues infinitely (timing). An uneven annuity is a series (frequency) of uneven payments (amount) that continue for a finite period (timing). An uneven perpetuity is a series (frequency) of payments (amount) that increase based on the growth rate (of inflation) and which continues infinitely (timing).

Once you have the counting money part down, telling time for an even annuity is easy. Take for example an even annuity that calls for semiannual payments. For this annuity, the time span *in* between periods or payments (on the timeline) represents six months. But telling time for a lump-sum or single payment isn't always straightforward.

How you tell time for a lump-sum payment will depend on the situation and whether you're given latitude in terms of telling time. Consider the situation that involves withdrawing a certain amount of money from a savings account eighteen months from today. In this lump-sum payment example, you might have the option of telling time with monthly periods, quarterly periods, or six-month periods. I say "might" because if the true investment yield for any one of those time spans is given, then it just makes sense to use that number.

From time to time, there will be situations where you will have some latitude regarding how you decide to tell time as it relates to the time span *in* between periods or payments (on the timeline). In other words, when you're not dealing with an even annuity and when you need to calculate the true investment yield.

Whether you get to determine how to tell time on the timeline, one thing that will always be given with certainty is the amount of one or more payments. What you do with that information will determine your future success in answering the question. Here I'm partly referring to the *different* payment signs.

A great illustration for the *different* payment signs is the bird in the hand and the two in the bush visual. A negative sign denotes money—when I say "money," you think "payment"—leaving your hand. In other words, money invested or deposited. A positive (no sign) value denotes money—you know the drill—coming into your hand. In other words, money received or withdrawn.

Time (*TVM Rule #1*)

As described above, telling time in the context of the Mathematics of Finance starts with counting money. In other words, knowledge of what you're dealing with in terms of the time span *in* between the periods or payments (on the timeline).

The opening quote tells us that "Time is money." But we can also learn something from George Gissing's take on this wisdom. He said, "Time is money, says the proverb, but turn it around and you get a precious truth. Money is time."

In addition to picking up what George was putting down, this reminds us that it takes 3 and 1 to get to 2. First you count money, next you tell time, and then you can "read and write" the true investment yield. You'll find an entire chapter in this user manual on the topic of reading and writing "i," which is the ultimate goal of the *312* warm-up routine.

In a hot minute, I'll teach you the importance of not only being able to read or interpret the true investment yield but also being able to write it out so that you know you're fully warmed up and ready to work out the math. It takes being able to count money or consider the *different* payment types (*TVM Rule #3*) to be able to tell time with respect to the timeline (*TVM Rule #1*) before you can read and write or determine the true investment yield (*TVM Rule #2*).

In the TVM Rules, notice that "*in* between periods or payments (on the timeline)" wasn't written "iN between periods or payments (on the timeline)." In the context of the Mathematics of Finance, there's "n," and then there's "N." It's "n," not "N," that must correspond with "i."

The TVM Rules are based on the mnemonic *indifferent*, which isn't spelled "iNdifferent." The variable "N" represents the number of consecutive periods, or payments for an even annuity, that are subject to the same true investment yield and the same time span *in* between periods or payments (on the timeline). This may or may not be equal to the total investment period.

The building block Future Value equation, which you've seen already in this book and that will also be covered in the chapter titled Technical Specifications, sheds further light on how "N" may not equal the total investment period. In all but one of the building block Time Value of Money equations, there's a direct or indirect mathematical relationship between "i" and "N": while "N" isn't a variable in the building block Time Value of Money equations for a perpetuity, you could get the same value using the corresponding building block Time Value of Money equation for an annuity, which includes both "i" and "N."

For example, if you're telling time on the timeline with semiannual periods, and then you need to switch it up and tell time using annual periods at some point during the total investment period, you can see that one Future Value equation will only get you so far down the line into the future.

The mathematical relationship also carries over to any one of the building block Time Value of Money equations for an annuity.

For an even annuity, "N" represents the number of consecutive payments that are subject to the same true investment yield and the same time span *in* between periods or payments (on the timeline). So if there's any change with regard to the *money* you're counting or the *time* you're telling or what you're reading and writing for *value* or the true investment yield, you're going to need at least one more equation to get to a certain point in time.

Even in situations where there is no change with respect to the even annuity, "N" might only represent a portion of the total investment period. In both these even annuity examples, you can see how "N" will represent a period of time that is less than the total investment period. In other words, the variable "N" may not be within one number of the rightmost period marker on the timeline.

And what about that one building block Time Value of Money equation for which there isn't a mathematical relationship between "i" and "N?" Well, that's the building block True Investment Yield equation. In the building block True Investment Yield equation, the mathematical relationship is between "i" and "n." This is why the mnemonic *indifferent* is spelled the way it is and the reason being able to read and write "i" is so crucial.

A whole lot of "n's" will likely go into determining "N." Let's say you are analyzing a situation that contemplates an even annuity with receipts or payments every six months over a fifteen-year period.

Let me say that again.

Let's say you are analyzing a situation that contemplates an even annuity (frequency) with receipts (+) or payments (amount) every six months (timing) over a fifteen-year period (N). The time span *in* between payments or periods (on the timeline) is six months.

Now let's change it up since not every situation contemplates an even annuity. For the second example, let's pretend you are analyzing a situation that contemplates a lump-sum (frequency or lack thereof) payment (amount) to be received (+) thirty (N) years (timing) from today. Go back and locate "(timing)" in this and the preceding paragraph, and you'll see what I mean by "telling time" as it relates to the Mathematics of Finance.

A timeline for the first example would include at least thirty periods (N) each with a six-month time span (n) *in* between payments (on the timeline).

A timeline for the second example would include at least thirty periods (N) with an annual time span (n) *in* between periods (on the timeline).

The total investment period, which is visually represented by the timeline and consists of one or more "N's," will include one or more "n's":

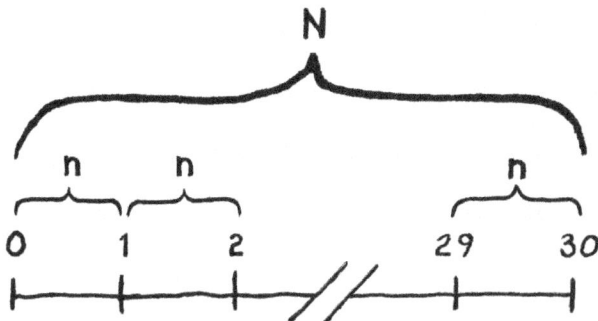

Just as there are seven days of the week, there are also seven common time spans *in* between periods or payments (on the timeline). Time span is typically measured in years, semiannual periods, quarters, months, weeks, days, and even odd periods that are greater than one year or less than one year but not one of the aforementioned periods.

There are countless possibilities for odd periods. For example, a two-year period, one that covers five years and two days, etc.

Without an understanding of the time span *in* between periods or payments (on the timeline), it's impossible to understand what true investment yield you need to circle.

Again, notice I didn't say "iN"; rather, "in." It's the time span *in* between periods or payments (on the timeline) (n) that must correspond with the time span of the true investment yield (i).

Value (*TVM Rule #2*)

Here's the skinny on value as it relates to the Time Value of Money. Value can be summed up with one letter. That letter is "i." To show you what I mean by *TVM Rule #2* being all about value and "i," let's once again reframe the TVM Rules, this time to include the five primary TVM financial calculator keys and the variables in the building block Time Value of Money equations:

1. N: money *in different* points in time;
2. i: correspond the time span *in* between periods or payments (on the timeline) (n) and the time span of the true investment yield; and
3. PV, PMT, and FV: consider *different* payment types and signs.

Again, each of the TVM Rules has a major and minor point. A cursory review of the TVM Rules might lead one to incorrectly interpret the major point of *TVM Rule #2* as anything but value. As a result, as it relates to the Mathematics of Finance, "i" is the manifestation of *TVM Rule #2*.

Before we go any further, I have a True or False statement for you to respond to:

The effective or equivalent investment yield is the true investment yield.

True it is. See what I mean about terminology? The effective or equivalent investment yield is just another way of referring to the true investment yield.

Investment yields are typically stated in annual terms. Regardless of the time span of the investment yield, the *true*—not *false*—investment yield is what you're after. A nominal investment yield is an approximation that doesn't consider the effects of compounding. Because a nominal investment yield doesn't consider the effects of compounding, it's also called a simple investment yield.

You expected this, right?

Since when is terminology something that we would call "simple?" There are at least three terms used to describe a true investment yield, so it seems par for the course to have at least three names used to describe the *false* investment yield. But there is a twist. A simple investment yield will be either a *false* investment yield or a *true* investment yield. The *simple truth* with respect to investment yields is that a simple investment yield with a time span that is equal to the time span of the compounding period is also a true investment yield. In this case, compounding hasn't had time to work its "magic" to produce return *on* return *on* investment.

Every nominal investment yield is a simple investment yield; however, sometimes a simple investment yield will be a true investment yield. For example, a simple annual investment yield with annual compounding is both a *simple and true* annual investment yield. Likewise, a simple quarterly investment yield with quarterly compounding is both a *simple and true* quarterly investment yield. Conversely, a simple annual investment yield with semiannual compounding is a *simple and false* annual investment yield. In summary, a true investment yield will always consider the *effects* of compounding, but whether there are *effects* of compounding depends on whether there is more than one compounding period within the time span of the true investment yield—which isn't the case for a simple and true investment yield. This relates directly to the definitions of "n" and "c" in the **TVM Formula**™. In other words, there's a difference between the number of compounding *periods* and the number of times compounding *occurs* within the time span *in* between periods or payments (on the timeline) or the time span of the simple investment yield.

Can you recite *TVM Rule #2* word for word? It's not that long, and I'd like to think that the words are somewhat rhythmic and roll off the tongue. If you can't yet, don't worry. The component of the mnemonic that relates to *TVM Rule #2* is the "in" of *indifferent*. *TVM Rule #2* reminds you to correspond "n"—the time span *in* between periods or payments (on the timeline)—and "i"—the time span of the true investment yield. The purpose of the *312* warm-up routine is to do just that. Without the correct true investment yield "i," you're wasting your time trying to analyze and evaluate a real-world Time Value of Money situation. So there you have it. That's the *312*!

All this talk about elementary school reminds me of another blast from my past which also related to PE—the Presidential Fitness Test, which as of this writing had been replaced with the Presidential Youth Fitness Program. One of the tests I dreaded was pull-ups.

All these years later, I hear people say that if you want to get better at pull-ups, you should do pull-ups. This chapter explains with mostly words how the *312*—the TVM Rules rearranged—is the warm-up required to get in a position to work out or analyze and evaluate real-world Time Value of Money situations using the 3-Step Systematic Approach to apply the Mathematics of Finance. But it's called the Mathematics—not *Words*—of Finance! Using the same logic that it takes doing pull-ups to get better at doing pull-ups, from this point forward, our primary focus is going to be on mathematics.

Chapter 8: Introduction: True Investment Yield

"Give me six hours to chop down a tree, and I will spend
the first four sharpening the axe."
—Abraham Lincoln

Fly fishing is a hobby that many people enjoy. Why wouldn't they? Time outdoors, the sounds of nature including water crashing against the shore, trees blowing in the wind, and birds conversing are all soothing and appealing. Add the excitement of catching a fish that you tricked into believing that the artificial fly was an actual insect, and I can see why people get hooked on this hobby.

Fly fishing is something that I've wanted to take up for some time ever since first learning how to tie a Palomar knot when I was bait fishing for walleye in northern Minnesota with my father-in-law while on an early summer trip with family. It's not that the Palomar knot is really a go-to knot in fly fishing, but learning how to tie this knot led to an interest in wanting to learn other knots that naturally led me to fly fishing, which is all about knots and more.

Accountability has tremendous value, so you heard it here. Once this book gets published, I plan to finally take up the hobby of fly fishing. Life is too short not to do what we dream about. Time is a nonrenewable resource.

Let's talk about time. Whenever we plan trips, whether around fly fishing getaways—what I might be doing while you're holding this book in your hands when my summer 9 to 5 is a 9-foot 5-weight fly rod—or getting together with family or friends, time is an important consideration. A weekend getaway looks a lot different than a two-week vacation in terms of needed groceries, the amount of clothes one needs to pack, etc. An important consideration that we'll be unpacking in this chapter is that of making sure to correspond "n"—the time span *in* between periods or payments (on the timeline)—and "i"—the time span of the true investment yield. A person who likes fly fishing but doesn't have an extensive knowledge of knots is like an aspiring or current finance professional who doesn't have a handle on the Mathematics of Finance.

What follows is an extension of the *312* warm-up discussion introduced in the Setup Instructions, which focused mostly on the *3*—counting money—and the *1*—telling time—since there wasn't any math in the last chapter. With the background of the *312*, now it's time to apply it.

Once you comprehend the material in this chapter, you'll be ready to learn how to work out or analyze and evaluate real-world Time Value of Money situations using the 3-Step Systematic Approach to apply the Mathematics of Finance. One of the benefits of the *312* warm-up routine is that it also serves as a crosscheck as you work through a situation.

Before you can progress through the steps in the prescribed 1–2–3 manner, you'll have to have completed the *312* warm-up routine, the primary purpose of which is to determine the true investment yield.

Without the correct true investment yield, don't waste your time. The *312* warm-up routine to the 3-Step Systematic Approach helps to mitigate the risk of "Garbage *in*, garbage out." You don't want "garbage *in*" for the "in" of *indifferent* or the true investment yield.

Match the Hatch: TVM Rule #2

In fly fishing, they talk about the need to match the hatch. This means that the person fishing needs to present an artificial fly that matches the hatch of insects that fish are currently feasting on. In other words, present a fly lure that matches the current hatch of emerging insects. It takes a little bit of prework to see what's on a fish's menu.

You match the hatch with respect to the Mathematics of Finance when you correspond or match the time span *in* between periods or payments (on the timeline) and the time span of the true investment yield. You may need to manipulate the stated investment yield to determine the true investment yield, which we've already established can also be referred to as the effective or equivalent investment yield.

While in practice terms such as effective investment yield or equivalent investment yield are oftentimes used interchangeably to describe the true investment yield, for some—including me—there are implied meanings in these terms which can, but need not, muddy the water. Right or wrong, whenever the time span *in* between periods or payments (on the timeline) is equal to the time span of the simple investment yield and there is more than one compounding period during that time span, I tend to think of the true investment yield as an effective investment yield. The number of compounding periods within the time span of the simple investment yield will determine the delta between the simple investment yield and the true investment yield.

Moving on.

Whenever the time span *in* between periods or payments (on the timeline) is greater than or less than the time span of the simple investment yield, I like to think of the true investment yield as an equivalent investment yield. It's kind of like extrapolation and interpolation, respectively.

This process of determining the effective or equivalent investment yield is somewhat like trying to fit a square peg in a round hole. Anyone who has knowledge of the Apollo 13 space mission will likely know the mayday communication that was sent on a day in April 1970: "Houston, we've had a problem" is the famous line, but this was actually the first part of the second communication from space after the astronauts were asked to, "Say again please." In the hours that followed the message from space, NASA had to figure out how to connect a square filter to a system that only used round air filters using only available material aboard the spaceship that was a sitting duck. I think it's safe to call this the 1,001st use for Duck Tape. There is a saying: "If it quacks like a duck, it's a duck." Whether one chooses to call it an effective investment yield or an equivalent investment yield, it quacks like a true investment yield. This is the one word that gets the point across, and as the saying goes, "Less is more."

Telling Time: "n"

We need to take a short detour to discuss "n" before we can continue the discussion regarding "i." Just as the astronauts aboard the Apollo 13 spaceship used their trusty OMEGA Speedmaster Professional chronograph watches to manually perform precision maneuvers in the depths of space, aspiring and current finance professionals need to be cognizant of the time span *in* between periods or payments (on the timeline) in order to determine the true investment yield.

There is an artistic element to the Time Value of Money through the pen scratches that are put down on paper and become timelines. Obviously, there is no scale to timeline drawings. For example, a timeline with an annual time span *in* between periods or payments would not be twice as long as a timeline that has the same number of periods but a semiannual time span *in* between period markers. That said, to illustrate a point, the below timelines should be considered to be drawn to scale:

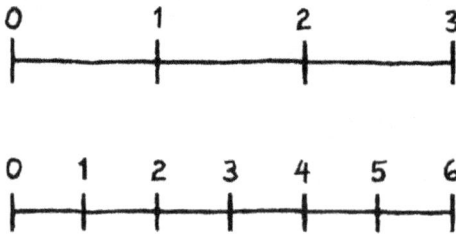

Again, for the sake of this discussion, we need to imagine for a moment that scale with respect to the timeline matters. Since we're already in imagination mode, further assume that the time span *in* between periods or payments (on the timeline) is represented by a narrow drawbridge that has been lowered to a horizontal position. When each drawbridge is in its upright or vertical position, it is exactly in line with the period marker on the timeline. It would take turning a make-believe crank for these make-believe drawbridges to be rotated down by 90 degrees to form the timeline.

Now that you have that in your mind's eye, I need to reveal that the drawbridge is the stem of the letter "n" that just happens to be as tall as it is wide. In the vertical position, the "feet" or serifs rest on the period markers that the serifs form when they are lowered to create the timeline. What you're left with is what you know to be a timeline—I don't know about you, but from now on, I'm always going to see lowered "drawbridges" or stems of the letter "n":

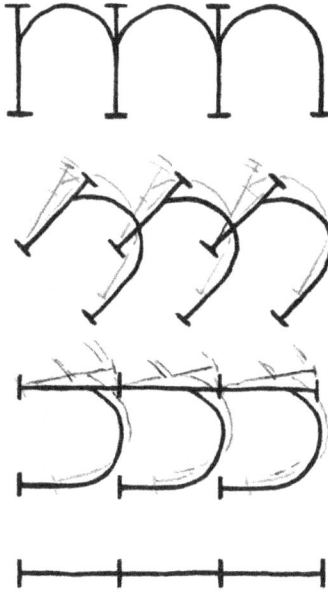

Similarly, the lowercase "i" can be thought of as a parallel drawbridge that is just as narrow:

With that visualized, now let's revisit the concept of scale as if it were a thing with respect to timelines. The longer the time span *in* between period markers on the timeline, the longer the required drawbridges (plural). If the time span *in* between periods or payments (on the timeline) represented twelve months, for example, a true semiannual investment yield won't get you to where you need to be (as you can see from the X-ray view through the "n" drawbridges which reveals the dot of the "i" drawbridges):

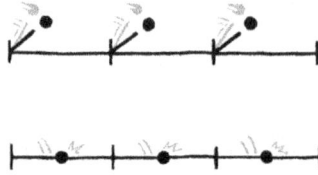

In the above illustration, the "i" drawbridges stopped short. Why is this a problem? We'll be discussing why this is a problem from a Time Value of Money perspective, but there's also a *drawbridge* perspective.

If you were in charge of moving something from one drawbridge to the next and needed use of the parallel drawbridges, think again. It's not happening in this illustration: halfway in, you'd run out of drawbridge. There'd be a crash, but I'll leave it up to your imagination as to whether the "and burn" part is applicable.

Similarly, a true annual investment yield won't cut it if the time span *in* between periods or payments (on the timeline) represented six months:

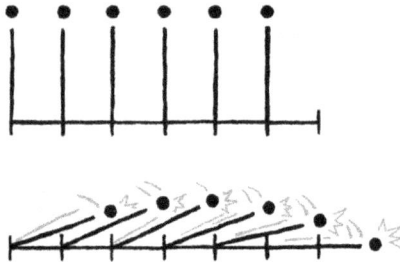

In the above illustration, the "i" drawbridges wouldn't lie flat since each "i" drawbridge is longer than the distance *in* between period markers (on the timeline), which causes a pile-up.

In both of these examples, you wouldn't have a *line*, so you wouldn't have a timeline. The critical reader might say, "Since when is the letter 'i,' dot included, the same height as the letter 'n'?" Well done, critical reader! For this illustration to work, we need to assume that the letter "i" with its dot is the same height as the letter "n," so the font size of the letter "i" is slightly smaller than that of the letter "n." When both the "n" and "i" drawbridges match in terms of height and are lowered, they form a timeline, and the dot of the letter "i" will be in the crosshairs of the serif of the letter "n" that forms the period markers:

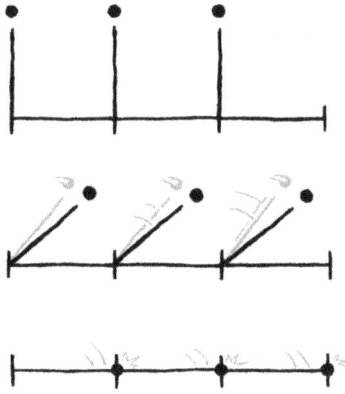

The above illustration shows the mental image you're going for with the dot of the letter "i" in the crosshairs of the serif of the letter "n." In this example, the time span *in* between periods or payments (on the timeline) is twelve months and you're working with a true annual investment yield. You match the hatch with respect to the Mathematics of Finance when you correspond or match the time span *in* between periods or payments (on the timeline) and the time span of the true investment yield, and this is how it's represented with an illustration of the timeline.

Remember that "n" refers to the time span *in* between periods or payments (on the timeline), not to be confused with "N" which represents the number of consecutive periods, or payments for an even annuity, that are subject to the same true investment yield and the same time span *in* between periods or payments (on the timeline). A timeline will be made up of one or more "n's" and one or more "N's" and will represent the total investment period.

Reading and Writing: "i"

In the Technical Specifications portion of the user manual, the building block Time Value of Money equations are presented together. If there's only one equation you choose to memorize, the building block True Investment Yield equation is it:

$$\left[1+\left(\tfrac{s}{c}\right)\right]^n - 1 = i$$

Here is the notation for the above equation—the TVM spin on the "s Corp.":

s: simple investment yield

i: true investment yield

n: number of actual or as if compounding periods within the time span *in* between periods or payments (on the timeline)

c: number of compounding periods within the time span of the simple investment yield

The notation, in particular "s," recognizes that the stated investment yield will be a simple and false investment yield or a simple and true investment yield. This is why "s" stands for the simple investment yield and not the stated investment yield. It's also why reference to "nominal" wouldn't work. That and "n" was taken already. You'll notice that here "n" has an expanded definition from how its defined in *TVM Rule #2*. It still includes the piece about "the time span *in* between periods or payments (on the timeline)" so consistency is maintained.

There is a relationship between the unit of time for the variables "c" and "n." It's important to recognize this fact because the time span *in* between periods or payments (on the timeline) will be equal to, greater than, or less than the time span of the compounding period of the simple investment yield. From time to time the value for the variable "n" will be a fraction. Left alone, a value of "1/3" for the variable "n" doesn't mean much. In fact, you may be asking, "If 'n' represents the number of actual or as if compounding periods within the time span *in* between periods or payments (on the timeline), what kind of time span is '1/3'?" With the knowledge, for example, that there are four compounding periods within the time span of the simple annual investment yield, then you would interpret a value of "1/3" for the variable "n" to mean it's as if there is one compounding period within the one-month time span *in* between periods or payments (on the timeline): see the P.P.S. at the end of this chapter to learn more about the 30/360 day-count convention. In summary, you need to know the time span of the compounding period of the simple investment yield to be able to interpret the value for the variable "n" and ultimately the time span *in* between periods or payments (on the timeline).

Something you will encounter in the "trees" as you work through the fundamentals of the Mathematics of Finance — although likely with more regularity than Sasquatch sightings — is a simple investment yield that is in fact a true investment yield in disguise. For example, a simple investment yield with annual compounding that some people — not you because you'll be following the **TVM Formula**™ — will refer to as a simple or nominal annual investment yield: we talk in terms of the "simple investment yield" and the "true investment yield."

In the building block True Investment Yield equation, when "c" and "n" both take the value of "1," that's when you're dealing with an "s" that could be thought of as the "Sasquatch investment yield" since Sasquatch starts with the letter s. Put another way, a simple investment yield that is in fact a true investment yield.

From time to time, the stated investment yield will be a not simple and true investment yield with all the associated information that would allow you to back into the simple investment yield using the building block True Investment Yield equation. At other times, the stated investment yield will be a true investment yield for a certain time span without any related information, so you won't be able to use the building block True Investment Yield equation other than to determine the equivalent or simple investment yield based on a given number of compounding periods; i.e., "c" will be the plug number.

Regardless of whether you have enough information to run the numbers through the building block True Investment Yield equation, there's nothing stopping you from "playing" with the numbers by changing up "c" to move from the simple investment yield to determine a certain true investment yield and vice versa.

When the stated investment yield is a simple and false investment yield, make sure to put the stated investment yield in the placeholder for the variable "s" in the building block True Investment Yield equation.

When the stated investment yield is a simple and true investment yield make sure to put the stated investment yield in the placeholder for the variable "i" in the building block True Investment Yield equation. Likewise, when the stated investment yield is a not simple and true investment yield make sure to put the stated investment yield in the placeholder for the variable "i" as well. Remember, it's a question of whether the stated investment yield *is* true (i) or false (s). No need to write me if you encounter in the wild—as I'm sure you will—a simple investment yield that is a true investment yield in disguise, but feel free to send me any photo you take of a Sasquatch while walking through real trees!

Investment Yield Manipulation

This chapter opened with a story about fly fishing, but people have been fishing by casting bait (minnows, worms, leeches, grasshoppers, etc.) for a lot longer than by casting flies. There's an ancient proverb that says, "Give a person a fish and you feed them for a day. Teach them how to fish and you feed them for a lifetime." And this, my friends, leads us into the discussion about how to complete the *312* warm-up routine and determine the true investment yield. Determining the TIY (true investment yield) is a DIY (do it yourself) exercise. Sure, every once in a while, you'll be given a true investment yield, but this saying applied to the Mathematics of Finance teaches us that you need to learn how to fish the true investment yield out of a simple investment yield to thrive and survive in the finance industry.

Simple yield manipulation

Simple yield manipulation is required to determine the true investment yield when the time span *in* between periods or payments (on the timeline) matches the time span of the compounding period for the simple investment yield.

Performing this mathematical operation is *simple* and involves dividing the simple investment yield by the number of compounding periods within the time span of the simple investment yield. For example, if the situation in question contemplates quarterly periods *in* between periods or payments (on the timeline) and you're working with a simple annual investment yield of 10% with quarterly compounding, simply divide the simple investment yield by 4 to determine the true quarterly investment yield.

Even though it's this simple, I still recommend that you follow through with the mathematical operations of the building block True Investment Yield equation and work it out to "i." In other words, divide 0.10 by 4, add 1, raise 1.025 to the power of 1, and then subtract 1 to solve for "i."

This is good form, and the reps will help to burn the building block True Investment Yield equation into your mind. Going back to the fishing analogy, think of this like the *actual* insect, worm, or fish used in bait casting.

Complex yield manipulation

Complex yield manipulation is required to determine the true investment yield when the time span *in* between periods or payments (on the timeline) does not match the time span of the compounding period for the simple investment yield. This can go one of two ways. The time span *in* between periods or payments (on the timeline) will be greater than or less than that of the compounding period. When this is the case, what you need to do is determine the true investment yield *as if* there were a match. Think of this like the *artificial* fly used in fly fishing.

Time span *in* between periods or payments (on the timeline) is greater than that of the compounding period:

Let's consider a situation that contemplates an annual time span *in* between periods or payments (on the timeline) and a simple annual investment yield of 10% with quarterly compounding. You'd need to manipulate the simple investment yield as follows to determine the true annual investment yield:

$$[1+(\tfrac{.10}{4})]^4 - 1 = .103813$$

In this example, there are four compounding periods within the time span of the simple investment yield. In other words, there are four *actual* compounding periods within the time span *in* between periods or payments (on the timeline). The simple annual investment yield or the true quarterly investment yield won't do you any good in this situation—other than helping you to determine "i."

Time span *in* between periods or payments (on the timeline) is less than that of the compounding period:

Next let's consider a situation that contemplates a monthly time span *in* between periods or payments (on the timeline) and the same simple annual investment yield of 10% with quarterly compounding. You'd need to manipulate the simple investment yield as follows to determine the true monthly investment yield:

$$[1+(\tfrac{.10}{4})]^{1/3} - 1 = .008265$$

In this example, since the time span *in* between period markers on the timeline is represented by monthly periods, it's *as if* there is one compounding period within the time span *in* between periods or payments (on the timeline), which is why I refer to this as *artificial*. As a result, you need to determine the true monthly investment yield.

While not that complex, complex yield manipulation requires exponential operation along with lower-level mathematical operations to solve for the true investment yield, as opposed to simple yield manipulation which requires simple division along with other basic mathematical operations.

And know that there's a difference between an *annualized* investment yield and a true annual investment yield. The former just might be a kind of hybrid investment yield that started off as an effective or true investment yield but was made "false" by simple multiplication. For example, the quoted yield for a treasury note or bond is usually an annualized yield, which because of the semiannual interest payments quacks like a simple investment yield with two compounding periods within the annual time span.

Making the complex simple

You can also use *simple* multiplication to annualize the true monthly investment yield—for example, to determine the simple annual(ized) investment yield of 9.9178%. For example, say you knew that the true monthly investment yield was 0.8265% but wanted to express the (simple) annualized investment yield.

Working backward to determine the simple investment yield:

Have you ever lost something, such as a wallet, and thought to yourself or been advised to backtrack your steps through where you've been? The mathematical operations required to "undo" or adjust a given true investment yield to determine the simple investment yield is kind of like that in terms of backtracking steps.

Working backward in the true investment yield equation involves performing mathematical operations in reverse order, which means moving mostly right to left in the equation: when it comes to the values within the brackets, you'll be moving left to right; however, you'll still be performing the mathematical operations in reverse order. You'll be adding instead of subtracting, raising to the inverse power rather than the whole number, subtracting instead of adding, and multiplying instead of dividing. The following example shows how to work backward from a true quarterly investment yield of 2.5% to calculate the unknown simple annual investment yield with monthly compounding:

$$\left[1+\left(\tfrac{s}{12}\right)\right]^{3}-1=.025$$

$$\left[(.025+1)^{\frac{1}{3}}-1\right]\times 12=.099178$$

That's how you reverse engineer a true investment yield using the building block True Investment Yield equation. Pretty slick, huh? Up until this point, you'd been working with a simple annual investment yield of 10% with quarterly compounding. The only difference has been the time span *in* between the periods or payments (on the timeline), which gave rise to the discussion regarding simple and complex yield manipulation. A simple annual investment yield of 9.9178% with monthly compounding was added to the mix. The next group of illustrations provides a double-check to the math up until this point:

$$\left[1+\left(\tfrac{10}{4}\right)\right]^{4}-1=.103813$$

$$\left[1+\left(\tfrac{.099178}{12}\right)\right]^{12}-1=.103813$$

Here *indifferent* takes on a meaning outside of the **TVM Formula**™ and provides a slightly different angle as to why investors are *indifferent* between values of money *in different* points in time, which further supports the reason why this one-word mnemonic was selected. All else equal, investors would be *indifferent* over a one-year investment period between a simple annual investment yield of 10% with quarterly compounding and a simple annual investment yield of 9.9178% with monthly compounding. Said another way, investors would be *indifferent* over a three-month investment period between a true quarterly investment yield of 2.50% and a true monthly investment yield of 0.8265%:

$$\left[1+\left(\tfrac{10}{4}\right)\right]^{1}-1=.025$$

$$\left[1+\left(\tfrac{.099178}{12}\right)\right]^{3}-1=.025$$

Here's the math in support of the fact that investors would be *indifferent* over a three-month investment period between a true quarterly investment yield of 2.50% and a true monthly investment yield of 0.8265%. Here, rather than comparing the two on the basis of the true annual investment yield, the true quarterly investment yield is used to show that investors would be *indifferent* between these two simple annual investment yields with their different compounding periods.

Here's the kicker. For a given true investment yield, you can determine the simple (and true) investment yield for which an investor would be *indifferent* without needing to know the number of compounding periods within the time span of the simple investment yield. Given a true quarterly investment yield of 2.50%, for example, you could use the building block True Investment Yield equation to determine the simple (and true) investment yield for any time span. In other words, the simple (and true) monthly investment yield of 0.8265%, the simple (and true) weekly investment yield of 0.2060%, the simple (and true) daily investment yield of 0.0274%, and so on and so forth. In each one of these examples, the variable "c" indirectly takes the value of "1" which is to be interpreted that it's *as if* there was one compounding period within the time span of the simple investment yield, which in this case is a simple *and* true investment yield. So, when you work backward using the building block True Investment Yield equation and you don't know the value for the variable "c," you'll be solving for a simple or equivalent investment yield for which you'd be *indifferent*. But since we're always focused on "i" rather than "s," it would be good form to add 1 and raise the simple (and true) investment yield to the power of 1 and then subtract 1 to determine the given true investment yield.

That's a lot of 1's.

Could you technically use the value of the variable "s" here? You could, but I'm advising that you take it from "s" to "i." While it's the same value, you can rest comfortably knowing that it's in the proper place in the building block True Investment Yield equation. Remember, "i" is what you're after.

Naming convention

Writing: "i"
Many people enjoy writing with and collecting fountain pens. Like anything, one can spend as much or as little as they'd like when getting into the hobby. From a few dollars—really—up to four figures and beyond—*really*! One of the most recognizable fountain pens is the Montblanc Meisterstück 146. Reference is made to this particular make and model because of its naming convention,

which we'll piggyback off of to get about the business of reading and writing "i."

With respect to the naming convention for the Montblanc Meisterstück 146, the *1* is reference to the (Meisterstück) product line; the *4* is reference to the (piston) filling system; and the *6* is reference to the (#6) nib size. The **TVM Formula**™ calls for a similar naming convention, which I refer to as the inc shorthand.

Pens aren't the only writing instruments or tools of the trade that have numbers. From the 146 to the 602. The Blackwing pencil, that is. Don't think you know the Blackwing 602? Think again. From John Steinbeck to John Williams, from Quincy Jones to Chuck Jones… the list of current or former fans—you read this right—of this pencil goes on and on. We're talking about creative works such as *Of Mice and Men*, *Star Wars*, *Thriller*, and *Looney Tunes*, just to name a few. Pencils are still in, and this pencil is a go-to writing instrument of people who create something from scratch. This brings us to why we're talking about the mother of all pencils, which may add insult to injury for some former students who thought the financial calculator was a dinosaur. "Does it pen?" doesn't have the same ring nor the meaning and industry recognition as "Does it pencil?" Pens like the 146 might be used to ink business deals, but finance professionals pencil-out investment opportunities using pencils like the 602. As if terminology wasn't enough for us to wrap our heads around. We could go on and on about idioms or sayings in finance, in particular those relating to investment opportunities.

Before going any further, I should point out that the inc shorthand is not to be confused with the subscript for "i." Just like the subscript for "N," subscripting "i" is prescribed in the 3-Step Systematic Approach. When I talk about writing "i" in the context of the 3-Step Systematic Approach, I'm referring to subscripting "i" using a pen or pencil and paper. The subtle difference between the inc shorthand and the subscript for "i" is that the former is a continuous string of values: one for "i," one for "n," and one for "c." The acronym "inc," spelled differently than the ink used in a fountain pen, is composed of the primary variables in the building block True Investment Yield equation: only the "s" variable is missing, and with all but one variable, we can solve for the unknown simple investment yield. In this context, "reading" refers to interpreting the true investment yield using the inc shorthand or the building block True Investment Yield equation. Each of the numbers in the aforementioned 146 reference means something to people who enjoy fountain pens, and similarly, each of the numbers in the inc shorthand or in the subscript for "i" will mean something to the aspiring or current finance professional applying the Mathematics of Finance using the 3-Step Systematic Approach.

Here's an example to help you see how the inc shorthand relates to the building block True Investment Yield equation:

$$\left[1+\left(\tfrac{\$}{\mathcal{C}}\right)\right]^{n}_{\wedge}-1=i$$

$$i, n, c$$

$$.103813, \ 4, \ 4$$

As you can see, the inc shorthand provides a summary of the primary variables in the building block True Investment Yield equation, which can be used to back into the simple investment yield, if needed. Your goal should be to replicate the building block True Investment Yield equation using only the inc shorthand and vice versa. The inc shorthand helps you with your longhand math!

One of the following true investment yields also doubles as a simple investment yield: this is the "Sasquatch investment yield" that was referenced earlier. From reading the inc shorthand, can you spot the investment yield that would show up twice in the building block True Investment Yield equation? In other words, a stated investment yield that is both a true investment yield and a simple investment yield?

.103813, 4, 4

.10, 1, 1

If you said, "The inc shorthand for the true investment yield of 10%." you're correct. Here's the supporting math:

$$\left[1+\left(\tfrac{10}{4}\right)\right]^{4}-1=.103813$$

$$\left[1+\left(\tfrac{10}{1}\right)\right]^{1}-1=.10$$

Without spoiling the new content in the Quick Start Guide, this is the time to mention that just as you'll be using the subscripts for "N" and "i" in tandem in the 3-Step Systematic Approach, you also need to consider the subscript for "N" to accurately read what has been written about the inc shorthand. This is a kind of second line of defense, since the true investment yield will not always be written in annual terms. You'll be fluent in reading and writing "i" when you also consider the subscript for "N." Interpreting the following inc shorthand is made possible when read in conjunction with the subscript for "N":

$$.638616, 20, 4$$

$$N_{5A}$$

We'll get into the specifics regarding the subscript for "N" in the Quick Start Guide, but suffice it to say that "5A" is used to denote a five-year time span *in* between periods or payments (on the timeline). With this information, you can read the inc shorthand and, as a result, understand that you're working with a true 5-year investment yield with quarterly compounding. Stated differently, you could interpret this to say that there are twenty quarters or five years *in* between period markers on the timeline. The building block True Investment Yield equation supports this and could be used to back into the simple annual investment yield of 10% with quarterly compounding:

$$\left[1+\left(\tfrac{s}{4}\right)\right]^{20}-1=.638616$$

$$\left[1+\left(\tfrac{10}{4}\right)\right]^{20}-1=.638616$$

Now that you know how to read an inc shorthand for a true investment yield with a time span greater than one year, let's go the other way. You'll recognize the inc shorthand, but this time you'll also find the associated subscript for "N":

$$.025, 1, 4$$

$$N_{Q}$$

The subscript for "N" tells us that there is a quarterly time span *in* between periods or payments (on the timeline), so when read together, you can interpret the inc shorthand. In other words, you understand you're working with a true quarterly investment yield of 2.5%.

Reading: "i"

Around the time of the Great Recession, I attended a presentation given by a colleague, a head portfolio manager who was responsible for investing billions of dollars each year on behalf of institutional investor clients. If this guy had a superpower, it was his ability to read or interpret graphs and the like and see what others might not. That particular day, he was sharing with us that his read of the graphs told him that we were in for a bull market run like never before experienced. Now remember the time. We were in the shadow—and it was a long one—of the Great Recession, the effects of which lingered. His presentation got a lot of us talking, and I'd be lying to you—which I wouldn't do—if I told you that the takeaway as we debriefed on the way back to our respective offices was anything but, "Yeah, right."

It turned out he was right! He and others like him are living proof that the saying, "It's who you know, not what you know" isn't an absolute truth.

You would be well served by developing an ability to read not only the inc shorthand and subscripts for "i" and "N" but also the building block Time Value of Money equations, which will be presented in the next chapter. As it relates to the inc shorthand, first you should be looking for how to tell time for the time span *in* between periods or payments (on the timeline).

Let's revisit inc shorthand we've worked with already to show you what I mean:

.103813, 4, 4

.10, 1, 1

We've already covered that most investment yields are stated in annual terms, but that's where the subscript for "N" comes in handy. Assuming you were working with a subscript for "N" that reads "A" to represent an annual time span *in* between periods or payments (on the timeline), here's how you would pair it with the inc shorthand. You can read the first inc shorthand—reading from right to left—to say that there are four (three-month) compounding periods within the time span of the simple investment yield (12 ÷ "c" = 3) and that there are four *actual* compounding periods within the time span *in* between periods or payments (on the timeline).

It's *as if* you're working with a true annual investment yield of 10.3813% with annual compounding—which is one example of where the *artificial* reference comes in because we know there are 4 *actual* compounding periods within the year. You would interpret this inc shorthand to say that 10.3813% is a true annual investment yield for the *artificial* one-year compounding period.

You can read the second inc shorthand—again, reading right to left—to say that there is one compounding period within the time span of the simple investment yield and one *actual* compounding period within the time span *in* between periods or payments (on the timeline). You would interpret this inc shorthand to say that 10% is a true annual investment yield for the *actual* one-year compounding period.

In case you're wondering, the inc shorthand for the true monthly investment yield of 0.8265% which was presented earlier would be written "0.008265, 1/3, 4." You would interpret this inc shorthand to say that 0.8265% is a true monthly investment yield for the *artificial* one-month compounding period.

Now let's analyze an investment opportunity that contemplates an even annuity to keep this conversation going about the importance of being able to read or interpret both the inc shorthand and other building block Time Value of Money equations.

What follows is the building block Present Value of an Ordinary Annuity equation, which is a sneak peek for the Technical Specifications, as well as a completed equation based on investment assumptions:

$$PVOA = PMT \times \left[\frac{(1+i)^N - 1}{(1+i)^N \times i} \right]$$

$$500 \times \left[\frac{(1.06)^{18} - 1}{(1.06)^{18} \times .06} \right]$$

Have you picked up on the fact that without the inc shorthand — or the subscript for "i" which will be introduced in the Quick Start Guide — and subscript for "N," you can't tell how we're telling time? In other words, the time span *in* between payments (on the timeline) is unknown. In the following illustration, you'll see how the inc shorthand and subscript for "N" complement the building block Present Value of an Ordinary Annuity equation:

$$500 \times \left[\frac{(1.06)^{18} - 1}{(1.06)^{18} \times .06} \right]$$

$$.06, 12, 12$$

$$N_A$$

With the information obtained from the inc shorthand and the subscript for "N," now you know that the eighteen even payments will be made over eighteen years, not some other investment period consisting of eighteen evenly spaced periods. Here you're "telling time" with annual periods. You would interpret the inc shorthand to say that 6% is a true annual investment yield for the *artificial* one-year compounding period. In other words, there are twelve *actual* compounding periods within the annual time span *in* between payments (on the timeline). If the middle 12 or the "n" of the inc shorthand were changed to 1 and the subscript for "N" changed to "M," then the even annuity would call for eighteen monthly payments over the eighteen-month investment period. Again, you can use the inc shorthand to back into the simple investment yield using longhand math:

$$.06, 12, 12$$

$$\left[1 + \left(\tfrac{S}{12} \right) \right]^{12} - 1 = .06$$

$$\left[1 + \left(\tfrac{.058411}{12} \right) \right]^{12} - 1 = .06$$

When an investment "comes back" and is returned, an investor expects to have something to show for having delayed consumption, opportunity cost, and for having taken on exposure to risk including the risk of inflation. That's where "i" or the return *on* investment comes in. The true investment yield is not to be confused with the real investment yield, the latter of which is the investment yield net of or adjusted for the impact of inflation. That said, the **TVM Formula**™ considers that at times you'll need the real investment yield. For example, when calculating the Present Value of an Ordinary Perpetuity or the Present Value of a Perpetuity Due. So how do we differentiate the real investment yield from the true investment yield? If we weren't so focused on consistency then it would have been easy to call "r" off the bench, since it's not a variable in the **TVM Formula**™, to explain the mathematical expression "i – g" where the variable "g" represents the growth rate of inflation. Underlining "i" seemed like the natural expression of this investment yield. That and "rndifferent" isn't a word, so there's no room for "r" in the TVM Wallet or elsewhere in the **TVM Formula**™.

As we're winding down the discussion related to the inc shorthand, here's another interesting observation. Outlining the inc of the building block True Investment Yield equation looks like a boomerang:

$$\left[1+\left(\tfrac{s}{c}\right)\right]^n - 1 = i$$

See what I mean by connectivity, this being one big "TVM puzzle," and the importance of not only having all the pieces but making sure they fit together? With the boomerang visual and a little practice, you can read into the situation to discover what you're dealing with in terms of the time span *in* between periods or payments (on the timeline) and ultimately the time span of the true investment yield. In other words, the relationship between "n" and "c," which are the two components of the subscript for "i" that you'll be using when it comes to the 3-Step Systematic Approach.

Take another look at the building block True Investment Yield equation but this time with grayscale:

$$i = \left[1+\left(\tfrac{s}{c}\right)\right]^n - 1$$

Notice how the variable "N" is nowhere to be found in this equation. Now you can really see how "n" leads to "i" and why they must correspond or match. When it comes to "i" in the Mathematics of Finance, you're fishing for the true investment yield—not the simple investment yield. The purpose of the *312* warm-up is to ensure that the time span *in* between periods or payments (on the timeline) matches the time span of the true investment yield. To do that is going to require that you be able to manipulate investment yields using longhand math and basic calculator functions.

P.S.

You might be wondering why I didn't reference continuous compounding in this chapter. Let's get real. When's the last time you actually worked with—I'm talking about outside a classroom—or know someone who worked with continuous compounding? Exactly. You could still use the building block True Investment Yield equation to approximate continuous compounding. How's that song go, "525,600 minutes…" That or some multiple is your "c" and then go about solving for whatever true investment yield you need; e.g., the approximate of the true three-year continuous investment yield. In terms of time measurement and compounding, minutes is pretty close to continuous. More often than not, a ballpark estimate may do the trick.

And if you've ever wondered where the *e* comes from, here's an explanation using the Time Value of Money. The FV of $1 after 1 year assuming a simple annual investment yield of 100% and continuous compounding is $2.718282…, which minus the dollar sign is *e*…a number that has no end in that it keeps going on and on with no repeating decimals. Easy, with a capital *e*, peasy.

P.P.S.

The dream of fly fishing goes way back to my early days in Corporate America when I was working as a commercial mortgage loan officer for the real estate arm of a global life insurance company. Still to this day, one of my favorite mortgage bankers and someone I'm proud to call a friend is Peter Dailey. Peter and I just see the world and business in a similar way—and both of us like math! Peter would routinely talk about "circling" a certain (interest) rate.

I tell you this story because I'd be remiss if this chapter ended without some discussion about day-count conventions. Since my former life was in commercial mortgage lending, and because the day-count convention is an important financing consideration or mortgage loan term, I'm going to break my own "rule" for a short few and start referring to the true investment yield as the "true interest rate."

This postscript focuses on a debt asset—yes you read that right, a financial instrument that fits into the debt or fixed income box is an asset from the lender or owner's perspective—so interest rate is more applicable for a couple reasons. You'll likely encounter day-count convention language for the interest rate out in the "wild."

Before we dive into the math related to day-count conventions, it's helpful to start by calling out the difference between accrued interest, simple interest, and compound interest.

Accrued interest is interest that has been incurred since the day of the last regular loan or debt service payment. In other words, the accumulated interest that hasn't been paid—in cash money—by the borrower. Accrued interest comes in two varieties: simple accrued interest and compound accrued interest. This doesn't need to be overly complicated. You know that the word *simple* implies that the effects of compounding were not considered. Simple accrued interest implies that there hasn't been return *on* return *on* investment during the accrual period.

This is typically how this provision of the loan documents would read, and it's worth pointing out that most mortgage loans require regular partial repayment of the outstanding principal balance over the loan term. In other words, the "snowball" of interest would only "roll" during the month if compounding occurred between regular loan debt service payments, which is compound accrued interest, or on a monthly basis if simple accrued interest were not repaid every month and capitalized or added to the outstanding principal balance of the loan.

The latter refers to negative amortization, which is not that common in the industry. Accrued interest is not to be confused with compound interest. Left unpaid, accrued interest would ultimately be compounded; however, as stated already, most loans require regular monthly debt service loan payments based on an amortization schedule. This results in a partial principal repayment each month.

If you're the borrower, can you see why you'd rather have simple accrued interest rather than compound accrued interest? The accrual method, just like the day-count convention, ultimately factors into determining the true investment yield or the effective cost of borrowing. But since interest *on* interest *on* the outstanding principal balance of the loan is not commonplace in the market, the focus of this discussion is on the day-count convention.

Before we back up the last claim with math, let's discuss day-count conventions. The most common day-count conventions are 30/360, Actual/360, 30/365, Actual/365, and Actual/Actual. For each day-count convention, the last number or word represents the agreed-upon number of days in a given year, and the first number or word represents the assumed number of days in a given month. The day-count convention 30/360 is also known as the "banker's year."

The "banker's year" assumes that there are 360 days in a year and 30 days in each month. The 30/360 day-count convention makes the math easy. Not all mortgage "bankers" are as good with math as Peter and need some help!

A mortgage loan is an example of a negotiated agreement, and the borrower and lender agree that for the purpose of calculating the simple daily interest rate, the assumption will be that there are 360 days in a year, and that for the purpose of calculating the simple accrued interest, it will be assumed that there are 30 days in each month.

In the inc shorthand for most mortgage loans, "c" would be 12 and the "n" would be 1. But this is really a 30/360 "banker's year" day-count convention in disguise, since you could divide the simple annual interest rate by 360 (/360) and then multiply by 30 to ultimately get the true monthly interest rate: the "c" isn't 360 because the loan document doesn't call for daily compounding or 360 compounding periods within the time span of the simple interest rate.

Now let's run the numbers using the inc shorthand "0.005, 1, 12." If this were a mortgage loan that required monthly debt service payments with interest calculated and accrued based on a 30/360 day-count convention, you could back into the simple annual interest rate of 6% in an unconventional way using the day-count convention:

$$[(.005 + 1)^{\frac{1}{1}} - 1] \times (360 \div 30) = .06$$

$$\left[1 + \left(\frac{.06}{(360 \div 30)}\right)\right]^{1} - 1 = .005$$

While we're on a roll, let's revisit the simple annual investment yield of 9.9178% with monthly compounding. Using the unconventional approach using the day-count convention math, if you were to plug "(360/30)" for "c," which is just another way of saying divide the simple annual investment yield by 360 and then multiply by 30, you'd ultimately get the true monthly investment yield of 0.8265%: in the building block True Investment Yield "c" is equal to 12 not 360, and "n" is equal to 1 not 30, so the inc shorthand would read, "0.008265, 1, 12." But for this fixed income asset, turning over the right rock would reveal that this loan is subject to a 30/360 day-count convention. If you wanted to really show that you know what you're doing, you could write the inc shorthand "0.008265, 1, 360/30."

So there you have it. You've been working with a 30/360 day-count convention and may not have realized it until now. If not already, there's no better time than now, since a finance professional who doesn't know about day-count conventions is a finance professional whose days in the industry may be numbered.

The key takeaway from this discussion is to show how dividing the (stated) simple annual investment yield by 12 in the denominator of the building block True Investment Yield equation is essentially the same thing as dividing by (360/30): the inverse of the day-count convention name, and the product of which is 12. In other words, the 30/360 day-count convention is widely used in practice and the go-to day-count convention of the Time Value of Money.

I feel the need to let you know that I'm not anti-spreadsheet; however, I'm a big proponent of using financial calculators and longhand math, as needed, to analyze and evaluate real-world Time Value of Money situations.

It always makes me laugh when one of my students—even if the student has experience in the industry—tries to tell me that financial calculators are rarely used anymore. Are you kidding me?

In my former life, with the help of Peter Dailey and others like him, our shop regularly originated an annual CML volume around $2 billion. We put those deals together using mostly pens or pencils, paper, and *financial calculators.*

I've heard all sides of the argument: one can't email work product using a financial calculator. I didn't say that we didn't use computers and spreadsheets. But real money managers use financial calculators. My experience is that people who use an HP-12C have likely been around the block a time or two. I'm just saying that the "Fincalc" is the original Fintech, and they're far from out of favor!

Soon we will dive into the Quick Start Guide, where the 3-Step Systematic Approach is presented. First, there is one more chapter, and more information from where the building block True Investment Yield equation came.

Before you consider skipping forward in this user manual, it's worth restating with a question my goal for you as it relates to the Time Value of Money.

When do you think you will have "arrived"? I think the question can also be phrased, "Can you teach it?"

That's true learning and one of the four pillars of my teaching philosophy, which is why I believe there are as many teachers as people in any one of my (physical or virtual) classrooms. It takes a higher level of understanding to teach, and that's why this teacher believes students should be put in a teacher's shoes as much as possible.

It's for this reason that in my classrooms, students regularly "switchback" between passive and active engagement in what I call the "See, Do, and Review." Students "See" me answer a math question, "Do" the math for a similar question on their own, and then a student will "Review" the math as a teacher walking through the question and providing step-by-step instruction or feedback.

Spreadsheet software has its place, but as it relates to the Mathematics of Finance, I think of spreadsheets more as a path of least resistance that hinder learning. As children grow up to become adults and go out on their own and do their own thing after they turn eighteen, you do you and use whatever tools you want to use to apply the Mathematics of Finance—that is *after* you've graduated to that point on Bloom's "mountain," where you know enough to be dangerous.

Until then and since you're still within the comfortable confines of the cover of this book, you'd do well to follow the prescribed path. At this point, there stands one chapter between comprehension and application.

Chapter 9: Technical Specifications: Building Block Time Value of Money Equations

"If you want something you've never had, you must be willing to do something you've never done."
—Thomas Jefferson

Ben Hogan—one of the greatest golfers of all time—claimed to have a swing secret. Like a lot of people who choose finance as their day job, I can golf, but I don't consider myself a golfer, if that makes sense. But even I'm mesmerized by watching old video clips of Ben Hogan's swing. It's truly something to behold.

Some will say that even more impressive—and possibly not present in today's game—was the crack sound that was produced when he made contact with the ball. Between the effortless and beautiful swing, the sound at impact more like a lumberjack striking a tree, and the fact that he could hit the ball a country mile without today's technology, many people are convinced that he did in fact have a swing secret.

Maybe we'll never know. Ben Hogan passed away in 1997.

He supposedly said that the secret was under his shoes or in the dirt.

Some have speculated that he might have had another shoe spike in one of his shoes.

I don't think so. Instead, was he simply referring to good old-fashioned hard work and the dirt of the practice range?

Of all the fundamentals of golf, Ben Hogan believed that developing a good grip was the place to start. Knowledge of the Mathematics of Finance starts with a good grip of the building block Time Value of Money equations.

I genuinely care about each of my students, which now takes on a new meaning that includes readers. If you're reading this book, then I'm one of your biggest fans even if we haven't formally met. I have a "dog in the hunt," as they say. I wouldn't be a teacher and author without students and readers. This is something I think about often.

Clayton John, a former colleague, helped me realize this back in the day. Clayton John was a living legend in the commercial real estate industry, but he didn't let that go to his head. He realized that he wouldn't have had the opportunity to underwrite, structure, negotiate, and originate new commercial mortgage loan product for the life insurance company—and make a great living to support his family—without life insurance salespeople.

This is why it was not uncommon to hear him telling people to find a life insurance salesperson, shake their hand, and say "Thank you." He meant it.

Sometimes we can overcomplicate things. Life is really pretty simple when you stop and think about it. I remember another one of Clayton John's lessons like it was yesterday. In classic Clayton John fashion, one day he asked a group of us a rhetorical question: "How is the date of Easter determined?" What he taught us that day was that you have to care enough to know how things work and not be afraid of the hard work it might take to figure it out. There's no "kind of" or "maybe." It's yes or no. You get it or you don't.

Because of this lesson, I can think of a handful of people who still to this day could tell you how the date of Easter is determined. You don't forget a lesson like that. For those who want to know it's the first Sunday, after the first full Moon, on or after the Vernal (Spring) Equinox. Kind of rolls off the tongue, doesn't it?

Since I gave you the answer, do me a favor and don't lose the important lesson here. The lesson is one of caring enough to do the work.

Before Clayton John made the trek to Cedar Rapids, Iowa, financial calculator in hand, responding to the job posting he saw in the Wall Street Journal and would later get, he was a high school math teacher in Albert City, Iowa.

I love this story for a lot of reasons. First and foremost, it showcases an important sequence that many people outright ignore. First comes the math, then comes the finance.

If my lesson from the not-so-widely known Clayton John—who back in his heyday was "The Man" when it came to commercial real estate finance—didn't get your attention, hopefully you'll take heed from the "father" of astronomy.

Galileo Galilei said, "If I were again beginning my studies, I would follow the advice of Plato and start with mathematics." Sad as it is, some people view the Mathematics of Finance as good-to-know information rather than fundamental to the profession.

I've said it before, and I'll say it again. In a perfect situation, I'd divide the Time Value of Money unit into two lessons. The first would focus on the building block Time Value of Money equations and students would only be allowed to use a pen or pencil, paper, and basic calculator functions. In other words, we'd work longhand math.

This is the foreign language class equivalent of not being able to speak your native language during certain classes. Math is a kind of language, so this isn't too much of a stretch. I get that not many people are going to work out real-world Time Value of Money questions using nothing but longhand math. I'm quick to raise my hand and recognize that this skill seems a better fit to double-check math related to more advanced real-world Time Value of Money situations.

In the second lesson, we'd work through real-world Time Value of Money questions using the tool of the trade: the financial calculator. Understanding the building block Time Value of Money equations and being able to visualize money flows (cash inflows and outflows over time) go hand in hand.

Unfortunately, not a lot of people get to the point of being able to visualize cash flows using only the building block Time Value of Money equations because they're in too much of a hurry. This isn't a race. Golfers don't just walk up to a ball and swing. No, the first part of taking the stance is getting the feet and legs—the foundation of the body—in the right position. There's also a pre-swing warm-up routine that involves getting set and likely includes visualization. Jack Nicklaus—another one of the greatest professional golfers of all time and an avid fly fisherman—swore by visualization and has essentially said that he hit every shot twice: first with his mind and then with his body. It's been said that there's no such thing as practice makes perfect, but that there is such a thing as perfect practice.

That's what dividing the Time Value of Money unit into two lessons would do, and that's essentially what you'll find in this book since you'll wrestle the building block Time Value of Money equations to the ground before you cut loose and use a "rescue tool" such as a financial calculator.

Tools of the trade, like financial calculators and software programs obviously have their place, but they can be good and bad. They're good in that they save time and perform certain tasks that would be nearly impossible for people—like determining the true annual investment yield over the investment period. They're bad when they become too much of a crutch. A crutch only comes in handy when one already knows how to walk. Think about that for a moment. First you need to walk through the math, so that you can run the numbers in your financial calculator later.

Sometimes people can create mountains out of molehills. There are only nine—count 'em, nine—building block Time Value of Money equations that stand between you and the real-world Time Value of Money questions you'll encounter in the classroom or in industry. Sound too difficult? If you're thinking, *no*, I like your enthusiasm! If you're thinking, *yes*, then I've got something you'll want to hear.

You could get by with committing only five of the building block Time Value of Money equations—those in italics—to memory. How's this possible? For two reasons.

First, remember the "Post-it Note event." There's a reason why Mike Trotter didn't need another Post-it Note to write out the building block Present Value equation. This is because the building block Future Value equation can be rearranged using algebra to reveal the building block Present Value equation. The building block Present Value equation is "hidden" in the building block Future Value equation.

Second, because of what I call the *Flux Capacitor of Finance*, the mathematical expression "$(1 + i)^N$." This is the mathematical expression that permits time travel in the context of the Mathematics of Finance. In the Hollywood blockbuster *Back to the Future*, whether it was the plutonium (think the building block Present Value equation) or a flash of lightning (think the building block Future Value equation) time travel was made possible because of the flux capacitor. In addition to the one example of rearranging using algebra, this one mathematical expression, $(1 + i)^N$, or more precisely (1 + i), what I like to call the add-on expression, is the only thing that differentiates the mountain—the nine building block Time Value of Money equations—from the molehill—the five fundamental building block Time Value of Money equations.

Earlier, we noted the **TVM Formula**™ considers that at times you'll need the real investment yield. For example, when calculating the Present Value of an Ordinary Perpetuity or the Present Value of a Perpetuity Due. In such situations where you need to consider the real investment yield or the true investment yield net of the growth rate of inflation, i – g, simply underline "i" in the building block Time Value of Money equations for a perpetuity. That's right, even if the growth rate of inflation is equal to zero, in which case "i" would be equal to "i." In a situation where you are dealing with a growth rate of inflation for a perpetuity, on the timeline, following the first payment the amount of each subsequent payment will increase by the growth rate of inflation. The variable "i" in the building block Time Value of Money equations for a perpetuity reminds you that you need to subtract the growth rate of inflation or "g" from the true investment yield or "i."

You can even adapt the building block True Investment Yield equation to calculate the growth rate of inflation. If, for example, you're quoted a growth rate of inflation, simply plug a "1" for the "c" variable in the building block True Investment Yield equation. In other words, what you have is a simple growth rate of inflation. Let's assume you're quoted a semiannual growth rate of inflation of 1.5%. You know the drill as it relates to the variable "c." And just as with calculating a true investment yield, you'd raise 1.015 to the power of 1/2 to determine the real quarterly growth rate of inflation or to the power of 2 to calculate the real annual growth rate of inflation and so on and so forth.

First, a word about mathematical variables. Below you'll find some variables that may differ slightly from others you've seen in *other* Time Value of Money literature. This topic was first covered in the Disclaimer, but there's more to add since the math is top of mind. Whether a variable is shown in uppercase or lowercase matters in the **TVM Formula**™.

As discussed previously, the *312* warm-up routine is part of the **TVM Formula**™ and a prerequisite to applying the Mathematics of Finance using the 3-Step Systematic Approach. Think about the *312* as the golfer's warm-up routine to get set in their power stance and in a position to take their best swing. You know that you must determine "n" to calculate "i." That's what the *312* is all about: counting money and telling time for the ultimate purpose of reading and writing "i."

The variable "n" is not to be confused with "N." The former is the time span *in* between periods or payments (on the timeline). The latter represents the number of consecutive periods, or payments for an even annuity, that are subject to the same true investment yield and the same time span *in* between periods or payments (on the timeline).

The variable PMT in the building block Time Value of Money equations for an annuity and perpetuity represents the next payment in the series—whether that next payment occurs one period into the future or immediately. In the case of an uneven perpetuity, on the timeline, following the first payment the amount of each subsequent payment will increase by the growth rate (of inflation). Unlike with an uneven annuity, for an uneven perpetuity you can use the five primary TVM financial calculator keys to solve for the Present Value of an Ordinary Perpetuity or the Present Value of a Perpetuity Due.

In addition, if you've been around finance for any period of time, you're likely used to seeing "r" or "i" in the building block Time Value of Money equations. I've already made my justification for why "i" was chosen over "r" in the **TVM Formula**™, but it's also fitting since on many financial calculators you'll commonly find the key "i" or "i/y" to denote the investment yield.

A fun aside is that just as there's no "i" in *team*, you won't find an "r" or a "y" in *the Mathematics of Finance*. The contrarian might say, "Yeah, but there's a 'y' in the Time Value of Money."

I would provide a real estate analogy by saying, "The Time Value of Money is to the power of eminent domain as the Mathematics of Finance is to condemnation." One is conceptual and the other is about action.

The new take on the Time Value of Money continues in this chapter in the form of handwritten building block Time Value of Money equations. Why handwritten equations? Because I need to lead by example. The 3-Step Systematic Approach requires a pen or pencil and paper in addition to your preferred "rescue tool."

Here are the building block Time Value of Money equations:

building block Future Value equation

$$FV = PV \times (1+i)^N$$

building block Present Value equation

$$PV = \frac{FV}{(1+i)^N}$$

building block Future Value of an Ordinary Annuity equation

$$FVOA = PMT \times \left[\frac{(1+i)^N - 1}{i}\right]$$

building block Future Value of an Annuity Due equation

$$FVAD = \left\{PMT \times \left[\frac{(1+i)^N - 1}{i}\right]\right\} \times (1+i)$$

building block Present Value of an Ordinary Annuity equation

$$PVOA = PMT \times \left[\frac{(1+i)^N - 1}{(1+i)^N \times i}\right]$$

building block Present Value of an Annuity Due equation

$$PVAD = \left\{PMT \times \left[\frac{(1+i)^N - 1}{(1+i)^N \times i}\right]\right\} \times (1+i)$$

building block Present Value of an Ordinary Perpetuity equation

$$PVOP = \frac{PMT}{i-g} = \frac{PMT}{i}$$

building block Present Value of a Perpetuity Due equation

$$PVPD = \left[\frac{PMT}{i-g}\right] \times (1+i) = \left[\frac{PMT}{i}\right] \times (1+i)$$

125

building block True Investment Yield equation

$$\left[1 + \left(\tfrac{s}{c}\right)\right]^{n} - 1 = i$$

With just a little effort, you can commit these building block Time Value of Money equations to memory. Sure, there's a memorization component here, but once you realize the purpose of certain components of the building block Time Value of Money equations, you can start to piece them together. This must be what it's like for a traveler in a foreign land being able to pick up what little they know about the language to make sense of spoken or written words.

Don't be like many aspiring or current finance professionals who are trying to run the numbers before they can walk through the building block Time Value of Money equations. These are the people who are "taught" to plug in values in their financial calculators with little or no knowledge of the TVM Rules, building block Time Value of Money equations, and the "Need to Knows" and "Good to Knows." This is a recipe for disaster and what causes people to freeze like a deer in headlights.

The willingness to work harder than others is a secret weapon used by people—students and professionals alike—every day. This was at the heart of Clayton John's lesson. Putting too much trust in a financial calculator is selling yourself short. This is a bigger issue, but if you believe in yourself more than you trust your financial calculator, great things are bound to come your way.

The mental aspect of sport can get overshadowed by the physical nature of the activity. When I think of two activities that are as much or more mental than physical, I think of golf and running. Not many people have tamed their mind more than the "mind trainer" himself, retired Navy SEAL turned endurance athlete and ultramarathoner David Goggins. This guy is the real deal. He pushes the limits as it relates to what the human body can do. It's his belief that people are capable of so much more than they may believe possible. His list of accomplishments is downright amazing.

One day the doorbell rang. It was Tony Trotter, who had stopped by on his bicycle. It was good to catch up, and somehow the conversation turned to what Mike Trevino, a friend from back home, was doing. Years earlier, and not that long after graduating high school, Tony and Mike and I were having a conversation back in our hometown on the Wednesday before Thanksgiving. Mike, a super humble guy, was sharing with us how he had participated in a few races and was training for others. Fast forward about ten years, Tony in bicycle getup is telling me how I should check out what Mike has accomplished. Since YouTube is right in my wheelhouse late on a Friday night, I was soon caught up. Come to find out, around the time when Tony and Mike and I were in conversation in Fort Dodge, Iowa, Mike was doing some big time training and racing. In 2001, Mike not only participated in the Badwater 135 Ultramarathon, which is known as "the world's toughest foot race" but won the race! In case you're wondering, "135" is a reference to the number of miles from start to finish — and this isn't a stage race. It is a race that David Goggins has run multiple times. Ironically, the start line is at the lowest elevation in the *high desert* that is the Mojave Desert and North America at 282 feet below sea level: the Badwater Basin. Let's just say the race isn't flat: from the start line in Death Valley, California to the highest point for a finish line in the Lower 48, which is the trailhead to the summit of Mt. Whitney. If the distance and course aren't enough, the temperature in degrees Fahrenheit can be within single digits below the race distance in miles. No doubt, the mind can have a tendency to play tricks on runners in endurance events such as this one.

As Whitt likes to say, "If your mind is playing tricks on you, take it out of the equation." The lesson here is that we can get in our own way.

If you're reading this book, you've probably used a financial calculator quite a bit in the past. You've been "running" the numbers. Ultramarathons like the ones David Goggins participates in can't be run the whole way. Even the best in the world have to do their fair share of walking from time to time. There are going to be times when the building block Time Value of Money equations will save you from making a wrong decision.

There's something here aspiring and current finance professionals can learn from the professional golfer and ultramarathoner alike. Professional golfers are required to walk the course during rounds of play. They aren't allowed to ride in golf carts, which would make playing a lot easier. While not required during an ultramarathon, walking is part of the running event and likely needed to accomplish the goal. David Goggins talks about huge reservoirs of potential that most people don't tap into because they're not willing to experience a little discomfort or because they don't think they're capable of extraordinary feats.

When you figure out how to apply the Mathematics of Finance to analyze and evaluate real-world Time Value of Money situations using only a pen or pencil, paper, and basic calculator functions, you will have found the other side.

In 2001, I completed my first Chicago marathon. It's hard to put into words what I was feeling as I waited for Sarah to meet me in Grant Park. In addition to tremendous gratitude, I felt like I could do anything I put my mind to. I mean it, anything! I was so excited for our future. If you've had this experience, you know exactly the feeling I'm talking about. That's the kind of confidence that awaits you if you train with the building block Time Value of Money equations.

Ben Hogan reportedly said that the secret was obvious if one knew where to look. Why are people so enamored by the mystery that surrounds his golf swing? I'm sure some are looking for a shortcut or hack, and others are hard workers who would apply it while developing blisters on their hands.

Those are the lifelong learners who have "the eye of the tiger" mindset. They are the professionals who are predictable in many ways including the way they structure their days, which start with a morning routine. They know what works, and they're not afraid of work, so they work—hard.

Regardless of the field, there is value in consistency. Ben Hogan found it in a repeatable swing that was so good that people are still talking about it. Someone looking to gauge your understanding of the Time Value of Money and ability to apply the Mathematics of Finance would be right to look under your financial calculator to paper and pen scratches for your knowledge of the building block Time Value of Money equations.

Part of the "perfect practice" of the Time Value of Money consists of the building block Time Value of Money equations. While clearly the less glamorous side of the profession, most everyone in the know about Ben Hogan would agree that, swing secret or no swing secret, hard work and dogged persistence didn't hurt come Sunday—the potential payday.

A golfer's worst enemy isn't a course or a competitor; rather, it is having bad fundamentals. The building block Time Value of Money equations are fundamental to the Mathematics of Finance. Memorizing math equations isn't one of those things that many people would call easy. As the saying goes, "If it were easy, everyone would do it."

The knowledge that not everyone is going to invest the time should be music to your ears, because that's a way for you to be better, to work harder, and to get a leg up on the competition.

Whether it's the game of golf or industry of finance, it's competitive in the field. For what it's worth, I'll take the hard worker over the smartest person in the room ten times out of ten. It's hard, if not impossible, to teach something to someone who thinks they know everything. If memorizing the five fundamental building block Time Value of Money equations still sounds like too much, then at least do yourself the favor of memorizing the building block True Investment Yield equation. If you can't calculate the true investment yield, then even the best financial calculator or spreadsheet in the world isn't going to help you get the right answer. In the rearview mirror of life, hard work is easier than learning a hard lesson.

I'd hazard a guess that most golf coaches would prefer to train someone who has never swung a club before because bad habits can be hard to break. But the reality is that people who have been golfing for years still take lessons. Look at the pros. They have swing coaches. If you're completely new to the Time Value of Money, then you're like a swing coach's ideal student who hasn't developed bad techniques over time.

As for me, I was the golf student who had developed improper techniques over years of playing around from not perfectly practicing. But like clockwork, I always hit the ball better while on the range under the instruction of a coach. It's funny how that works. Golf coaches seem to bring out the best in students. One of the reasons could be because of how they slow you down and get you "third personing" the shot before you step up to take your stance.

If Ben Hogan had a swing secret, he likely pictured his swing thought in his mind's eye before or during every swing of the club. Over time, bad habits can be corrected with perfect practice. Regardless of whether you've studied the Time Value of

Money before, what follows is the closest thing I can give you to a secret for applying the Mathematics of Finance in a solid and repeatable manner.

Chapter 10: Quick Start Guide: 3-Step Systematic Approach

"The most popular systems are those that apply a
disciplined systematic technique…"
—William McKinley

Have you ever lost the hood to your car on the interstate? Yes, you read it right. Well, I have! It makes for a great story because it ended well with no loss of life, injury, or damage to other people's property. Talk about humbling: fishing your car's—or should I say hooptie's—hood out of its temporary resting place in the ditch only to be put in your other car's trunk, which should be reserved for golf clubs and the like.

It goes without saying that my wife and I were in the market for a new vehicle. Another colleague at the time, Darrel Carlson, was a car guy, so I went to Darrel with a simple list of needs and wants. Sarah and I were already parents at the time, so safety and reliability were at the top of the list. Thanks to Darrel's advice, we ultimately ended up purchasing a brand-new Honda Odyssey. We had officially become a "minivan family." It was a great vehicle. But what made the decision easy was how Darrel framed it. He said something to the effect that, "Honda makes a very good vehicle that is built around a great engine." Sold!

Few things are more frustrating than car troubles. When a car engine is running as it should, we pay no mind. We expect the vehicle to work. But when things go south, car troubles, especially engine issues, make for a difficult day. Most people, if asked to match the words *safe* and *reliable* with *car* and *engine* might pair them in the order presented: cars are thought to be safe or not, and engines reliable or not. But what if I told you that engines can bring about safety? One of the most unsafe moments in my driving history was brought on indirectly by a car engine. Let's just say that one of the best ways to keep yourself and others safe on the road is to change your engine oil as recommended. That fateful day, I was trying to be cute and save a buck by buying a case of motor oil a few miles down the road at a department store instead of paying the sky-high price for a single quart at the gas station. I can be cheap at times. When I left the office, the dashboard indicator light for low engine oil lit up. Sarah's Grandpa Vinson once said that if the check engine light turns on, it might be too late. What I failed to remember as I was coming out of the gas station and still stewing over price gouging realized was that I had popped the hood. As I was entering the interstate from the onramp, I was reminded of this when it was too late. This wind sound that I had never heard before while driving—and that I hope to never hear again—was the precursor to the hood ultimately flying off my car and for a brief moment turning into a metal kite—no strings attached.

Would it surprise you to find out that I remember what I was wearing the day the hood flew off my car? Some people have amazing memories, but this isn't me. I'm lucky if I can remember what I ate yesterday for lunch. That's just the way my brain works. Early in my career in Corporate America, Lonnie Sundell got me onto white dress shirts. Every day at the office, he wore a nice white Oxford shirt. White-collar uniforms are nothing new and have been a thing for some time, although not widely accepted and definitely not required like their blue-collar counterpart. It's a shame more people aren't onto this style. As someone who went from a required dress code in high school to a job at night that required khakis and a red shirt—you may have guessed where I was trying to find a deal on motor oil—I'm sold on the value of limiting the number of decisions one needs to make in a given day. A "uniform" approach to business is nothing new. Some of the most successful business leaders choose to wear the same style of clothes every day. Steve Jobs was known for wearing jeans and a black turtleneck. Richard Branson can be seen sporting a white shirt and jeans—my favorite of the two. Clean and comfortable. And jeans, come on. Who doesn't love a pair of jeans that fit like a glove? I'd go with the "Branson uniform" if it wasn't for my wife not liking white dress shirts. So I go with the white-collar uniform that includes jeans and a dress shirt with a blue collar.

My "white-collar blue-collar uniform" reminds me that like blue-collar jobs, there are tools to the "trade" of finance. These being a financial calculator, pen or pencil, and paper. One of the main reasons cited for wearing a "uniform" when one isn't required is brainpower conservation, and not wanting to waste time on trivial decisions. These successful people have figured out that part of the battle is reducing "manual" brain transmissions in favor of the automatic "no-brainer" variety. In other words, these big hitters see value in setting themselves up for success with a system that provides for conservation and allocation of brain waves for the decisions that really matter.

You may find it hard to believe given how this chapter opened, but I'm actually a good driver. In fact, like most of the people reading this book, I consider myself an *above-average driver*. Rarely do I speed. And my friends tell me I drive like a Grandpa. True, true, and true. Prior to trading in my office in Corporate America for a classroom in academia, my work regularly involved traveling to markets to inspect real estate. Whether a due diligence trip involved traveling solo or with a colleague, one thing I knew was that there was going to be a lot of windshield time on the ground. That's the way real estate inspections work. You've got to "Kick the tires." Odds are you've been a passenger in a car in a new city. Are you with me in thinking that it's difficult to get to know the lay of the land as a passenger? On those trips, I always wanted to get as much driving time in as possible because that's how I could get to experience an area like a local would and burn images on my mind. I didn't want to be like a former colleague who fell asleep on a stranger's shoulder in the backseat after lunch on a hot day—drool and all.

Have you ever been in a place that's new to you? Driving the vehicle yourself is the best way to remember how to get from one point to another. Benjamin Franklin said, "Tell me and I forget, teach me and I may remember, involve me and I learn." Fads come and go, but learning by doing will never go out of style. In the classroom, I'm always looking for ways to engage students. As it relates to the Time Value of Money, I needed a vehicle for teaching others how to effectively apply the Mathematics of Finance in a reliable, safe, and repeatable manner.

With most of the specialized knowledge of this book in the rearview mirror, it's almost time for you to show off your comprehension of the Time Value of Money through application of the Mathematics of Finance. This is where the rubber meets the road on the switchbacks up "Bloom's mountain." And if you've been tracking, you probably sense that it's about time for you to take over the wheel.

You're not going to be alone. I'll be your wingman, although instead of riding shotgun you'll find me in the words of this book and user manual, which is probably more apt to be stored in your backpack than your car's glove compartment. Even though I'm with you in spirit, rest assured, because this vehicle is outfitted with the best the market has to offer.

When you're lost, you'll find a visual navigation solution (aka road map) in the visual aid and template that is the TVM Wallet. Safety is of utmost importance, which is why you'll find indicators in the TVM Wallet for each of the five primary TVM financial calculator keys that relate to variables in the building block Time Value of Money equations. If you find yourself stuck, you can call up the audible aid in the mnemonic *indifferent* to recall the TVM Rules. The engine that gets you from one point to the next—the 3-Step Systematic Approach—is automatic, so anyone with specialized knowledge can take it for a spin. You shouldn't have a cold start, so always remember to warm up the engine: use the *312* warm-up routine. You can't miss the key to unlock it, which has a safety button and is stamped with the word *reliability*. Reliability is where word of mouth comes from, and soon there will be one word on the tip of your tongue. The vehicle model— the **TVM Formula**™—is complete with the components mentioned above and offers you piece of mind when it comes to applying the Mathematics of Finance to analyze and evaluate real-world Time Value of Money situations.

The TVM Formula™

An equation includes an equal sign as opposed to a formula that provides instructions for how to achieve a desired result. If you're big into math, you're probably thinking, *Yeah, duh.* But there are people out there who are going to mix words like *equation* and *formula* even though they aren't exactly the same thing. Terminology is important.

Speaking of multiple uses for words, let's turn our attention to the mnemonic *indifferent*. This is one to be happy about given that it has multiple uses. Within the **TVM Formula**™, you can use the mnemonic *indifferent* to remember the TVM Rules and step through the TVM Wallet to apply the Mathematics of Finance using the 3-Step Systematic Approach after you've completed the *312* warm-up and a quick cool-down.

Before coining the name, I gave some thought to the "Indifferent Formula," but that idea lasted for about two seconds. The **TVM Formula**™ is held together in part by consistency and connectivity, and *indifferent* isn't capitalized. Why mess it up at this point? The *"indifferent* Formula" just doesn't look right. I think Apple has the market cornered on most things with a lowercase "i." That and some people would undoubtedly write it out "Indifferent Formula," which was a no-go to start. More importantly, TVM is an acronym that is understood in finance circles. Just as important and as described above, *indifferent* and "TVM" both relate back to the original TVM Rules: the "T" is associated with remembering not to "add or subtract or compare money *in different* points in time"; the "V" is associated with making sure not to "fail to correspond the time span *in* between periods or payments (on the timeline) and the time span of the true investment yield"; and the "M" is associated with needing not to "neglect to consider *different* payment types and signs." Our intellectual property attorney thought that the "Pritchard Formula" might work, but that's a little too vain and not my style.

The TVM Wallet

The first thing you need to do is draw your wallet. Not that wallet. This isn't a robbery in progress. But before you get out a pen or pencil and paper, let me give you some guidance for what you will need to include in this rough sketch since there is an exact way you'll need to draw the TVM Wallet. If you've ever seen a bifold wallet that includes a window for a driver's license on one side and slots for debit cards and the like on the other, then with a little imagination, you might recognize the below image, which is what you're shooting for:

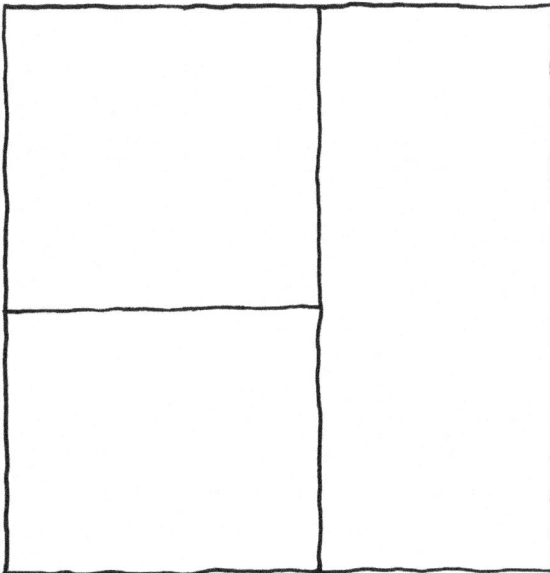

If a picture is worth a thousand words, then you have 999 to go because one of those words, the mnemonic *indifferent,* is taken already. You'll be using this template and visual aid in conjunction with the mnemonic *indifferent* to step through the 3-Step Systematic Approach as you apply the Mathematics of Finance to analyze and evaluate real-world Time Value of Money situations.

It's also important to draw a distinction between the first and second pass through the TVM Wallet. The first pass through the TVM Wallet consists of the warm-up and quick cool-down that involves initially visiting each window of the TVM Wallet in a counterclockwise manner—the left side and right side of the TVM Wallet is where the warm-up and quick cool-down will happen, respectively. In the second pass, you will work out the math using the 3 simple steps: the 3-Step Systematic Approach. In other words, you'll be in a position to work out or run the numbers using the 3-Step Systematic Approach once all of the known primary TVM variables are listed in the TVM Wallet.

Step 1: The 1ˢᵗ window of the TVM Wallet represents *TVM Rule #1*

At this point, you're setting things up and wrapping your head around the situation.

By drawing a timeline, you're using visualization, which can only help you. The best of the best—athletes at the top of their game and other peak performers—include visualization in their routines, so why shouldn't aspiring and current finance professionals do the same?

The visualization provided in the first window of the TVM Wallet will help you get ready to run the numbers.

When you get to the point of using the 3-Step Systematic Approach, you may find—as I have—that the first window of the TVM Wallet is where you'll spot an error in your thinking, which will save you from tripping up later.

Here you continue to unleash your inner artist, but this time you're drawing a timeline in the upper left window of the TVM Wallet:

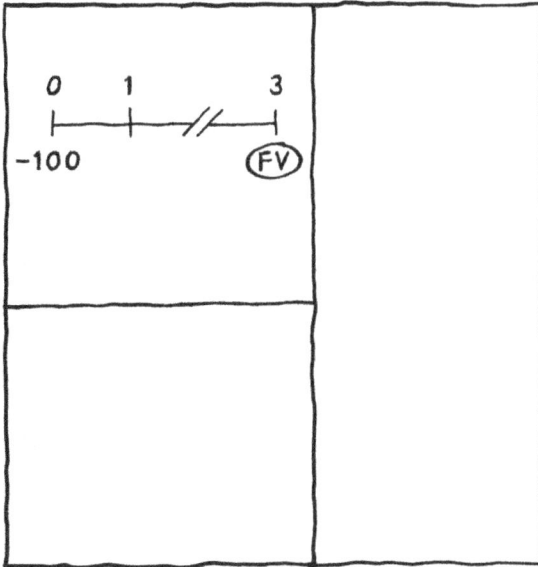

Well, that was easy. Now we're on to Step 2.

Step 2: The 2nd window of the TVM Wallet represents *TVM Rule #2*

The first two primary TVM variables that you'll be working with are "N" and "i":

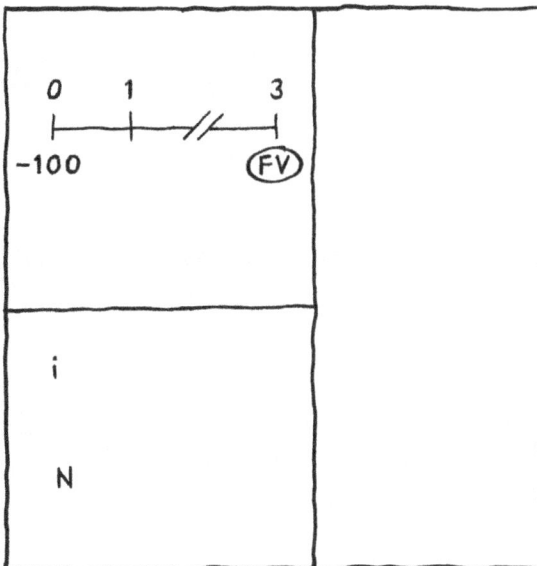

With visualization behind you, you follow another play from the athlete's playbook and now get about the business of completing the warm-up routine.

This is the step where you do the *312* to identify the true investment yield, unless that's the unknown variable. It may be helpful to start by subscripting "N" with how you'll be telling time on the timeline. The subscript for "N" represents the time span *in* between periods or payments (on the timeline).

As it relates to subscripting "N," I recommend choosing from the following self-explanatory list: A, S, Q, M, W, or D, which stand for annual, semiannual, quarterly, monthly, weekly, and daily, respectively.

Additionally, if you're dealing with a time span *in* between periods or payments (on the timeline) which is greater than one year, I suggest inserting the pertinent number in front of the letter.

For example, "3A" when the time span *in* between periods or payments (on the timeline) is equal to three years. Since you're still working to warm up, here's what you'll have for a completed TVM Wallet at this point:

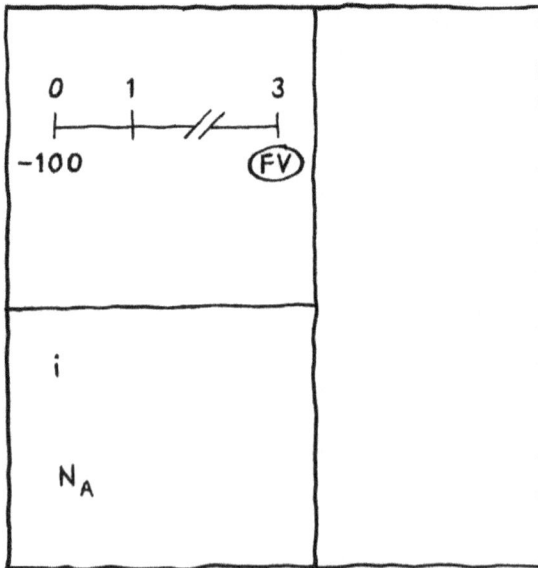

Next, it's about completing the second window of the TVM Wallet, which involves subscripting "i" and ultimately determining the true investment yield for the time span in question, which completes the *312* warm-up:

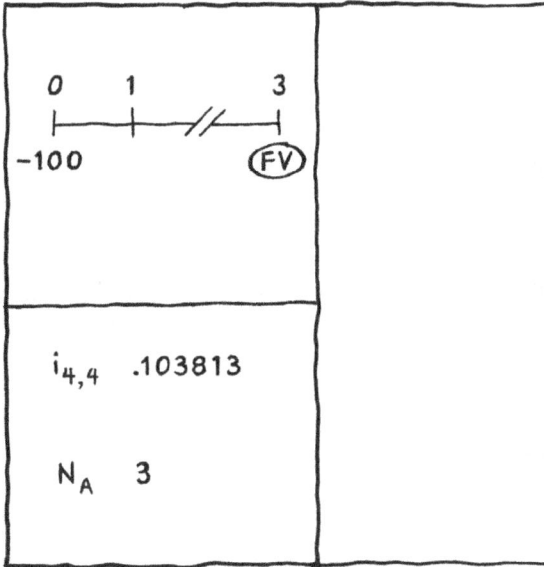

The subscript naming conventions aren't just for show. As with all the components of the **TVM Formula**™, there's a purpose for everything. By following the subscript naming convention for "N" that involves letters and that of "i" which involves numbers, you'll be able to read or interpret the true investment yield. If you forget how you're telling time in the question, all you have to do is read the subscripts together—assuming all is correct, of course.

Let's see how they work together. The subscript for "N" that reads "A" and the "3" for "N" tells you that there are three consecutive annual periods that are subject to the same true investment yield and the same time span *in* between periods (on the timeline).

In this example, the total investment period is three years, as represented by the period markers on the timeline in the first window of the TVM Wallet. There are three "n's," and the subscript for "N" needs to correspond with your reading of the subscript for "i."

By reading the subscripts for "N" and "i" together, you can tell that there are four *actual* compounding periods within the annual time span *in* between periods (on the timeline). The subscript for "N" that reads "A" matches the descriptor for the investment yield. In other words, the true *annual* investment yield.

From reading the subscript for "i," it's apparent that we're working with a true *annual* investment yield: there are four *actual* (three-month) compounding periods within the annual time span *in* between periods or payments (on the timeline).

With two windows of the TVM Wallet completed and one to go, not only can you write and read the true investment yield, but you can also circle back to the first window of the TVM Wallet and interpret the timeline and the time span *in* between period markers (on the timeline) based on the subscripts for "N" and "i." In other words, you could also read someone else's work.

Step 3: The 3rd window of the TVM Wallet represents *TVM Rule #3*

With the warm-up behind you, it's to the quick cool-down before working out the math. The three primary TVM variables that you'll be working with are PV and PMT and FV:

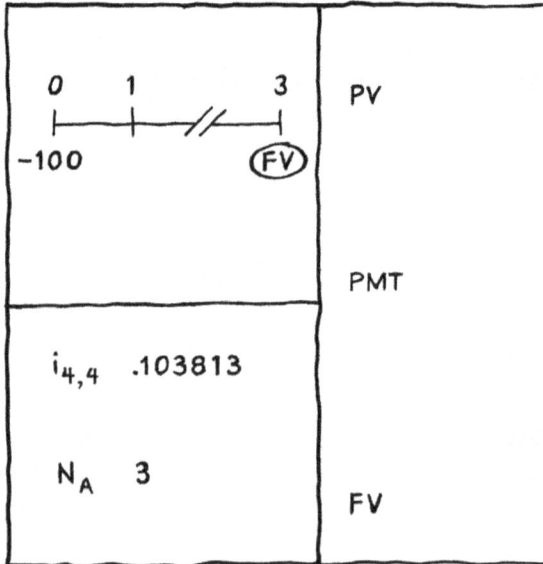

With placeholders for each of the five primary TVM variables, the only missing information relates to the payment(s):

0 1 3	PV −100
⊢──┼──//──┤	
−100 (FV)	
	PMT 0
$i_{4,4}$ .103813	
N_A 3	FV

Now that the TVM Wallet is complete with all but the unknown primary TVM variable and the warm-up and quick cool-down is behind you, it's time to work out or analyze and evaluate the real-world Time Value of Money situation by applying the Mathematics of Finance and stepping through the 3-Step Systematic Approach in a 1–2–3 manner:

0 1 3	PV −100
⊢──┼──//──┤	
−100 (FV)	
	PMT 0
$i_{4,4}$ .103813	
N_A 3	FV 134.49

This method involves a warm-up and quick cool-down before the workout that is the 3-Step Systematic Approach. It helps to mitigate the risk of making a mistake, which will inevitably happen from time to time.

Some situations are going to require multiple operations or sets of the "3-Step" reps. The TVM Wallet still works for these types of situations. If you've ever seen a movie or show where an FBI agent flashes his or her badge from a wallet that includes a piece that flops down, flipping the book on its side with this page up will provide the visual you are going for in more ways than one:

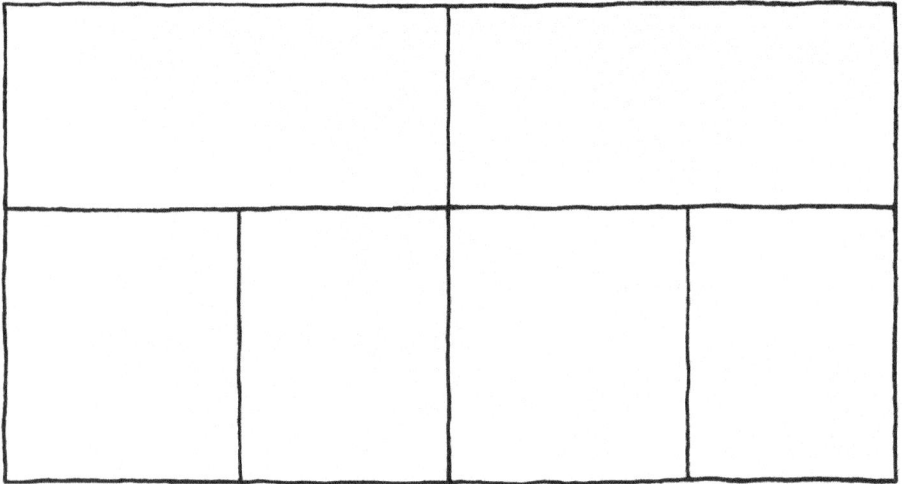

There's no limit to the number of drop-down TVM Wallets you could find yourself working with. It will just depend on the situation.

There you have it. When you use the information presented in this user manual and the simple tool that is the **TVM Formula**™, you can put together all the parts and use the 3-Step Systematic Approach to analyze and evaluate real-world Time Value of Money situations. The 3-Step Systematic Approach is the engine that the **TVM Formula**™, the vehicle, was built around. This is how to confidently apply the Mathematics of Finance. In the same way that you don't want to leave home without your wallet, you're not going to want to analyze and evaluate real-world Time Value of Money situations without the TVM Wallet and 3-Step Systematic Approach. So many people consider themselves visual learners. I know I'm in this group. It's about time a meaningful visual aid was incorporated into learning and teaching the Time Value of Money.

In this book, I believe I've proven that the concept of the Time Value of Money is easy to comprehend and that applying the Mathematics of Finance is really not that hard thanks to the **TVM Formula**™ and the 3-Step Systematic Approach. The first order of business was clearing up any possible confusion regarding terminology, which was addressed in the What section. At the heart of the How section is the **TVM Formula**™ and the 3-Step Systematic Approach, which is the cornerstone of the book. But you haven't come to the end. There's still more great content in the pages that follow.

You will find real-world Time Value of Money situations in the Frequently Asked Questions chapter along with answers in the Troubleshooting Instructions. Don't feel bad if you get off to a shaky start. Are you a better driver today than you were the first time you hit the road with your driver's ed instructor? I don't know about you, but my driver's ed instructor had to use the chicken brake a time or two when I drove.

To effectively apply the Mathematics of Finance requires that you have all the important or essential information at your fingertips. Information I like to refer to as the "Need to Knows" and "Good to Knows" is also key. Depending on your level of comprehension, you can use the Instructions for Normal or Intended Operations chapter and the Where to Find Further Help chapter before test driving the **TVM Formula**™, given the horsepower under the hood!

Chapter 11: Frequently Asked Questions: *Q* of Q&A

> "Take time to deliberate; but when the time for action
> arrives, stop thinking and go in."
> —Andrew Jackson

Back in the day, before he became a household name, my mom was big into Tony Robbins. He has been quoted as saying, "Repetition is the mother of skill." In this chapter, you'll be immersing yourself in real-world Time Value of Money situations that will challenge you. Through "reps," you will develop the mental muscle required to apply the Mathematics of Finance in the classroom and beyond in practice. In the spirit of this wisdom, this chapter is organized such that you can exercise your knowledge of the concept of the Time Value of Money and refine the hard skill that is the Mathematics of Finance with questions—no *problems* here—that will test comprehension and application of this all-important topic.

One of the value propositions of this book is the user manual that is self-contained and includes all the important or essential information related to the Time Value of Money in one place. In that spirit, I've also created space for you to keep your notes and track your progress. Below you'll find twenty-three Q's, each of which is followed by three blank pages so that you can work out the A's.

Let's revisit the baseball analogy. Think about each question as an at bat against a certain pitcher, and try to avoid striking out. For those who might not know how the count in baseball works, it starts at 0–0. The number on the left represents the number of balls, and the number on the right the number of strikes. In the baseball count, zero is commonly pronounced "oh." For example, 1-0 is "one and oh" or "a one-oh count." That's one ball and no strikes. Each blank page includes the count options so that you can gauge your success as you face each "pitcher." You can keep track of how well you're keeping your "eye on the ball" by circling which count applies. For example, if the first time you faced the "pitcher" or Q you got a "strike" or incorrect answer, you would circle 0-1. If the next time you make the connection or get the A, then you would circle 1-1. I hope there are no strikeouts! Let the immersion begin.

Q1. Your family is just wrapping up a weeklong vacation on Sanibel Island in Florida. All the rest and relaxation has you wanting another vacation. You start thinking about how nice it would be to live on island time most of the year. As you review a local real estate guide, you start putting ink to paper. At this point, you're only interested in "quick math." To this end, you assume a true monthly investment yield based on an historical investment yield for another one of your accounts that has earned a simple annual investment yield of 7% with semiannual compounding. What level amount would you need to deposit at the end of each month over the next ten years to have $650,000 saved if you started with initial savings of $75,000?

Q1 Count: 1–0 or 0–1

Q1 Count: 1–1 or 0–2

Q1 Count: 1–2 or 0–3

Q2. Five years and six months from today, you would like to have $65,000 in your savings account. The account is expected to earn a simple annual investment yield of 5.25% with quarterly compounding. What amount would you need to have in savings today to achieve this goal with no additional deposits over the investment period?

Q2 Count: 1–0 or 0–1

Q2 Count: 1–1 or 0–2

Q2 Count: 1–2 or 0–3

Q3. Your mom calls you while on her way to the bank. Your parents are getting ready to deposit a lump sum of $18,000 into a new savings account for your benefit. She tells you that they expect this account will earn a simple annual investment yield of 3.75% with monthly compounding. Three and one half years from now, they want you to use the balance of this savings account to fully fund a trip to Hawaii, which at that time is estimated to cost $20,000. Don't let them down—they did support your education after all—or the next time you hear them say "Aloha," it might not mean "Hello." What do you expect the account balance will grow to after three and one half years?

Q3 Count: 1–0 or 0–1

Q3 Count: 1–1 or 0–2

Q3 Count: 1–2 or 0–3

Would Your Boomerang Return?

Q4. You have the choice to receive $5,000 today or $12,000 seven years from today. What is the implied true annual investment yield?

Q4 Count: 1–0 or 0–1

Q4 Count: 1–1 or 0–2

Q4 Count: 1–2 or 0–3

Q5. You have decided to start taking investing seriously. A year from now, you want to increase your rate of savings. In addition to a regular salary, your current compensation package includes an attractive bonus plan. Based on your total compensation history, you conservatively estimate that the take home from each annual bonus over the next ten years will be $40,000 net of required withholdings and income taxes. The bonus is paid on the same date each year. You expect you'll be able to make ten consecutive annual deposits of $20,000 at the end of each of the next ten years. The first deposit will occur one year from now. The account is expected to earn a true annual investment yield of 6% with annual compounding. How much do you expect to have saved in this new retirement account after eleven years?

Q5 Count: 1–0 or 0–1

Q5 Count: 1–1 or 0–2

Q5 Count: 1–2 or 0–3

Q6. Over the next twenty-nine years you plan to receive payments totaling $450,000. The annual payments are expected to be received at the beginning of each year with the first of thirty consecutive payments of $15,000 to be received immediately. Assume a true annual investment yield of 4.25% with annual compounding. What do you estimate for the present value of this even annuity?

Q6 Count: 1–0 or 0–1

Q6 Count: 1–1 or 0–2

Q6 Count: 1–2 or 0–3

Q7. Close your eyes for a second and imagine that your hard work has paid off. (Really, this is a great exercise! A person can be what they see.) In addition to tremendous success, you also have accumulated a significant net worth. You want to establish an endowment that will fund higher educational opportunities at your alma mater and pay tuition for qualified individuals. The semiannual distributions from this endowment will be financed solely with the fund's annual return *on* investment while preserving the real value of the endowment. The semiannual growth rate of inflation is assumed to be 1%. Assume a true semiannual investment yield of 3.5%. What is the minimum amount needed to fully fund this endowment based on the investment objectives of real value preservation and the expectation that the first semiannual distribution starting in six months will be equal to $100,000 and will increase thereafter based on the rate of inflation?

Q7 Count: 1–0 or 0–1

Q7 Count: 1–1 or 0–2

Q7 Count: 1–2 or 0–3

Q8. Your friends are planning to work for twenty more years before retiring to a beach somewhere. Their plan is to invest $12,000 at the end of each of the next ten years and $24,000 at the end of each of the last ten *working* years. Funds will be invested in an account that is expected to earn a simple annual investment yield of 6.785% with monthly compounding. This is one of a few savings or retirement accounts that your friends have and will be used solely for "walking cash." Your friends have come to you because they know you have studied the Mathematics of Finance. The first monthly withdrawal will be made at the same time as the final deposit. Your friends plan to fully exhaust this account balance with the last withdrawal. Today, the balance of this account is $25,000. What level amount can they plan on withdrawing at the beginning of each month over the thirty-year retirement period?

Q8 Count: 1–0 or 0–1

Q8 Count: 1–1 or 0–2

Q8 Count: 1–2 or 0–3

Q9. You have volunteered to show a team member how to calculate a mortgage loan's balloon payment at maturity. The initial principal loan amount of $350,000 is subject to a simple annual interest rate of 3.65% with simple accrued interest based on a 30/360 day-count convention. The monthly required debt service payment of $2,056.94 is based on a 240-month amortization schedule. The mortgage loan matures after 120 months, at which time the unamortized loan amount, the balloon payment, is due. What would the loan documents reference for a balloon payment at maturity?

Q9 Count: 1–0 or 0–1

Q9 Count: 1–1 or 0–2

Q9 Count: 1–2 or 0–3

Q10. Your friends, who are real estate partners, are considering whether to renovate the kitchen in one of their investment properties. Quotes for the work suggest that it could cost as much as $15,000 to complete the renovation. Currently, they have a tenant who is paying monthly rent of $1,540. The ownership group would require that the tenant sign a new three-year lease if they are to undertake this improvement project. Monthly rent is payable in advance, not in arrears like the monthly required debt service payments. How much would the owners need to increase the monthly rent over a three-year investment period if they require a simple annual investment yield of 7.50% with monthly compounding on the new investment of $15,000?

Q10 Count: 1–0 or 0–1

Q10 Count: 1–1 or 0–2

Q10 Count: 1–2 or 0–3

Q11. Your company plans to make lump-sum payments of $12,081,977 in one year, $9,142,005 in two years, $11,172,007 in three years, and $4,292,009 in four years. Assume a true annual investment yield of 8% with quarterly compounding. What do you estimate for the aggregate value as of today of these future payments?

Q11 Count: 1–0 or 0–1

Q11 Count: 1–1 or 0–2

Q11 Count: 1–2 or 0–3

Q12. Now that you know the Mathematics of Finance like the back of your hand, you are excited to tell your closest family and friends about the "Eighth Wonder of the World": compound investment yield. This beats other topics that people like to bring up around the table at Thanksgiving! You want people to understand that becoming a multimillionaire is within most people's reach. You're especially excited for what this knowledge means for those people closest to you who will be starting a family before too long. Assume that new parents were to make semiannual deposits of $3,000 starting today and every six months for the next eighteen years into an investment account that is expected to earn a simple annual investment yield of 8% compounded quarterly. What would you estimate for the future value of the investment account fifty years from today?

Q12 Count: 1–0 or 0–1

Q12 Count: 1–1 or 0–2

Q12 Count: 1–2 or 0–3

Q13. You like surrounding yourself with big thinkers who plan ahead. Two of these people—your closest friends—are coming to you because they want their child to have college fully funded by the time that rolls around. They're expecting that their child will start college eighteen and a half years from now and that it will take four and a half years for their child to complete college. Starting in one month and at the end of each subsequent month until one month before their child is expected to graduate college, they will be depositing $400 into an investment account to be used primarily for a college fund. At the start of college and each six-month period thereafter and ending six months prior to graduation, they expect their then-college student will withdraw $15,000 to pay for tuition and related expenses. As an added bonus, upon their child's graduation, they want to give their child the remaining balance to be used to buy a new car and to establish an emergency fund for life post-graduation. Assume a simple annual investment yield of 6% with monthly compounding. How much money do you expect will be available in this account to provide for a new car and emergency fund upon their child's graduating from college?

Q13 Count: 1–0 or 0–1

Q13 Count: 1–1 or 0–2

Q13 Count: 1–2 or 0–3

Q14. In five years, you expect to have $60,000 in a savings account. Starting at the end of the sixth year and continuing through the end of the eleventh year, you expect you'll be able to save $5,000 annually. At the beginning of the eleventh year, you will make annual withdrawals totaling $7,500 through and including the end of the twentieth year. Assume a true annual investment yield of 2.25% with quarterly compounding the first eleven years and a true annual investment yield of 2.00% thereafter. What do you expect to have for a remaining balance in your saving account twenty years from now?

Q14 Count: 1–0 or 0–1

Q14 Count: 1–1 or 0–2

Q14 Count: 1–2 or 0–3

Q15. You have a friend who would like to retire thirty-three years from now. During retirement, your friend will take monthly withdrawals of $12,500 over thirty years. The first monthly withdrawal will occur on the same day as the last quarterly deposit. Deposits will start three months from today. Assume a simple annual investment yield of 9.5% with semiannual compounding. The plan is to fully exhaust savings over the retirement period. What level amount would your friend need to deposit at the end of each quarter over the next thirty years to fund the retirement plans?

Q15 Count: 1–0 or 0–1

Q15 Count: 1–1 or 0–2

Q15 Count: 1–2 or 0–3

Q16. The last thing you remember before you woke up was the news that you would be receiving $5,000 today and every subsequent four years in perpetuity. Assume a true annual investment yield of 4.79% with annual compounding. What is the present value of this perpetuity as of today?

Q16 Count: 1–0 or 0–1

Q16 Count: 1–1 or 0–2

Q16 Count: 1–2 or 0–3

Q17. You are comparing investment accounts at two financial institutions. A credit union has a simple annual investment yield of 5.00% with quarterly compounding. A bank has a simple annual investment yield of 4.98% with monthly compounding. What is the true monthly investment yield for each financial institution?

Q17 Count: 1–0 or 0–1

Q17 Count: 1–1 or 0–2

Q17 Count: 1–2 or 0–3

Q18. Your parents have come to you for general financial advice. They plan to deposit $5,000 today and at the end of each of the next eight years into an investment account that is expected to earn a simple annual investment yield of 6.25% with quarterly compounding. At the end of the ninth year, they would like to take the first of five consecutive annual withdrawals of $2,500. How much do you expect to have for a remaining balance in the account after the last withdrawal?

Q18 Count: 1–0 or 0–1

Q18 Count: 1–1 or 0–2

Q18 Count: 1–2 or 0–3

Q19. The balance of your investment portfolio is currently $35,000. You expect that you'll be able to earn a true annual investment yield of 4% with quarterly compounding over the investment period that spans the next five years. What simple annual investment yield with quarterly compounding would you need "to circle" or expect to earn between the end of the fifth year and the end of the ten-year investment period to have $56,000 saved?

Q19 Count: 1–0 or 0–1

Q19 Count: 1–1 or 0–2

Q19 Count: 1–2 or 0–3

Q20. Assuming you can earn a simple annual investment yield of 3.50% with quarterly compounding, how many years would you expect it to take for an investment of $10,000 to double in value?

Q20 Count: 1–0 or 0–1

Q20 Count: 1–1 or 0–2

Q20 Count: 1–2 or 0–3

Q21. You are considering an investment opportunity that is expected to produce $500 in consecutive monthly payments. The first payment would be received one month after the investment is made. Assume a true annual investment yield of 4.15% with monthly compounding. The future value of this investment at the time of the last payment is estimated to be $8,734.77. What is the duration of the investment period?

Q21 Count: 1–0 or 0–1

Q21 Count: 1–1 or 0–2

Q21 Count: 1–2 or 0–3

Q22. You have been asked by your manager to double-check an estimate for the prepayment premium calculation for a commercial mortgage loan that was originated ten years ago. This is a rush since the estimate needs to be sent to the borrower before they leave the country on vacation.

The mortgage loan in question had an original loan amount of $7,000,000 and is scheduled to fully amortize over a 360-month schedule. The contract simple annual interest rate is 3.45% with simple accrued interest based on a 30/360 day-count convention. The loan documents require monthly debt service payments.

In addition, in the event the mortgage loan is prepaid before maturity, the loan document requires a prepayment premium equal to the greater of 1% of the outstanding principal balance of the loan and the difference between 1) the present value of the remaining monthly loan payments, including any balloon payment at maturity, discounted at the true monthly investment yield that is calculated using the annualized yield for the on-the-run treasury note or bond with a maturity equal to the remaining term of the loan, and 2) the present value of the remaining monthly loan payments, including any balloon payment at maturity, discounted at the true monthly contract interest rate.

The instructions you have received are to assume that the borrower will make the 120th loan payment on the due date and that the prepayment will occur simultaneously. The on-the-run 20-year treasury bond currently has an annualized yield of 1.80% (with semiannual interest payments). What do you estimate for the prepayment premium?

Q22 Count: 1–0 or 0–1

Q22 Count: 1–1 or 0–2

Q22 Count: 1–2 or 0–3

Q23. You are analyzing an even annuity with monthly payments of $100 to be made at the end of each month over a three-month period. You're modeling a simple annual investment yield of 6.0301% with quarterly compounding. What is the future value of this even annuity at the end of the three-month investment period?

Q23 Count: 1–0 or 0–1

Q23 Count: 1–1 or 0–2

Q23 Count: 1–2 or 0–3

Chapter 12: Troubleshooting
Instructions: *A* of Q&A

"A well-adjusted person is one who makes the same
mistake twice without getting nervous."
— Alexander Hamilton

Below you'll find the A's to the Q's of the Frequently Asked
Questions chapter:

Q1. $2,909.13

Q2. $48,789.53

Q3. $20,520.35

Q4. 13.3224%

Q5. $279,432.85

Q6. $262,381.88

Q7. $4,000,000

Q8. $4,883.55

Q9. $206,540.69

Q10. $463.70

Q11. $31,048,265.61

Q12. $3,118,231.41

Q13. $79,243.13

Q14. $28,590.19

Q15. $1,752.66

Q16. $29,294.09

Q17. 0.4149% (credit union) < 0.4150% (bank)

Q18. $65,441.49

Q19. 5.5157%

Q20. 19.890723 years

Q21. 17 months

Q22. $885,885.29

Q23. $301.50

For additional information and resources, please visit this book's website, the official online home of the **TVM Formula**™, at www.WouldYourBoomerangReturn.com.

Chapter 13: Instructions for Normal or Intended Operations: "Need to Knows" and "Good to Knows"

"The circulation of confidence is better than the circulation of money."
—James Madison

There are TVM Rules, and then there are the "Need to Knows" and "Good to Knows." Math is best learned by doing math, but when that's not working for whatever reason, coming back to words before circling back to numbers can be an effective strategy.

Instructions for Normal or Intended Operations is a practical index for the Frequently Asked Questions with the "Need to Knows" and "Good to Knows" organized by each of the TVM Rules. Since the **TVM Formula**™ is about connectivity, which is bookended by the TVM Rules and the 3-Step Systematic Approach, you'll find information presented starting from the top, which is Step 1 of the 3-Step Systematic Approach or the first window of the TVM Wallet.

Because this is a reference it's not meant to be read from top to bottom. For that reason, there's no flow to the content like you'll find in other chapters in this user manual and book.

The only person I can think of who would have read—and memorized—a traditional index was Kim Peek. He was the inspiration for the character Raymond Babbitt, played by Dustin Hoffman, in the Hollywood blockbuster *Rain Man* and, in my mind, the real star of the movie—sorry, Tom. Kim Peek had amazing talents, including a memory like none other.

This book has already bucked the trend and proven that there is a user manual that can be read from start to finish, so I guess if you're so inclined to read this chapter as the others, have at it.

For each of the "Need to Knows" and "Good to Knows," you'll find reference to a particular Q of Q&A. I didn't see the value-add to referencing every single Q of Q&A that relates to each of these. For one, there are some "Need to Knows" that relate to every Q of Q&A. And there's value to working it all out on your own. As a result, this reference provides a starting point and is not a complete cross-reference.

The language used in this chapter is not only financial calculator friendly but also recognizes that eight of the nine building block Time Value of Money equations are for determining *Present Value* and *Future Value*, even if there are additional words used:

- *Present Value* (PV)
- *Present Value* of an Ordinary Annuity (PVOA)
- *Present Value* of an Annuity Due (PVAD)
- *Present Value* of an Ordinary Perpetuity (PVOP)
- *Present Value* of a Perpetuity Due (PVPD)
- *Future Value* (FV)
- *Future Value* of an Ordinary Annuity (FVOA)
- *Future Value* of an Annuity Due (FVAD)

The five primary TVM keys on your financial calculator relate to the primary variables in the building block Time Value of Money equations: i, N, PV, FV, and PMT. The PV and FV keys are also used to calculate the Present Value of an Ordinary Annuity, the Present Value of an Annuity Due, the Present Value of an Ordinary Perpetuity, the Present Value of a Perpetuity Due, the Future Value of an Ordinary Annuity, and the Future Value of an Annuity Due. Because of that, when applicable, you'll find parentheses used to correspond the building block Time Value of Money equation with what the PV or FV key is actually solving for. In other words, PV(OA), PV(OP), FV(OA), and FV(AD).

Since the **TVM Formula**™ doesn't advocate your using Beg. Mode on your financial calculator, another operation or set of the 3-Step rep and the FV key would be needed to determine the Present Value of an Annuity Due, the Present Value of a Perpetuity Due, and the Future Value of an Annuity Due.

The teacher in me and lifelong student in you could remember that solving for such values using the financial calculator will require another operation or step by thinking about the only letter grade that is worse than a D, which is an F. Notice how the Present

Value of an Annuity Due, the Present Value of a Perpetuity Due, and the Future Value of an Annuity Due each end with a word that starts with the letter *D*. So, the answer will ultimately be found with another operation or set of the 3-Step rep and the key that includes an *F*, the FV key.

It's important to be able to interpret the output from one of the five primary TVM financial calculator keys. All but "N" of the primary TVM keys on your financial calculator represents one or more of the building block Time Value of Money equations. As described above, sometimes it's not that obvious. While not original in the sense that it isn't a creative work like all the components of the **TVM Formula**™, this may be the first time you've been presented with such a connection between the five primary TVM keys on the financial calculator and the building block Time Value of Money equations.

Between the Frequently Asked Questions, Troubleshooting Instructions, and the Instructions for Normal or Intended Operations chapters, you will be able to identify any *question* giving you a *problem* and the instructions for how to course correct. Since this is an extension of the Troubleshooting Instructions, here you'll find the words that support an *answer*, which is stated in terms of a number.

Some of this information is presented in other parts of the user manual, but it's put here so that you can easily reference the specific concept. Below you'll find a question reference after one or more paragraphs that describe a concept. This is inside baseball as it relates to the Time Value of Money. With this information, you will continue to further build your confidence as it relates to the Mathematics of Finance so that you're ready for anything the Time Value of Money throws at you.

Step 1: *in different* (the 1st window of the TVM Wallet)

"Need to Knows"

The numbers or period markers on top of the timeline will always count up from 0 by 1 for each period or payment. For example, if a question calls for an annuity with even payments every three months, the 1 (period marker) on the top of the timeline represents the end of the first three-month period within the total investment period, which may also coincide with the timing of the first payment. In this example, the time span *in* between periods or payments (on the timeline) is equal to three months. Multiplication will help you tell time for the question. At the end of the fifth period, fifteen months are assumed to have passed: (period marker) 5 × 3(-month time span *in* between periods or payments).

You need not look any further than the dial on an automatic or mechanical wristwatch and the minute hand to see how this kind of numbering convention plays out in real life. While it doesn't start at zero, most dials have hour markers that step up by 1 clockwise with the time span *in* between the markers representing a five-minute or 300-second interval, depending on how you think about it.

Likewise, you can think about the numbers or period markers on the top of the timeline as the general unit of measurement and the time span *in* between the period markers as the unit of measurement specific to a particular situation. There won't always be a one-to-one relationship between period markers and the time span *in* between periods or payments (on the timeline).

Reference: Q15.

The end of one period is the same as the beginning of the next period. Imagine you're bringing in the New Year in New York City. For a split second, when the ball drops and it starts raining confetti, the end is the beginning. On the timeline, period marker 1 represents the end of the first period and the beginning of the second period, and so on and so forth.

Reference: Q14.

You may want to abridge the timeline when the total investment period is longer. You do this by inserting two parallel diagonal lines on the timeline. It's kind of like the ditto mark, which consists of two apostrophes, but bigger. The way to read the abridged timeline is that the last payment before the parallel diagonal lines continues throughout the period of time that has been abridged. See, it is a kind of ditto mark! This will save you time and ink.

Reference: Q1.

When analyzing and evaluating a real-world Time Value of Money situation, the present isn't always as of today or period marker 0. Similarly, a future point in time isn't always a certain number of periods from now. A better way to think about Present Value and Future Value is that both are as of certain points in time. For example, three years from now, you will find yourself in the then present, which is two years beyond one year from now.

Reference: Q14.

The Future Value at the end of one period on the timeline is the same thing as the Present Value at the beginning of the next period. For example, the Future Value at the end of the third period is the same thing as the Present Value at the beginning of the fourth period.

For questions that involve multiple operations or sets of the 3-Step rep, this is why PV can be switched to FV to solve for an earlier PV, for example. How can PV and FV be the same? Recall the building block Future Value equation: $FV = PV \times (1 + i)^N$. The equation shows you that $FV = PV$ when there's no time traveling below the timeline by way of *"indifferent* lines" and the *Flux Capacitor of Finance*, $(1 + i)^N$.

Reference: Q14.

The total investment period is represented by the timeline, which will consist of one or more "N's."

Reference: Q14.

For an even annuity, the last period marker on the timeline will not always sync up with "N." This disconnect will occur when the first payment in the series occurs immediately, at period marker 0, at some point in time beyond period marker 1 on the timeline, or when there is more than one investment period within the total investment period.

Reference: Q6.

For an even annuity, you could be dealing with a -1 period marker. In other words, if the first payment in the series is to be made at period marker 0, then I'm going to suggest that you add "real estate" to the leftmost side of the timeline since you will use your financial calculator to determine the PV(OA), which is as of one period before when the first payment is to be made. In this situation, odds are you'll be ultimately concerned with calculating the Present Value of an Annuity Due as of period marker 0. This will help you keep things straight since you'd need to use the FV key on your financial calculator to solve for the Present Value of an Annuity Due.

Reference: Q6.

Make sure you're drawing a complete timeline. For example, there may be investment period beyond when the last payment is made. In other words, you may need to add "real estate" to the rightmost side of the timeline. You don't want to stop short.

Reference: Q10.

Make sure you know the symbol for infinity: ∞. You'll write this above the last period marker above the timeline when you have a perpetuity. It's a Lazy 8: a horizontal figure eight.

Reference: Q7.

"Good to Knows"

When you are working with a total investment period that has two or more ways of telling time, there will be a point in time when the "time change" occurs. For example, you start telling time with annual periods, and then after twenty years, the time span *in* between periods or payments (on the timeline) switches to one month. In such situations, at and around the point on the timeline when the time change occurs, you might benefit by including the former way of telling time in parentheses above the period marker in question.

Reference: Q8.

For more complex questions that involve multiple ways of telling time, you may benefit from drawing multiple and parallel timelines. This is the TVM version of a "parallel universe." You'll probably only have these parallel timelines in the first TVM Wallet for a question that involves multiple operations or sets of the 3-Step rep. Try it out if you haven't already. This is a great way to further simplify complex questions.

Reference: Q13.

The fact that you will encounter situations where you need to tell time using a different time span *in* between periods or payments (on the timeline) means that you would also have to consider more than one true investment yield during the total investment period. In situations like this, you may want to consider using braces above the timeline to show which "i" relates to which investment period as represented by "N."

Reference: Q14.

For questions that involve multiple operations or sets of the 3-Step rep, you might want to use a square to identify one or more variables that are intermediate answers and a circle for the variable that you are ultimately seeking to answer. This is the Time Value of Money version of fitting a square peg in a round hole. I've found this to be a great alternative to subscripting the variables in the third window of the TVM Wallet or adding variables with subscripts to the first window of the TVM Wallet.

Even when a question doesn't involve multiple operations or sets of the 3-Step rep, this approach is a great alternative to using subscripts beyond the subscripts for "N" and "i." You wouldn't want to misinterpret a subscript for PV or PMT or FV for a value related to that variable.

Reference: Q8.

Do you still count on your hands? I do. It's saved me on multiple occasions, which is why I believe we're never too old for this technique.

Reference: Q14.

You may want to keep some space on the leftmost and rightmost sides of the timeline, since you might need to add a period marker for -1 or one or more on the rightmost side.

Reference: Q16.

Albert Einstein determined that time is relative. My lightbulb moment with respect to the Time Value of Money occurred when I realized that values can be kept in their own "lane." For example, say that you have a nest egg that is expected to have FV of $162,078.21 after 222 months. If at the end of the 222nd month you wanted to start taking semiannual withdrawals totaling $15,000 while also continuing to deposit $400 a month, you could keep each of the three in their own lane to determine how much you would have remaining after a certain amount of time. You would then add or subtract or compare money that has time traveled—been compounded—to that certain point in time.

Reference: Q13.

Step 2: *in* (the 2nd window of the TVM Wallet)

"Need to Knows"

How you think about or tell time for an investment period as denoted by "N" depends on the time span *in* between periods or payments (on the timeline). The time span *in* between periods or payments (on the timeline) is denoted by "n." You can't determine "i" or the true investment yield unless you know how you're "telling time" *in* between periods or payments (on the timeline).

Reference: Q1.

The variable "N" represents the number of consecutive periods, or payments for an even annuity, that are subject to the same true investment yield and the same time span *in* between periods or payments (on the timeline). There's a distinction between the investment period and the total investment period. For example, if a situation calls for two even annuities, then there are at least two investment periods within the total investment period, which is represented by the timeline. In this case, the variable "N" represents the number of consecutive payments for an even annuity that are subject to the same true investment yield and the same time span *in* between payments (on the timeline). It needs to be this way for there to be consistency across the building block Time Value of Money equations and the **TVM Formula**™.

Consider two of the most widely recognized building block Time Value of Money equations. In the building block Future Value equation and building block Present Value equation, "N" represents the number of consecutive periods that are subject to the same true investment yield and the same time span *in* between periods (on the timeline). Again, "N" may or may not explain the total investment period and is made up of one or more "n's."

Reference: Q18.

When you encounter a situation where the time span *in* between periods or payments (on the timeline) does not correspond with the time span of the true investment yield, that will require that the investment yield be manipulated using simple or complex mathematical operation.

As far as the Mathematics of Finance is concerned, we should think about division and multiplication as "simple" and exponential operation as "complex."

You can manipulate a simple investment yield to determine a true investment yield with simple division when the time span *in* between periods or payments (on the timeline) is equal to the time span of the compounding period for the simple investment yield. This is the lowest true investment yield that can be calculated with simple division.

You could go lower, but that would take a more complex exponential operation that involves a fraction. As it relates to simple yield manipulation, for example, dividing a simple annual investment yield of 6% with quarterly compounding by 4 (the number of compounding periods within the time span of the simple investment yield) produces a simple and true quarterly investment yield of 1.5%.

You could raise 1.015 to the power of 1/3 to determine the true monthly investment yield of 0.4975%: the true monthly investment yield *as if* there is one compounding period within the time span *in* between periods or payments (on the timeline). Annualizing a true monthly investment yield with simple multiplication, for example, will produce a simple annual investment yield.

Using the building block True Investment Yield equation, you can use a whole number exponent for "n" to determine the true investment yield with a time span that exceeds that of the compounding period for the simple investment yield. For example, you can raise 1.015 to the power of 4 to determine the true annual investment yield of 6.1364%: the true annual investment yield based on the *actual* number of compounding periods within the time span *in* between periods or payments (on the timeline). The time span *in* between periods or payments (on the timeline) will be equal to, greater than, or less than the time span of the compounding period for the simple investment yield.

Reference: Q8.

Most of the time the investment yield will be stated in annual terms. But this isn't always the case.

Reference: Q7.

While you likely won't encounter such a scenario in many real-world situations, it's not out of the question for the time span *in* between periods or payments (on the timeline) and the time span of the true investment yield to be greater than one year.

Reference: Q16.

Some financial calculators require that you key or input "i" with the percentage format like 0.5751%, while others require the decimal form: .005751. My trusty HP-12C requires the percentage input for the true investment yield. I can't tell you how many times students have asked me if I know how to operate their financial calculators. The answer is, "No, and I don't plan to." It is for the same reason I don't do much yard work. It's not that I think I'm better than anyone else; rather, it's an issue of how I value my time. My time is better spent doing other activities, so I'll gladly pay someone to help me out when I find someone with a time-value proposition that is a mirror image of mine. You need to know how *your* financial calculator works.

Reference: Q1.

The best practice is to consider both the subscripts for "N" and "i" together. Think this is overkill? Think again.

Let's assume you're working with a true investment yield of 20.5811% with a subscript for "i" that reads "4, 1." Without consulting the subscript for "N" you don't know the time span *in* between periods or payments (on the timeline), and as a result, the time span of the true investment yield. You could be working with a simple quarterly investment yield with quarterly compounding. There would be one compounding period within the time span of the simple quarterly investment yield of 4.79%.

With the knowledge that the subscript for "N" is "4A," you could rest assured knowing that "i" is in fact a true four-year investment yield, and that 4.79% is in fact the (stated) simple annual investment yield.

Reference: Q16.

At times, the time span *in* between periods or payments (on the timeline) is less than the time span of the compounding period for the simple investment yield. In this situation, the "n" of the subscript for "i" will be a fraction and less than the "c." For example, the subscript for "i" might read "1/6, 2" which when considered with the subscript for "N" that reads "M" tells you that "i" is a true monthly investment yield derived from a (stated) simple annual investment yield with semiannual compounding.

Reference: Q15.

At times, the time span *in* between periods or payments (on the timeline) is greater than the time span of the compounding period for the simple investment yield. In this situation, the "n" of the subscript for "i" will be a whole number. For example, the subscript for "i" might read "6, 12." When considered with the subscript for "N" that reads "S," it tells you that "i" is a true semiannual investment yield derived from a (stated) simple annual investment yield with monthly compounding.

Reference: Q13.

When the time span *in* between periods or payments (on the timeline) is greater than one year, it can help keep things straight by using a subscript for "N" that includes a number and letter combo. For example, "5A."

Reference: Q16.

When you're comparing true investment yields between financial institutions, for example, you have to make sure that you are comparing apples to apples. In other words, if one financial institution offers monthly compounding and the other offers quarterly compounding, then it would be natural to compare the alternatives in terms of the true monthly investment yield or the true quarterly investment yield.

Reference: Q17.

It's possible that the way of telling time within the total investment period will change. For example, the time span *in* between periods or payments (on the timeline) switches from years to months, etc. Of course, this will lead to a change in the true investment yield, because it would be a violation of *TVM Rule #2* to fail to correspond the time span *in* between periods or payments (on the timeline) and the time span of the true investment yield.

Reference: Q8.

From time to time, you'll be working with more than one true investment yield over the total investment period, regardless of whether that's a result of a time change.

Reference: Q14.

When performing simple or complex yield manipulation, unless stated otherwise, you should assume 52 weeks in a year, 30 days in each month, and 360 days in each year. I know that the product of 52 weeks multiplied by 7 days in a week is equal to 364 days; however, when you're dealing with estimates, "quick math" may suffice.

Reference: Q13.

This "Need to Know" is something you know already. You know that there are three months in each quarter. You also know that there are four quarters in a year. Sounds simple enough, but if this hasn't messed you up yet, it likely will at some point in time.

My favorite uncle, Jim Morrow, who loved aviation and flying small planes, used to say that there were those pilots who have had a belly landing and those who would. He spoke from experience having lived through a belly landing in his small plane that he piloted.

This is the way I feel about the issue of months in quarters and quarters in years. This can be tricky because there are four of these three-month periods in a year. Again, it sounds simple but just wait.

Reference: Q17.

Don't make the mistake of leaving out numbers. For example, if a situation requires that you divide 1 by 3, then don't try to shortcut the math and manually insert 0.33 or worse yet, 0.3. The best practice is to use the product of multiplication or division, in this case 0.333333, and not to plug such a number. In other words, input 1 and divide by 3 and then work with what the financial calculator gives you. This kind of error can leave you scratching your head for a long time trying to figure out where you went wrong.

Reference: Q17.

When working with a perpetuity—an annuity on steroids—"9999" is the financial calculator input for the variable "N."

Reference: Q7.

For some questions, the variable "i" or "N" won't be known, since that's what you're being asked to answer. When you solve for "i," you might be solving for an implied true investment yield. In some situations, you may not have enough information to complete the subscript for "i." The time span of the true investment yield will of course correspond to the time span *in* between periods or payments (on the timeline), but not enough information is provided such that you could complete the building block True Investment Yield equation. You still know enough to be dangerous, as they say.

Reference: Q4.

It's not always easy to discern the time span of the investment period or "N" when dealing with a single or lump-sum payment. If you use your financial calculator to solve for the variable "N," you may find that it rounds to the nearest whole number. For example, 20 instead of 19.890723. Solving for "N" using logarithmic operation and longhand math will produce a more precise number, which you may need.

This makes me think of all the committee proposals or white papers that I drafted and presented for investment recommendations in practice. In such a situation, rounding up wasn't acceptable. Detail was of utmost importance. Look, I like "quick math" as much as the next person does, but there's a time and place.

Reference: Q20.

Sometimes you'll catch people using the phrase, "It just takes money." As it relates to the Time Value of Money, we can also say that, "It just takes math." You can also calculate the variable "N" for an even annuity. The best way to solve for the exact value for the variable "N" for an even annuity is to use the building block Future Value of an Ordinary Annuity equation or the building block Future Value of an Annuity Due equation, provided the Future Value of an Ordinary Annuity or the Future Value of an Annuity Due is known.

Reference: Q21.

"Good to Knows"

You might want to get in the habit of subscripting "N" as soon as the time span *in* between periods or payments (on the timeline) is known. For example, as you're drawing the timeline in the first window of the TVM Wallet, you might choose to subscript "N" in the second window of the TVM Wallet. The subscript for "N" doesn't complete the second window of the TVM Wallet, but you'll be coming back to the second window of the TVM Wallet after you complete the first window of the TVM Wallet during the *312* warm-up. As you get more familiar with the TVM Wallet and the *312* warm-up and quick cool-down, you may discover that there is fluidity in the method.

Reference: Q1.

Since the real estate in the second window of the TVM Wallet is limited, you might want to use the margin on your paper to work out the building block True Investment Yield equation, which will keep the second window of the TVM Wallet clean. The second window of the TVM Wallet is for the subscripts for "N" and "i" and the associated values.

Reference: Q1.

Students have told me that some teachers want to see five digits to the right of the decimal point when solving for or writing an investment yield. Since this book is all about improving how the Time Value of Money is learned and taught, why not up the ante and make it six digits to the right of the decimal point for an investment yield?

That kind of reminds me of the "razor war" that played out on TV around the turn of the 20th Century as companies kept introducing more blades. I remember when a razor had just that—one blade.

There's also a practical aspect to rounding to six digits to the right of the decimal point for the investment yield as it relates to the decimal form for expressing the percentage. It prevents excessive rounding up or down. For example, 11% would not be how you would want to represent 0.106304 or 10.6304%. I've seen such careless rounding on exams more times than I would care to admit. Now if the investment yield has nothing but zeros on the other side of a non-zero number to the right of the decimal point or you're working with a whole number, save yourself some time and drop the zeros.

It's easy to *set it*—your financial calculator to six digits to the right of the decimal point—and *forget it*. Consistency is important, so whether it's keying in "i" in your financial calculator or working with longhand math and the building block Time Value of Money equations, I recommend you stick to six digits to the right of the decimal point for "i."

Setting up your financial calculator this way will also result in up to six digits to the right of the decimal point for a dollar value, depending on how big of a number you're working with. This isn't a big deal. All you need to do is round to the nearest penny or 1/100th of a dollar. For example, $125.20 instead of $125.201534.

Reference: Q3.

Here's one that I can't explain. You may want to stick to whole numbers for the financial calculator input for the variable "N."

You could use a non-whole number for "N" in the building block Time Value of Money equations and get the right answer, but that same non-whole number used as an input for the variable "N" in your financial calculator could lead to a number that is close but not exact. For example, $20,523.95 instead of $20,520.35. The best practice is to use a whole number for "N."

Reference: Q3.

There's no "N" in the building block Present Value of an Ordinary Perpetuity equation and building block Present Value of a Perpetuity Due equation. The stream of payments doesn't have an ending; however, it's worth noting that if you were to input "9999" for the "N" variable in the building block Present Value of an Ordinary Annuity equation or the building block Present Value of an Annuity Due equation, you'd get the same answer as if you used the building block Present Value of an Ordinary Perpetuity equation or the building block Present Value of a Perpetuity Due equation, respectively. This is evidence that "9999" is the correct financial calculator input for the variable "N" and yet another example of consistency in the **TVM Formula**™.

Reference: Q16.

Some questions allow latitude with respect to what true investment yield you can use. For a situation that contemplates an investment period including five and one half years and a single or lump-sum payment, you could choose to tell time monthly, quarterly, or semiannually. Five and one half years includes 66 months, 22 quarters, and 11 semiannual periods. Your subscript for "i" might read "1/3, 4" or "1, 4" or "2, 4," respectively. The subscripts for "N" would read "M" or "Q" or "S," respectively.

I'd be remiss if I didn't say that you could also use "22, 4" for the subscript for "i"; however, that runs contrary to how we should think of "N" as being the summation of all the "n's."

Remember that *TVM Rule #2* states that you must not fail to correspond the time span *in* between periods or payments (on the timeline) and the time span of the true investment yield. For *TVM Rule #2*, notice the references to periods and payments plural. While there's nothing wrong with telling time with a 66-month time span—using a subscript for "N" of "66M"—it's not how

I'm suggesting you do it, and it's also not how you'll see it done in practice.

The time span of the compounding period for the simple investment yield may influence how you choose to tell time on the timeline. When the time span of the compounding period for the simple investment yield is quarterly, it's simple to determine the true quarterly investment yield. Sometimes you have latitude as it relates to the time span *in* between periods (on the timeline)—just not payments!

Reference: Q2.

To save time, for questions that involve multiple operations or sets of the 3-Step rep, you may choose to use the word *same* for variables such as "i" when applicable.

Reference: Q19.

If you keep the TVM Rules front of mind, you'll mitigate the risk of making a mistake that could make someone question your competency. Here's an example that covers both those bases. Suppose you were analyzing an even annuity with monthly payments of $100 to be made at the end of each month over a three-month period. Further assume that you were working with a simple annual investment yield of 6.0301% with quarterly compounding. Don't do what I've seen some smart people do, which is plot $300 at period marker 0 on the timeline and then work with a true one-ninth of a quarter—what's this!—investment yield of 0.1664% to calculate the FV at the end of the three-month period, which is $301.50.

I hope you see the problems with this approach. First, it doesn't consider how *cash* is expected to *flow*. You can't add or subtract or compare money *in different* points in time. That's a violation of *TVM Rule #1*. Second, the time span *in* between periods or payments on *their* timeline fails to correspond with the time span of the true investment yield: a violation of *TVM Rule #2*. You can see this by reading the subscripts for "N" and "i" for this whacked-out way of solving this question.

But let's also point out that a person using such a messed-up approach is probably not going to be using the 3-Step Systematic Approach to begin with. For the sake of this discussion, the subscript for "i" would read, "1/9, 4" and the subscript for "N" would read "M." I hope you can see how the time span *in* between periods (on the timeline), which is monthly, as denoted by the subscript for "N" that speaks to "n," fails to correspond with "i." The interpretation of the subscript for "i" is that this is a true one-third-month investment yield, which doesn't match the subscript for "N." Such an approach as the one described above is wrong in so many ways—and, believe it or not, right in one way.

What makes this a Time Value of Money atrocity is that people who take this "approach" have to get the right answer first before going off on a crazy tangent to back into a true investment yield that makes the math hold. Talk about a Duck Tape job at best, and for having so-called 1,001 uses, this is clearly not one of them.

There's never a good reason to present the math this way. The most active "ingredient" in the **TVM Formula**™ is the TVM Rules! Keep them front of mind, and you'll do just fine.

Reference: Q23.

You know that the variable "N" represents the number of consecutive payments for an even annuity that are subject to the same true investment yield and the same time span *in* between payments (on the timeline)—so there's a relationship between "N" and PMT. But don't forget that "N" also represents the investment period. In other words, the variable "N" also represents the number of consecutive periods that are subject to the same true investment yield and the same time span *in* between periods (on the timeline).

You may encounter situations where you are analyzing both an even annuity and a single or lump-sum payment. The number of consecutive payments for an even annuity that are subject to the same true investment yield and the same time span *in* between payments (on the timeline) might not match the investment period for the lump-sum payment. In other words, the spacing in terms of periods (on the timeline) between PV and FV as represented by "N" needs to jibe with the number of consecutive payments for an even annuity if you are inputting both the PV and the PMT in the financial calculator and solving for FV.

You may need to compound or discount the value of the single or lump-sum payment to ensure that the investment period as denoted by "N" for both PV and PMT is consistent. In other words, that the number of consecutive periods that are subject to the same true investment yield and the same time span *in* between payments (on the timeline) applies to both the PV and PMT.

An alternative would be to keep the single payment and the even annuity series each in their own "lane" by determining the FV of the lump-sums before you add or subtract or compare money at the end of the total investment period, for example.

Reference: Q14.

Step 3: *different* (the 3ʳᵈ window of the TVM Wallet)

"Need to Knows"

There are two *different* payment types or classifications, and four *different* payment subclassifications. The acronym FAT, which stands for "Frequency, Amount, and Timing," will help you tell what kind of payment you are dealing with. A payment with no frequency is called a single or lump-sum payment, which is represented by the variable PV or FV. When there's frequency in the payment, you're dealing with an even annuity, even perpetuity, uneven annuity, or uneven perpetuity. Amount and timing of the recurring payments tell you whether you're dealing with an even annuity, even perpetuity, uneven annuity, or uneven perpetuity. A series of finite, even payments—even in terms of amount and timing—is considered an even annuity and represented with the variable PMT. An even perpetuity is a kind of even annuity with perpetual timing. When the number of the payments in the series is not even (equal) then you're dealing with an uneven annuity. An uneven perpetuity has perpetual timing but payments that increase based on the growth rate (of inflation).

Thinking in terms of the five primary TVM keys on your financial calculator or the variables in the building block Time Value of Money equations, each payment in the series for an uneven annuity can be thought of as being represented by the variable FV. If you didn't want to take the scenic route for solving for an uneven annuity this way, you could also use the IRR function of your financial calculator. This is likely the fastest way to an answer for an uneven annuity. Time is money, people! Furthermore, not every payment will be represented with the variable PMT, just as not every annuity will be represented by the variable PMT. If the payment is a single or lump-sum amount, then it is represented by the variable PV or FV. If there are multiple payments to be made or received in a series which are even in terms of amount and timing, then the payment is represented by the variable PMT. If you want to solve for an uneven annuity using only the five primary TVM keys on your financial calculator, then each payment will be represented by the variable FV, and it will be an iterative process to solve for the cumulative Present Value.

Reference: Q8.

A payment can either represent money received in the form of a withdrawal or cash inflow, or a deposit or cash outflow. If payment has a "negative" meaning to you, you need a "positive" mindset change and a different way of thinking about payments. Payment is a general term to describe a cash inflow or outflow: money received or withdrawn, and money invested or deposited. Payments will have a negative sign or a positive (no sign) value.

Reference: Q21.

Don't let the word *Present* of "Present Value" and *Future* of "Future Value" throw you off. The present isn't always as of today or period marker 0, and a future point in time isn't always a certain number of periods from now. To illustrate this point, think about a string. The leftmost side of the string represents the Present Value, and the rightmost side represents the Future Value. If this string were overlaid onto the timeline and the leftmost side of the string placed at period marker 5 and the rightmost side of the string placed at period marker 10, you can see what I mean by the Present Value not necessarily being as of today or period marker 0. If you needed to determine the Present Value as of period marker 0, the repositioning of the string which would now be overlaid from period marker 0 to period marker 5 explains why you'd need to input the PV as of period marker 5 after a switcheroo or sign change as the FV in your financial calculator before solving for the PV as of period marker 0.

Similarly, today you might be interested in calculating the compounded annual rate of inflation for a movie ticket since 1985. Today's price of a movie ticket would be represented by the variable FV, and the price of the movie ticket in 1985 would be represented by the variable PV.

Reference: Q14.

You use PV and FV for not only actual single or lump-sum payments but also for hypothetical single or lump-sum payments.

Reference: Q8.

The best guidance I can give you with respect to signs for payments is to think about whether the money effectively flows from or to your hand. Forget about assets and liabilities.

Remember, you're an aspiring or current finance professional... not an accountant! For example, at first, you might want to attach a negative sign to money borrowed from a bank, but since those funds would flow into your hand (or bank account) the appropriate treatment is a positive (no sign) value. Negative signs would be associated with a borrower's regular required loan payments.

For some situations, it's not always this clear. For example, let's say your parents give you $18,000. (Wouldn't that be nice?) From your parents' perspective, the $18,000 would have a negative sign associated with it. Initially, from your perspective the $18,000 would have a positive (no sign) value; however, we don't store money under a mattress. You're going to invest it somewhere. It would ultimately get a negative sign from your perspective so long as you invest it.

Similarly, another party directly depositing money on your behalf is effectively cutting you—the middleperson in this example—out and sparing you the time of needing to turn around and deposit those funds, as was described above. This is why you'd also assign a negative sign to money deposited or invested for your benefit, for example.

Negative signs only relate to certain TVM financial calculator inputs. Regardless of which way the money is flowing, you will always be working with positive (no sign) values for the variables PV, PMT, and FV in the building block Time Value of Money equations.

Reference: Q3.

If the question provides values for both the variable PV and FV, one must be negative. Think about it. To expect to have a certain amount of money in the future would require a deposit at a prior point in time. This is how you think about the situation that requires a decision between receiving an amount of money at one point in time or another point in time.

In these situations, you may be asked to solve for the implied or true investment yield that makes you *indifferent* between two lump-sum payments. Whether you like the implied or true investment yield depends on what you can earn for a return *on* investment or true investment yield for funds invested in an alternative investment with similar perceived risk.

Even though either one of these payments would be a positive in terms of a cash inflow, only one flows in. Do you want what's behind Door #1 or Door #2? You can only pick one. That's the way to think about this kind of situation.

Reference: Q4.

The financial calculator inputs for PV and PMT can share the same sign. For example, if you had $214,976.50 saved and wanted to save $24,000 at the end of each of the next ten years, both the current savings and the future expected deposits would be inputted into your financial calculator with negative signs.

Reference: Q8.

For questions requiring multiple operations or sets of the 3-step rep, the sign for the intermediate answer may need to be changed in the subsequent operation. Say you're working with a total investment period that spans fifty years, and during the first eighteen years there is an even annuity with thirty-seven consecutive semiannual payments of $3,000. If the first operation requires that you calculate the FV(OA) at period marker thirty-six, the second operation would involve switching—this is why I call this the "switcheroo"—the FV(OA) from a positive (no sign) value of $247,221.57 to being keyed as a PV with a negative sign for the subsequent operation or set of the 3-Step rep.

Reference: Q12.

Just because there's an intermediate operation, it doesn't mean that a value needs to take on its mirror image. For example, a positive (no sign) FV could stay a positive (no sign) FV because the situation requires that you go back in time to determine the PV one period prior. Say you calculated an FV of $754,487.59 as of the end of the twentieth year, but you need to calculate the PV as of the end of the 239th month. When FV stays FV, then the sign remains unchanged. You'll encounter this no sign change—what I call the "two-step"—when you are working to determine the payment series for an even annuity, for example.

Reference: Q8.

For an even annuity, it's ordinary for the PV(OA) to be as of one period before the first payment and for the FV(OA) to be as of the timing of the last payment. But you shouldn't dwell on the words *ordinary annuity* and *annuity due*. Why? Because what appears to be an annuity due might be an ordinary annuity in disguise and vice versa. Pay more attention to what you're trying to solve for and the relevant building block Time Value of Money equation for an annuity. Suppose you're working with an even annuity that calls for $10,000 payments starting one year from today and at the end of each of the following nine years. If you're asked to calculate the value of this even annuity at the end of the eleventh year, then what at first might appear to be an ordinary annuity really quacks like an annuity due.

Most people associate an annuity due with an even annuity for which the first payment is made immediately. What I just described above is just like that but pushed out one period into the future. In other words, instead of a payment series stretching from period marker 0 to period marker 9 with the value as of period marker 10 on the timeline, this even annuity series spans from period marker 1 to period marker 10 with the value as of period marker 11. The FV(OA) as of the end of the tenth period might be $263,615.90, but that doesn't consider that there's one additional year in the total investment period for funds to earn a return *on* investment. This operation would require the switcheroo that involves the positive (no sign) value for FV(OA) being keyed as PV with a negative sign so that you can solve for the FV(AD).

Reference: Q5.

Watch out for the "lag period," which signals that you're really dealing with the underlying building block Future Value of an Annuity Due equation. In other words, you're asked to estimate value for an even annuity one year after the last payment in the series is made. This is one more year that the investment will be earning a return *on* investment.

Reference: Q5.

When an even annuity contemplates the first payment being made immediately at period marker 0, you'll need to add "real estate" to the leftmost side of the timeline since your financial calculator will determine the PV(OA), which will be as of period marker -1. You'll need to two-step it from the PV(OA) to solve for the FV which is the same number that you'd find using longhand math and the building block Present Value of an Annuity Due equation.

Reference: Q6.

Since a perpetuity is an annuity on steroids, just like its close relative the even annuity, the PV(OP) will be as of one period before the first payment in the perpetual stream. The add-on expression $(1 + i)$ in the building block Present Value of a Perpetuity Due equation gets the PV(OP) value *back to the future* and one more period down the line. (Technically, the add-on expression is the same thing as the *Flux Capacitor of Finance*, but there's not really a reason to include the exponent "N" and raise the expression to the power of 1.)

The difference between the Present Value of a Perpetuity Due and the Present Value of an Ordinary Perpetuity is the timing of the first perpetual payment. As with the building block Present Value of an Ordinary Annuity equation, the building block Present Value of an Annuity Due equation, the building block Future Value of an Ordinary Annuity equation, and the building block Future Value of an Annuity Due equation, the add-on expression $(1 + i)$ is the only thing that differentiates the building block Present Value of an Ordinary Perpetuity equation and the building block Present Value of a Perpetuity Due equation.

Reference: Q16.

When working with an uneven perpetuity, on the timeline, following the first payment the amount of each subsequent payment will increase by the growth rate (of inflation).

Reference: Q7.

The building block Time Value of Money equations for an annuity or perpetuity have something on your financial calculator. When you use your financial calculator to solve for the PV(OA) or FV(OA) for an even annuity, you'll get to the same place as if you used the building block Present Value of an Ordinary Annuity equation or the building block Future Value of an Ordinary Annuity equation, respectively. Similarly, when you use your financial calculator to solve for PV(OP), you will get to the same place as if you used the building block Present Value of an Ordinary Perpetuity equation. And that will be enough, or it won't in the case of needing the sister building block Time Value of Money equation with the add-on expression. Put differently, the building block Present Value of an Annuity Due equation, the building block Future Value of an Annuity Due equation, or the building block Present Value of a Perpetuity Due equation.

Using the financial calculator, two of these intermediate operations will require the two-step, and one will require the switcheroo. In other words, keeping the sign the same and using the two-step for PV(OA) to determine the Present Value of the Annuity Due using the FV key, keeping the sign the same and using the two-step for PV(OP) to determine the Present Value for a Perpetuity Due using the FV key, and changing the sign or what I call the switcheroo for FV(OA) and keying the value as PV so to ultimately determine FV(AD).

Reference: Q6.

For an even annuity, "N" always represents the number of consecutive payments, PMT, that are subject to the same true investment yield and the same time span *in* between payments (on the timeline) regardless of whether the first payment occurs immediately or one period into the future or whether you're using your financial calculator or longhand math and the building block Time Value of Money equations for an annuity. There's a relationship between "N" and PMT for an even annuity, so long as the fine print is satisfied. In other words, those even payments are subject to the same true investment yield and the same time span *in* between payments (on the timeline).

The building block Present Value of an Annuity Due equation and the building block Future Value of an Annuity Due equation, which include the add-on expression, $(1 + i)$, recognize that one more period of time needs to be considered. For the Future Value of an Annuity Due, that gets you one period further down the line of the timeline. As it relates to the Present Value of an Annuity Due, it does the same, although it might not be as apparent. It gets you right back to the beginning of the investment period for the even annuity, the point in time when the first payment is made or received.

Reference: Q6.

If the question requires that you move the Present Value of an Ordinary Annuity or the Present Value of an Ordinary Perpetuity or the Future Value of an Ordinary Annuity to one or more different points in time, you need to think about the value as a kind of hypothetical single or lump-sum payment.

Reference: Q5.

When calculating the payment for an even annuity such as a loan, keying in "$0" for FV assumes a full return *of* investment over the investment period, which is equal to the value that is keyed for the variable "N." In other words, it's the amortization schedule, which may or may not equal the loan term, that is keyed as the variable "N." When dealing with a loan, whether the loan actually fully amortizes over the loan term or if there is a balloon amount due at maturity will depend on whether the loan term matches the amortization schedule.

Reference: Q22.

Since the last payment in a series for an even annuity is assumed to be made or received at the end of the investment period as represented by "N," there's no need to key for FV the same value that was inputted for PMT. Remember that the values for PV and FV are used to represent single or lump-sum payments. For example, if an even annuity called for consecutive even annual payments of $20,000, you'd be double counting the last payment if you keyed "$20,000" as FV in your financial calculator.

Reference: Q5.

When dealing with an even annuity that calls for the first payment to be made immediately, I don't suggest you key the first payment with PV. Why? Because this contradicts the consistency that the **TVM Formula**™ is built upon: "N" represents the number of consecutive payments for an even annuity that are subject to the same true investment yield and the same time span *in* between payments (on the timeline), while PV is the variable used for a single or lump-sum payment, and the like.

Reference: Q6.

Related to the last point, when you're dealing with an even annuity and first and last payments that overlap each other, I don't suggest netting out the value since doing so would require that you break the **TVM Formula**™ and then be forced to key for "N" a value that is one fewer than the number of consecutive payments for an even annuity that are subject to the same true investment yield and the same time span *in* between payments (on the timeline).

Reference: Q14.

Say you were analyzing two even annuity series and the only difference was the timing of the payments. One series contemplates the first of ten even payments to be made today, and the other series contemplates the first payment being made one period into the future. If you were using the building block Future Value of an Ordinary Annuity equation to support your financial calculator answer, you'd get the same value for each cash flow series…but not really, because one value is as of the end of the ninth period, and the other is as of the end of the tenth period.

Reference: Q5.

Knowing all the building block Time Value of Money equations will save you in a pinch. You wouldn't want to overpay for borrowed funds and the like: $466.59 and $463.70 are different numbers.

Reference: Q10.

When applicable, it's easy to update the placeholders for PV and FV in the third window of the TVM Wallet when you're working with one of the offshoots by adding letters in parentheses: PV(OA), PV(OP), FV(OA), or FV(AD), for example.

Reference: Q5.

When you follow the **TVM Formula**™, you'll be calculating "OA" values with your financial calculator; i.e., Future Value of an *Ordinary Annuity* and the like.

Since the investment period spans thirty-six months you may first want to calculate the FV of the investment at the end of the investment period before using the PV key on your financial calculator to calculate the Future Value of an Ordinary Annuity at the end of the thirty-fifth period. From there, you'll need to do a switcheroo and key the value as the FV(OA) to ultimately determine the PMT—which here is an additional amount.

Or you could add real estate to the leftmost side of the timeline, calculate the PV(OA) as of period marker -1 and two-step it to ultimately determine the PMT.

Reference: Q10.

"Good to Knows"

Using an equal sign can potentially mess you up, since one of the lines could be misinterpreted for a negative sign for a payment when a positive (no sign) value is what you're working with.

Reference: Q1.

Just as an equal sign could be misinterpreted for a negative sign, so too could the vertical line in a plus sign or dollar sign be misinterpreted for the number 1. This is why I don't recommend use of the "$" or "+" symbol in the TVM Wallet.

Reference: Q2.

One of the ways you'll know you've "arrived" in your comprehension of the Time Value of Money is when you can explain using the building block Future Value of an Ordinary Annuity equation why the value can be the same as the variable PMT when "N" is equal to 1. This sentence is here to let you know that the answer follows. Don't read the next paragraph if you still need to figure out why this is and you're up for a challenge. This is your last notice or "spoiler alert."

The reason why the FV(OA) is the same as PMT when the variable "N" is equal to 1 is because while one period is assumed to have passed, the PMT that was received at the end of the period hasn't had any time to compound. Technically, this isn't even an even annuity since it only contemplates one payment. In other words, the payment is not frequent or recurring. Since this is technically a single or lump-sum payment, you can also look to the building block Future Value equation and the building block Present Value equation to see that when no time passes Future Value is equal to Present Value.

This last point is what allows you to use the switcheroo for situations that involve multiple operations or sets of the 3-Step rep.

Reference: Q14.

Remember, "If it quacks like a duck, it's a duck." A series of uneven cash flows quacks like more than one single or lump-sum payment. You're really just being asked to calculate more than one Present Value or Future Value.

For these kinds of questions, it may be helpful to drop all the negative signs from the intermediate answers when calculating the cumulative PV, for example, before you add all the values together. I find this to be more intuitive than using the negative number to add negative values.

Reference: Q11.

Sometimes you'll need to work backward to find the answer.

Reference: Q15.

There will be times when you can attack a question from multiple angles or directions. For example, when calculating the outstanding principal balance of a loan, you have two conventional paths to the answer. You can consider the number of remaining even annuity payments as represented by PMT as well as FV and then solve for PV(OA). Or you can consider the number of even annuity payments that have been made already as represented by PMT and solve for FV: the initial loan amount would be represented by PV. A third approach, although unconventional, would keep the values in their own "lane." In other words, you would determine the FV of the money lent, the PV, and the FV(OA) of the payments made, and add them together at a certain point in time to determine the outstanding principal balance of the loan. My preference is the first approach, since investors "buy" future expected cash flows and because the PV(OA) (or PVAD) can be determined at any time using the then current market true investment yield.

Reference: Q9.

A negative sign or value for PV can be interpreted as the investment needed to buy a future expected cash flow or series of cash flows.

Reference: Q22.

For questions involving multiple streams of cash flows, you can think bigger than the information provided in the question. For example, if you are asked to determine the amount of a savings account balance at a certain point in the future, you can extend the future value of deposits and even the future value of withdrawals to that point in time. You're keeping the *different* payment types in their own lane so that you can get to a point in time where you can add or subtract or compare money. When you wrap your head around this point, it opens things up and makes thinking about Time Value of Money questions more manageable. Remember that you possess the *Flux Capacitor of Finance*, $(1 + i)^N$, which allows time travel in the context of the Time Value of Money by way of "*indifferent* lines."

Reference: Q14.

This "Good to Know" takes a slightly different form. You *need to know* that I've heard of the financial calculator Beg. Mode; however, I'm not a fan. Why don't I recommend using Beg. Mode?

First, I like that I can tell you that "N" will always represent the number of consecutive payments for an even annuity that are subject to the same true investment yield and the same time span *in* between payments (on the timeline) — regardless of when the first payment is made: "N" will be equal to the total number of payments in the series when both conditions are satisfied. Beg. Mode is inconsistent with this definition as it relates to the building block Future Value of an Ordinary Annuity equation since its version of "N" considers the number of consecutive payments less one: the amount of the even annuity payment would need to be added manually to determine the FV(OA). Consistency is one key to success in life, so it seemed appropriate to set you up for success as you go about applying the Mathematics of Finance to analyze and evaluate real-world Time Value of Money situations. Using Beg. Mode and needing to remember to manually add the amount of the even annuity payment to ultimately determine the Future Value of an Ordinary Annuity would be a solution in search of a problem. By now, you should have picked up on the fact that exceptions are not found in the **TVM Formula**™.

There is tremendous value to a principled approach. That's why Dave Ramsey's program for helping people get out of debt is so successful. Once the Baby Steps are memorized, you know what to do. And when it comes to budgeting, every dollar has a name. It's genius. Dave Ramsey is so smart that he was able to take the brain out of personal finance. In a nutshell, that's what the **TVM Formula**™ is all about. Stick to the principled approach, and you'll do just fine.

Second, it's easy to forget to switch back to End Mode. This is like being one question off on a standardized test. Not good.

Reference: Q6.

All Together Now

For more complex problems, you may want to sketch out the extended TVM Wallet before wrestling with the math.

Reference: Q13.

Sometimes there is going to be so much going on in the extended TVM Wallet that it may make sense to spread out the squares for the intermediate answers and the circle for the variable you're ultimately answering in the appropriate TVM Wallet. In other words, there's not always going to be enough space in the first window of the TVM Wallet to show all the squares and the circle.

Reference: Q14.

Don't forget to clear some or all of the registers in your financial calculator when working with questions with multiple operations or sets of the 3-Step rep that is the TVM Wallet. You wouldn't want stragglers in the financial calculator input for the variable PMT or N, etc. The best practice is to use the recall button on your financial calculator when working with questions that require multiple operations or sets of the 3-Step reps to ensure that there aren't any numbers left behind from the previous operation that would ultimately lead to an incorrect answer.

Reference: Q13.

Once you get your legs under you, what you may find is that you bounce back and forth between the windows of the TVM Wallet as you organize information from the question. Now that I know my way around the TVM Wallet, one of the first things I do after a quick sketch of the timeline in the first window of the TVM Wallet is to subscript "N." Then it's back to the timeline sketch.

Once I have one or more variables squared and the ultimate variable I'm solving for circled, then it's off to complete the rest of the second window of the TVM Wallet by writing the subscript for "i" and the values for "N" and "i." Even when I'm jumping around between the windows of the TVM Wallet, after the warm-up and quick cool-down, I'm always stepping through the 3-Step Systematic Approach as prescribed in the 1–2–3 manner when it comes to solving the math.

Chapter 14: Where to Find Further Help: Final Frontier Mathematics of Finance

"Honor lies in honest toil."
—Grover Cleveland

My wife and I love Indian food. In fact, I've loved Indian food for about as long as I've loved my wife: we are high school sweethearts. It wasn't until years after I was introduced to Indian food that Sarah finally agreed to try it. Now it's her favorite cuisine. How do I know? Our favorite Indian restaurant is the only place around town where we have regular status: we're on a first-name basis, and our friend Sunny knows Sarah's order—Malai Kofta. When I'm walking through a lunch buffet or scanning a menu at an Indian restaurant, I really don't always know what is in a dish. Sometimes I can't even pronounce what I'm eating. Sunny helps us with this as well. This is not a knock against Indian food. Pronunciation just isn't my jam.

In terms of math, solving exponential equations using exponential and logarithmic functions or operations isn't something that comes naturally to me. Regarding the latter, I'm talking about solving for "N" or "n" using logarithmic operation.

Don't ask me how some of the rules for logarithms work; I just know they do. Even though I can't explain all of the rules that govern algebra and logarithms, I can still enjoy math just like I can enjoy Indian food I can't pronounce.

I'm going to be straight with you as I have been from the first word, which is the only way I know how to do it. Higher-level algebraic operations can be a little tricky. But as with anything, it becomes easier with time and hard work.

Once you conquer solving for exponential equations using exponential and logarithmic operations, you will be in a class all your own and able to apply the Mathematics of Finance to analyze and evaluate real-world Time Value of Money situations with only a pen or pencil, paper, and basic calculator functions.

While I'm not a bona fide math instructor, I'm not completely off base leading you into this higher-level math lesson. As of the time of this writing, not only have I lectured about the topic of the Time Value of Money for years, but I've practiced what I teach having made a living applying the Mathematics of Finance in industry for over two decades. Two of the variables that relate to the building block Time Value of Money equations which you'll be solving for using logarithmic and exponential operations are "N" or "n" and "i," respectively. Both "N" and "i" are found in the *Flux Capacitor of Finance*, $(1 + i)^N$.

Time travel may just be the ultimate final frontier. This is fitting since the *Flux Capacitor of Finance* is the mathematical expression that makes time travel possible with respect to the Time Value of Money. Let's start with how to write and read a logarithmic equation:

$$\text{Log}_b\ a = N \text{ or } n$$

You read this logarithmic equation, "Log base 'b' of 'a' is equal to 'N' or 'n.'" The inclusion of "n" is not a typo. What you see here isn't a deviation from the precise notation presented in the user manual. Instead, this equation has been adapted for the Mathematics of Finance to recognize that you can use logarithmic operation to solve for either "N" or "n."

You may also encounter other ways of expressing this logarithmic equation in the "wild." But you know the drill. Use this one! I like the above logarithmic equation for more than the fact that it was adapted for the Mathematics of Finance. It also fits within the **TVM Formula**™. In the equation, "b" represents the "base" number and *base* starts with a *b*. In the equation, "a" represents what's known in math circles as the "argument," which is just a fancy way of saying that's the answer to the base number raised to the power of "N" or "n." Again, it's fitting because *argument* starts with an *a*. Some people choose to write this logarithmic equation with "ln," which is short for "Log," and use "c" for the "N or n." Can't blame them: makes sense for them to start at the beginning of the alphabet.

You're likely to even find other equations that switch "b" for "a" or "c" and vice versa. Seems natural to me to stick with "b" for the base number, "a" for the argument, and to scrap "c" since that variable is taken already in the building block True Investment Yield equation, where "c" represents the number of compounding periods within the time span of the simple investment yield.

All this to say that the way I've presented the logarithmic equation is consistent with the three overarching goals of the **TVM Formula**™, which are simplicity, consistency, and connectivity: "1, 2, 3" but not "a, b, c."

Let's put some numbers to these words as it relates to the variable "N." Say you have an opportunity that is expected to provide a true annual investment yield of 10%. Your client has $100,000,000 to invest. How many years do you expect it will take for the investment to grow to $164,025,308? Here's an example of how to solve for "N" using algebra and logarithmic operation:

$$FV = PV \times (1+i)^N$$

$$164,025,308 = 100,000,000 \times (1.10)^N$$

$$\frac{164,025,308}{100,000,000} = (1.10)^N$$

$$1.640253 = (1.10)^N$$

$$Log_{1.10} 1.640253 = Log_{1.10} (1.10)^N$$

$$\frac{Log\, 1.640253}{Log\, 1.10} = N$$

$$N = 5.192001$$

Now let's put some numbers to these words as it relates to the variable "n." For a simple annual investment yield of 9.6455% with quarterly compounding, you want to know the number of compounding periods within the time span *in* between periods or payments (on the timeline) that produces a true annual investment yield of 10%. Here's an example of how to solve for "n" using algebra and logarithmic operation:

$$\left[1+\left(\frac{s}{c}\right)\right]^{n}-1 = i$$

$$.10 = \left[1+\left(\frac{.096455}{4}\right)\right]^{n}-1$$

$$1.10 = (1.024114)^{n}$$

$$Log_{1.024114}\,1.10 = Log_{1.024114}\,(1.024114)^{n}$$

$$\frac{Log\,1.10}{Log\,1.024114} = n$$

$$n = 4$$

Similar to how my wife trusted me when I told her Indian food is where it's at, you can trust me when I tell you that you can solve for "N" or "n" by dividing the logarithm of "a" by the logarithm of "b." In other words, the logarithm of the argument by the logarithm of the base number.

Algebra can be summarized as moving one value from one side of an equation to the other side of the equation. We have algebra to thank for the building block Present Value equation being "hidden" in the building block Future Value equation. You can obviously solve for PV using the building block Present Value equation. With a little bit of rearranging, you could also solve for PV using the building block Future Value equation and vice versa. You can also use algebra to determine the PMT variable in the building block Time Value of Money equations for an annuity or perpetuity.

But there's one more variable in the building block Time Value of Money equations that we have yet to cover. Using the building block True Investment Yield equation isn't the only way to solve for "i." In other words, you can also calculate "i" indirectly. Here's an example of how to solve for "i" using algebra and exponential operation:

$$FV = PV \times (1+i)^N$$

$$121 = 100 \times (1+i)^2$$

$$\frac{121}{100} = (1+i)^2$$

$$1.21 = (1+i)^2$$

$$(1.21)^{1/2} = 1+i$$

$$1.10 = 1+i$$

$$i = .10$$

There's longhand math, and then there is *long* longhand math! Trying to zero in on "i" using any of the building block Time Value of Money equations for an annuity or perpetuity can be done; however, in all but the building block Present Value of an Ordinary Perpetuity equation, all you can hope for is an approximation—and this is with even more complex mathematics. This is because the variable "i" shows up in both the numerator and denominator.

A related issue is present when trying to solve for "N" using the building block Present Value of an Ordinary Annuity equation and the building block Present Value of an Annuity Due equation, but this time the "double trouble" is brought on by "N" showing up in both the numerator and denominator.

This is really what financial calculators are for. But you can—and should know how to—solve for the exact value for "N" using the building block Future Value of an Ordinary Annuity equation and the building block Future Value of an Annuity Due equation, since "N" only shows up once in these building block Time Value of Money equations. Longhand math provides a great way to double-check math when it's feasible. The key word here is *feasible*. Longhand math can help you really dial in the hard skill that is the Mathematics of Finance, but *long* longhand math is not the be-all and end-all.

Will you do me a favor and try Indian food, if you haven't already? At the very least, it might help you get the real essence of this lesson. If you haven't tried Indian food already and you take me up on this offer, then you're in for a treat. If you haven't tried Indian food and you're passing, then I've got another analogy that you will understand. I'm talking about walking.

Most people walking this planet don't understand how gravity works, yet they still walk. If you're like me, you're in this category of people. But we still do it and it gets us from Point A to Point B. That's the way I feel about solving exponential equations using exponential and logarithmic operations, which is why I call this the "Final Frontier Mathematics of Finance."

You don't have to understand all the rules of mathematics to apply the Mathematics of Finance. This is a journey you're on, and things are to be discovered along the way. This is why it pays to be a lifelong learner and student of finance. The good news as proven above is that you don't always have to understand how something is made to understand it works. There are sprinklings of this in the

Mathematics of Finance just like there are for me in Indian food. I'd enjoy joining you for a great Indian lunch if we found ourselves close to each other and in search of food. If he were still alive today, we'd want to save a seat for another person, Brahmagupta. He'd fit right in and have a lot to say about both algebra and gravity: Brahmagupta was an Indian mathematician and astronomer who lived between 598 and 668 AD.

You did it! You've come to the end of this user manual. The fact that you're still with me proves that you not only have a high propensity for finance but also that you're a hard worker. That's a proven recipe for success in the field!

Part 3: The Why

New Take, Take Three: The End is The Beginning

Final Thoughts

"Perseverance and spirit have done wonders in all ages."
—George Washington

While I don't count myself among the many who frequent fast-food restaurants, when asked to think about a brand that has a face to the name, KFC (Kentucky Fried Chicken) comes to mind. Some people don't know the story behind Colonel Sanders's success. Let's just say it wasn't overnight. Colonel Sanders was sixty-five when he found his. Legend has it that he heard no 1,009 times before the sweet sound of yes. The rest, as they say, is history!

In every endeavor, people will meet obstacles and must persevere to be successful:

- Ultramarathoners talk about focusing on the next foot strike to get them through the "pain cave" late in a race and eventually across the finish line.
- Similar thoughts must have been going through Colonel Sanders's mind as he slammed his car door only to drive from one no to the next.
- Abraham Lincoln knew that a sharp axe would be needed to chop down a tree.

Work can have a binary component to it. So we deal in 0's and 1's, noes and yeses, and losses and wins. But we shouldn't misinterpret hard work that is associated with a "0" as a loss; instead, one step closer to a win.

One step takes a runner across a finish line. One swing of an axe chops down a tree. One yes turns an original recipe into one of the most guarded and highly prized secret recipes of all time. Colonel Sanders understood the value of having his recipe—a secret blend of eleven herbs and spices—dialed in before kicking the tires. Perseverance is born of belief, which stems from preparation.

I'm going to go out on a limb and unilaterally make the five-dollar bill, with Abraham Lincoln's face, the official bill of the Time Value of Money. I know the saying doesn't go, "A five-dollar bill in the present is worth more than a five-dollar bill in the future." While true regardless of the denomination, here's why I think the five-dollar bill is more fitting than the one with the likeness of the President who brought us the opening quote.

A five-dollar bill reminds us that there are five fundamental building block Time Value of Money equations. These and the other building block Time Value of Money equations can be used to double-check your work or to analyze and evaluate real-world Time Value of Money situations using nothing more than a pen or pencil, paper, and basic calculator functions.

A five-dollar bill also reminds us of the value of preparation. Colonel Sanders's face is trademarked, so that wasn't going to work. That and the chicken isn't the Time Value of Money mascot! Abraham Lincoln's association with money and preparation is just too perfect a match.

You can have a daily reminder of the value of prework and the five fundamental building block Time Value of Money equations with you in your wallet every day. So take Abraham Lincoln's advice—sharpen your axe that is the hard skill of the Mathematics of Finance—and swing until you get it down.

If ever I have an axe to grind, it's when someone clearly hasn't done the work and wants to "hack" their way through the Mathematics of Finance with a "dull blade." They're looking for a shortcut. Please don't misinterpret what I'm about to say because I genuinely care about the success of each person I interact with. I've just been around the block enough times to know how some of these interactions work.

I wish I had a dollar—wait, make that a five-dollar bill—for every time a person asked for five minutes of my time to ask a question related to the Time Value of Money without clearly having done any prework. In truth, there's a part of me that would rather give that person a five-dollar bill than let them take my most precious resource. When someone "steals" your time, they are essentially telling you that they value their time more than yours, which doesn't leave a good impression.

This book was written so that you can figure out the Mathematics of Finance while I sleep. Runners don't get fit by staring at a pair of running shoes in the corner, and aspiring and current finance professionals need to do the hard work.

Come to think of it, Colonel Sanders—in addition to being a model of the value of preparation, belief, and perseverance—can teach us a thing or two about the Mathematics of Finance. If we wanted to boil it down this way, there are eleven "ingredients" you need to solve Time Value of Money questions using longhand math: nine building block Time Value of Money equations and two higher-level algebraic operations. These eleven trade secrets are *not* guarded in a vault:

- building block Future Value equation
- building block Present Value equation
- building block Future Value of an Ordinary Annuity equation
- building block Future Value of an Annuity Due equation
- building block Present Value of an Ordinary Annuity equation
- building block Present Value of an Annuity Due equation
- building block Present Value of an Ordinary Perpetuity equation
- building block Present Value of a Perpetuity Due equation
- building block True Investment Yield equation
- solving for "i" using algebra and exponential operation
- solving for "N" or "n" using algebra and logarithmic operation

Like Colonel Sanders, I believe in my original recipe, the **TVM Formula**™, and all the supporting information included in the user manual that makes it possible to use the 3-Step Systematic Approach to analyze and evaluate real-world Time Value of Money situations. Mine doesn't involve chicken, but it can help you soar in the field as a finance professional, or at the very least help you understand this all-important topic where the rubber meets the road—via application. If you do the work and believe in yourself, with perseverance you can master the Time Value of Money using the new take on this age-old topic, which is provided in this book.

"I make myself rich by making my wants few."
—Henry David Thoreau

Afterword

"A resignation is a grave act; never performed by a right-minded person without forethought or with reserve."
—Salmon P. Chase

Prior to resigning from my position in Corporate America—which I held for twenty-two years to the day—I used to get asked quite regularly about my teaching. These questions were coming from my then-colleagues who were friends and more than anything else were just curious and wanted to pick my brain. I was also fielding similar types of questions from people who needed to know the answer, since they were considering my joining their ranks. It's an easy answer.

Teaching energizes me, whether that's lecturing or preparing for a lesson. It's the furthest thing from draining. When I prepare for class, I lose track of time—and it's not uncommon for me to forget to eat! I get lost in the work. Time truly flies when you're having fun. For most of my life leading up to *my* great resignation, I had been doing soul-searching for a gig that didn't feel like work. Don't get me wrong. I really enjoyed my time in Corporate America. It couldn't have been scripted any better—from the people to the work to the results, and the feather that I was able to put in my cap as I prepared to walk through another "door" being held open for me. Finally, I had found the place where my passion met what I believe to be one of my purposes here on Earth. The idea of teaching and the actual act itself puts me on cloud nine, which I guess explains why time bends—this is known as Gravitational Time Dilation and is supported by Albert Einstein's theory of general relativity.

Teachers quickly figure out that they can't be everything to everybody, but I'm not waving the white flag just yet! With engagement and open communication, however, it's possible to meet students where they are. Anyone who has ever taken one of my classes knows that I solicit feedback like it's going out of style. Why do I do this?

Because back when I was working in Corporate America, a wise man was known for saying, "Find a life insurance salesperson and shake their hand." Commercial mortgage loan officers lending on behalf of insurance companies wouldn't have any money to invest were it not for life insurance salespeople selling products that add value. Without students, I can't be a teacher.

I also consider teaching a great responsibility, which is another reason why I'm constantly looking for feedback from my students. What's working? What could I do better, etc.? Sure, end-of-course evaluations have a place, but why put off until tomorrow what's possible to do today? And end-of-course evaluations only benefit future students. On a regular basis, I'm asking students to rate the quality of my course and instruction on a scale of 1 to 10. If not a 10, then I want to know what it would take to make it a 10.

When I first heard of the book *What You Think of Me Is None of My Business* by Terry Cole-Whittaker, I had to stop and let that title sink in. What a great title! Some might think I'm crazy to expose myself to potential ridicule or harsh feedback. It's not all constructive, that's for sure. But when you understand that feedback comes in two forms, then some of the comments are trivial. There are opinions and then there is advice. I'd like to share a couple stories straight from the horse's mouth.

Two comments that were provided anonymously speak directly to the point I'm making as this book comes to a close. I'll never forget when one student was complaining that I shouldn't require writing assignments since "A finance class isn't a writing Gen Ed." Actually, I couldn't agree more. The writing finance professionals do is specific to business: nothing general about that! Well, I have news for you—and *you* whoever *you* are. Not mastering such a skill can potentially leave a person with more than a feeling of inadequacy. It has the potential to get a person fired! That's real life. The other piece of "advice" came from a student who felt like "There was too much math." Really?! What did this person expect?!

I think there are some people out there that use the Time Value of Money as a kind of euphemism for the Mathematics of Finance. John Kremer, "The Man" when it comes to book marketing and the person we consulted for the title critique for this book, picked up on this early. Look, some people are qualified to give advice, and some aren't. Opinions are a dime a dozen and don't carry as much weight as advice. But it's possible to value everyone, regardless of what they're dishing out. Feedback must be filtered. It's that whole "Until you've walked a mile in someone else's shoes" thing.

When I was in junior high school, my mom wanted to take ballroom dancing classes. A single mom at the time, she needed a dance partner. I became that partner on Wednesday evenings in downtown Fort Dodge, Iowa, with people who were twice *her* age. The class loved having a youngster around, and I quickly began to look forward to classes and the interactions with my fellow classmates.

This was before ballroom dancing was cool and made for prime-time television. My mom has always been one step ahead of mainstream. She was the first person to introduce me to Stevie Ray Vaughan and Double Trouble's music on the album *In Step*, which was released a little over a year before his tragic and untimely death in 1990. I quickly figured out that ballroom dancing is easier when both people have some idea of what they're doing. Still don't believe me that effective communication is an essential soft skill in finance? Read a poorly written letter, and then tell me what you really think.

Effective communication is far from the only soft skill that has value in industry, but there's a reason it's high on many a company's wish list. If there's one hard skill that is never going to fall out of favor for finance professionals, it's the Mathematics of Finance. But as I've lived, I'm convinced that people tend to be overconfident about certain abilities—whether that's driving, dancing, effectively communicating using the written or spoken word, or accurately applying the Mathematics of Finance.

Any teacher who takes teaching seriously feels a strong sense of responsibility for the position they have and the potential to—hopefully positively—influence the way their students think about things and experience the future.

Another thing I do to promote engagement in my classes and create an atmosphere that is conducive to learning is sharing stories from my professional and personal experiences—just as I've done in this book to drive home key points.

As in life, business isn't all wine and roses. My students get the hard truth from me. No sugar coating. In particular, I'm an open book and share what I've experienced, including the easy lessons and the hard lessons that I have experienced in practice.

One of my responsibilities as a teacher is to help my students potentially limit their exposure to hard lessons by learning from experiences that were far from my finest hours. Hard lessons that stemmed from then-underdeveloped skills which were both of the soft and hard variety and would have gotten me fired had not people seen something in me that I couldn't yet see at the time.

Hard lessons are no fun when they're happening to you. The good news about hard lessons is that, unlike soft lessons, they leave a mark: you don't forget a hard lesson learned. And scars are cool after you've lived to tell the story of what you have gone through. Some say, "What doesn't kill you makes you stronger."

As with an investment, it might take some time for specialized knowledge acquired to pay off. This might explain why I receive emails and calls out of the blue from former students sometimes months or years after we shared time together. Some of the lessons I'm teaching won't mature until you've journeyed a bit.

Positioning for success as a finance professional involves a passion for lifelong learning, hard work, and continuous improvement as it relates to both hard and soft skills, which set the stage for certain experiences.

My teaching philosophy has four pillars, one of which is helping students of finance to further refine and develop the skills that "pay the bills." See, what I've figured out is that if a person can effectively write a letter, then that person has the potential to make an effective verbal presentation, write a knockout email, etc. We're all "selling" something, and arguments must be persuasive. Writing effectively, it seems, is becoming a lost art. Just like a guitarist can't hide a wrong note coming from an acoustic guitar as easily as with an electric guitar, a finance professional's ability to communicate effectively is exposed when it comes to writing a business letter. The marketable or transferable skill of effective communication is transferable in more than one sense of the word.

This one pillar happens to have four sides to it because in addition to effective communication, I'm not alone when placing high value on analytical thinking, critical and independent thinking, and problem-solving skills. Success also involves being in the right place at the right time and surrounding yourself with people who bring up the average smarts in a room. Time and time again, I heard Steven Caldwell say that real estate can be taught. An extension of that thought is that the Mathematics of Finance isn't really that *hard* of a skill to learn. Soft skills can be learned, but they may be harder to acquire than hard skills, which is counterintuitive. Have you heard someone talking about how someone else "has it." Whatever "it" is, is a soft skill, such as the ability to light up the whole room. Just because soft skills may be hard to acquire, it doesn't mean you shouldn't give it your all.

Now I'm not a math instructor, any more than I'm an officially trained writer. But that doesn't stop me from constantly impressing upon people the importance of numbers and words in the day-to-day life of a finance professional. I think I'm qualified to give advice having logged more hours with the Mathematics of Finance and professional business writing on the job than many people.

But if you're one of those tough nuts to crack, I know a former high school math teacher who can support my position. I've talked about Clayton John before, so here's the rest of the story.

At Clayton John's retirement party, the then-head of our group shared that Clayton John contributed to the company's bottom line to the tune of roughly $10 million on average each of the twenty-seven years he was in the group. He loved wearing cowboy boots and was a kind of cowboy of a loan officer in addition to being deceptively smart. It was always fun seeing people's first reactions after meeting Clayton John because he was so much larger than life. Behind his aw-shucks demeanor stood a man who had more book smarts and street smarts than probably anyone whose hand he ever gently shook.

Clayton John was notorious for saying that what we (finance professionals) do is "just numbers and words." Roger that, Clayton John. What finance professionals do can be summarized as numbers—the Mathematics of Finance—and words—effective communication.

As I was writing the manuscript that later became this book, I was learning about the craft of writing through podcasts and the like. I had my go-to sources and would listen to advice from professionals in the field.

In addition to technical know-how, I also came across some advice that made me do a double take. For example, experts say that you could possibly become an authority in certain subjects by only having read a few books on the topic. At some level, this makes sense to me. Passion for a topic is the X factor that can bring about some amazing results.

Some people believe it takes 10,000 hours in a certain discipline to master something. Malcolm Gladwell, in his book *Outliers: The Story of Success*, popularized the 10,000-hour rule. Considering that I passed the "10 times 1,000-hour mark" around the fifth anniversary in practice and that I kept learning about the Time Value of Money as a finance professional, reading three books on the topic felt like overkill.

What really sealed the deal for me was when I heard an influencer in the field say something to the effect of, "We each have a unique set of experiences and thoughts that makes each of us—singularly—the only person qualified to write a certain book." It felt good to be reassured because I was sure of it that there was a better way to learn and teach the Time Value of Money. With my "10X," I was looking for a new place to hang my hat.

Seems like we've been in a kind of "bear market" as far as pedagogy with respect to the Time Value of Money is concerned. Whether you are an aspiring or current finance professional, college finance instructor, high school teacher, or employer in the finance industry—or even a person looking to gauge a prospective finance professional's aptitude as it relates to the Mathematics of Finance—I trust you'll embrace the "flight to quality" provided by this book.

Working backward from a problem can be a great way to find a solution. With a clean slate, I got to write the book that I would have wanted to have had when I was first learning about the Time Value of Money.

The book you're holding in your hands flips the script on how the hard skill of the Mathematics of Finance is learned and taught—fleshes out issues with terminology, includes the first-of-its-kind user manual for the Mathematics of Finance, and presents an original 3-Step Systematic Approach with an order of operations for applying the Mathematics of Finance to analyze and evaluate real-world Time Value of Money situations.

Speaking of mathematical order of operations, with a little bit of creativity, you can see the birds in the braces, the hurdlers jumping over the brackets, and boomerangs in the parentheses:

{ } [ ] ( ).

Who knew that improvements in learning and teaching the Time Value of Money would come through birds, hurdlers, and boomerangs? Business can and should be fun. So too can learning the Mathematics of Finance. Storytelling is an effective form of communication. Information is not effectively processed through facts alone. I hope you like the tale that I wove about the Time Value of Money.

As our time together is nearing the end, I'd be remiss and leaving you hanging if I didn't share with you that the soft skill of effective communication also relates to aspiring and current finance professionals' résumés. This seems obvious, but it also is something that could fall under the category of needing to see (in writing) to believe.

Most of the people reading this book are likely doing so because they want to put the hard skill of the Mathematics of Finance and certain soft skills to work in practice. If this is you, then you may also benefit from my thoughts on how to write a résumé right for an effective job search. Head over to the website for this book, and download your copy of the free bonus chapter—the QR code is below.

In the free bonus chapter, you'll find some common knowledge related to the job-search process along with some lesser-known information and an original take on the résumé, which has already helped countless students. What started as a separate project for collecting and organizing in one place my thoughts on the résumé and job-search process to share with the finance students I mentor, Seeing "i" to "I" ended up being the perfect extension of the Why section of this book.

This book started with a quote from my mom, who back in the day liked listening to John Mellencamp in our *small town*. Given how the subconscious mind works, I may never know if those profound words that I think about often can be traced back to John (Cougar) Mellencamp's "Small Town." Over the years, what she said to me that day when I left home in search of a future has taken on multiple meanings with the times, which has helped me on my life journey—both personally and professionally. But here's where it gets real. It took me twenty-five years and writing this book to learn what I believe to be the true meaning of her words. It wasn't until I literally hung my hat in an office on a university campus, jumped into the second chapter of my professional life with both feet, and doubled down on my passion that the real meaning of her words rang true.

You see, I think that never forgetting where you came from has more to do with mapping your course on the road ahead than where the road lies behind you. Where you came from is one of the reasons you're here now getting ready to finish this book and why you'll go down certain paths personally and professionally. How that plays out looks different for each person. All I know is that it took me serving *on call* or purpose to realize that, "The End is The Beginning."

Thank you for your investment in time, for the value you've placed on this work, and for supporting our family-owned-and-operated publishing company and educational content, products, and services with your hard-earned money. Like the Time Value of Money, this is sure to have a compounding effect for you . . . a different kind of future value!

The End: The Beginning

Postscript

The bird in the hand—heavy as it might have been—could have been a goose, and the holder…an aspiring or current finance professional. Seems like an odd picture—I know—and would have likely involved more cradling than hand holding: a goose is a heavy bird! Finance is the only field I can think of where teams are potentially okay with a big fat goose egg—that is, an NPV of $0. Since the only confirmed time travel is made possible by the *Flux Capacitor of Finance*, $(1 + i)^N$, and *"indifferent* lines," we may never know the true identity of the bird. But at least we can have fun speculating.

Acknowledgments

"There is no such thing as a 'self-made person.' We are
made up of thousands of others. Everyone who has
ever done a kind deed for us, or spoken one word of
encouragement to us, has entered into the makeup of our
character and of our thoughts, as well as our success."
—George Matthew Adams

I'm convinced as I have lived that there's no such thing as self-made. When I was younger, my mom sacrificed to provide for my sister and me. Later in life, my wife, Sarah, would do the same for our family. It's a shame that there's not a place on degrees for honorable mentions. Without the love and support of family and the love of my life, I wouldn't be where I'm at today, and you wouldn't be reading this book.

Here is a list of some of the people who have opened doors for me over the years. Some of the people on the list I've never met, and they don't even realize the impact they've had on my life and those around me. That impact ultimately led to the creation of this book. I guess we have the Information Age to thank for this conundrum that it's impossible to fully measure a content creator's impact. It's mind-boggling to think that influencers have no way of knowing exactly how far their reach extends.

Since any list like this is far from complete, I also need to extend an attaboy and attagirl to every person with whom I've had the good fortune of spending time over the years—whether we were on parallel paths or met as our paths crossed. Many of these friendships are what I call "bicycle friendships." You can pick up right where you left off no matter how much time has passed. Each encounter with individuals in my life has allowed me to do something the late, great Stevie Ray Vaughan did, which is borrow ideas and the like from others and then put my own style to it and make it my own:

Thank you, Jim Morrow, for the door you opened for me. When we weren't flying around the airspace of Council Bluffs, Iowa, you always kept me on my toes. I loved not knowing what was next in terms of what you would say or do but always knew that it was going to be extreme and fabulous.

Thank you, Mark Johnson (aka Johnny), for the door you opened for me. I can't imagine where I would be today if you hadn't offered me an internship and my first position in the real estate finance industry. I'll be forever grateful for all you've done for me and my family. Every dollar I earn has a little bit of Mark Johnson's fingerprints on it. *Johnny "B. Goode."*

Thank you to all the great people who made up the team in the real assets groups of the global asset management company where I formerly worked for the doors you opened for me. I couldn't have hand selected a better group of people to help me develop my own unique style as it relates to underwriting real estate transactions and credit (risk) analysis.

Thank you, Ashish Tiwari, PhD, for the door you opened for me. You inspired me to want to become a college finance instructor. It was in your classroom—one that I've taught in—at the Tippie College of Business at The University of Iowa where I first dreamed of teaching.

Thank you, Anand Vijh, PhD, for the door you opened for me. You helped me realize that education is a "two-way street." Your philosophy on student engagement and participation, which you shared with me and my fellow classmates all those years ago, laid the foundation for one of the pillars of my teaching philosophy: that there are as many teachers as people in any one of my classrooms.

Thank you, Colette Atkins, for the door you opened for me. In addition to offering me my first teaching job, you impressed upon me the power of a practical education, which would later become another pillar of my teaching philosophy.

Thank you to all the great people and amazing faculty and staff at the Tippie College of Business at The University of Iowa for the doors you opened for me. Being a faculty member in the Department of Finance is an honor I don't take lightly. I can't think of a better way to serve others and to give back to the university that gave me so much. There are days when I think about pinching myself because it could be a dream.

Thank you, Rich Roll, for the door you opened for me. The standout lesson you've taught me is that action comes before mood whatever the way every day. Your book *Finding Ultra: Rejecting Middle Age, Becoming One of the World's Fittest Men, and Discovering Myself* and your podcast, *The Rich Roll Podcast*, have inspired me to chase my best self.

Thank you, Steven Pressfield, for the door you opened for me. I'm not exactly sure where I found Steven. This guy is everywhere. It might have been down Rich Roll's rabbit hole. Thanks to you and your book *The War of Art: Break Through the Blocks and Win Your Inner Creative Battles*, I was able to identify and beat "Resistance" and type "The End."

Thank you, Ryan Holiday, for the door you opened for me. I found you down Rich Roll's rabbit hole. You've taught me a lot, including that "properly managing" is p.m. work after the "about making" in the a.m. Thanks to you and your extensive list of books, in particular *Perennial Seller: The Art of Making and Marketing Work that Lasts*, I found the courage to hit the Publish button. Speaking of courage, if you haven't done so already you might want to check out Ryan's book *Courage is Calling: Fortune Favors the Brave*.

Thank you, Matthew McConaughey, for the door you opened for me. You remind me that life is about living—and that teachin' is cool. It was your book *Greenlights* that helped me find my own writing voice and get through the dreaded "middle" of the manuscript, which allowed me to see the *green* light at the end of the tunnel.

Thank you, Dave Ramsey, for the door you opened for me. Because of you and your team, our family was able to find financial freedom. I'll never forget the feeling that day when we were, as you describe it, "sick and tired of being sick and tired." As our young family sat at a stoplight, my heart sank in my chest as I gazed through the rearview mirror at our happy-go-lucky daughters in the back of our van. They had no idea the financial mess their parents were in. Yeah . . . Dad was a *finance guy*. That real-life nightmare starring our young family in a van with fuel added by Dave Ramsey started us down the road to financial peace and hasn't stopped "burning" since that day. Dave, you've written a lot of books, but the two that changed my life are *Financial Peace* and *EntreLeadership: 20 Years of Practical Business Wisdom from the Trenches*. I'll be the first to raise my hand and admit that there's more that I don't know, but one thing I do know is that we're never going *back to* debt in *the future*. Thanks for helping us live a dream!

Thank you, Dan Miller, for the door you opened for me. I found you down Dave Ramsey's rabbit hole. Because of you and your team, I was able to see a future that included work and a life I love, and create it applying your 15-Hours a Week plan. Your *48 Days Podcast* is a go-to. Readers, if you haven't done so already, you need to read Dan's book *48 Days to the Work And Life You Love: Find It—Or Create It*. This is one of those books that I wish would have existed and that I had found when I was younger. Now each of our daughters has a standing opportunity every year to read this book and provide a short synopsis in exchange for $48. Our daughters also thank you!

Thank you, Jack Canfield and Mark Victor Hansen, for the door you opened for me. I found you two down Dan Miller's rabbit hole. Listening to a previously unopened 2007 version of *Mega Book Marketing University*, which I purchased in 2020, for the first time I was able to see the path that was created for me. Not only could I see a future as a teacher and author, but for the first time, I could see how every past experience in my life perfectly qualifies me for what lies ahead.

Thank you, John Kremer, for the door you opened for me. I found you down Jack Canfield's rabbit hole. We couldn't have asked for a better person to help us with the title critique for this book and for all the other book-marketing wisdom shared. You are a walking encyclopedia of book-marketing knowledge. I wouldn't be surprised if John's book *1001 Ways to Market Your Books* is still selling copies 1001 years from now.

Thank you, Kent Sanders, for the door you opened for me. I found you down Dan Miller's rabbit hole. You helped me realize that I was "the perfect person to write this book." Between the points in time when we first met virtually and this book was launched, your show *The Daily Writer Podcast* provided the much-needed daily inspiration I needed to write this book, and you provided a connection and referral that would solidify "Dream Team" status for this book project. You've got a lifelong listener in me.

Thank you, Jennifer Harshman, for the door you opened for me. I was introduced to Jennifer by Kent Sanders. If anyone reading this is a writer, the best first person to read your manuscript other than you is Jennifer Harshman. Jennifer is a fantastic editor and formatter, and as professional as they come. Thank you for preserving my writing voice, helping me tell the stories that needed to be told, and for turning my manuscript into a book that I'm 100% proud to own.

Thank you, Michael La Ronn, for the door you opened for me. You helped me realize that being an author is within anyone's reach. If I had to point to one piece of advice gained along the way that helped me create this book from a blank page, it would be your belief that "What gets measured gets managed." Over time, two "crappy pages" a day really does turn into a manuscript. I'm so glad to have found your *Author Level Up* YouTube channel and your countless nonfiction books that help authors like me.

Thank you, Eric Aitchison, for the door you opened for me. In addition to being a great friend, thank you for being the first person to put this book, then an edited manuscript, on a recommended summer reading list for a high school student.

Thank you, Tony Robbins, for the door you opened for me. Your morning priming exercise and daily cold showers have been game changers. Your positivity is infectious. The world is a better place, and I'm in a better place because of you.

Thank you, Ryan Van Duzer, for the door you opened for me. Sarah and I love watching your bicycling adventures on YouTube. You're like Tony Robbins on a bike. When you get out to wherever there is, the smile on your face reminds me that we are made for movement and that loving each moment in this one wild and precious life is important. It's 100% because of you that someday we want to start bikepacking.

Thank you, Dean Karnazes, for the door you opened for me. Your book *Ultramarathon Man: Confessions of an All-Night Runner* helped me rekindle my love of running and the great outdoors. Thanks for also modeling that it's possible to make a living doing what you are passionate about.

Thank you, David Pridemore, for the door you opened for me. In all my business travels that involved puddle jumping around America, you were the nicest person I ever met on the road. Thanks for that special book and the special note reminding me to

"Remember Ft. Dodge!!" The book you gave me on September 12, 2000, will always stay in my collection.

Thank you to my brothers and sisters "from another mother" for the doors you opened for me: Ryan and Erin Baker, Alan and Sara Cross, Jim and Anne Kelly, and Paul and Adina Pursley. Around you, I'm able to be 100% myself—a luxury not always found amongst "friends." I love you like family.

Thank you, Gary Whittington, for the door you opened for me. Where do I start? Where would I end? You're one of my best friends. Thanks for always telling me the truth, even if it was hard for me to hear. That, my friends, is a friend. Just like your Houston Astros retired the No. 5 jersey of Hall of Famer Jeff Bagwell, your friendship is one that is worthy of a retired "High Five" number. You've left an indelible mark on my life.

Thank you, Jim Humston, for the door you opened for me. I first met you at Gary's house. When I was younger, if I could have handpicked a father, you would have been it. And then in middle age, out of nowhere my life was blessed with your life and a dose of what I would have wished for. You are the only person in my life outside of family who tells me you love me. Thanks for helping make up for lost time, Jim. I love you.

Thank you to the monks and staff and all the people who support St. Meinrad Archabbey in one way or another for the doors you opened for me. Since visiting the "Hill" for the first time, it has always been my special place to unplug from the daily grind and tune into what's really important. In the peace and quiet on my first full day on the "Hill," I was given the gift of the word *give*, unsure of what that meant. My pilgrimage in August of 2021 is what allowed me to start the big (yearlong) push that ultimately led to bringing together the manuscript for this book.

Thank you, Father David, for the door you opened for me. I met you on the "Hill" that week in August of 2021. I would have never guessed that my search for solitude would bring me a friend. The imagery you shared on my last full day on the "Hill" of water pouring over the sides of one's hand is something I will never forget. Thank you for teaching me an important life lesson that we must *receive* before we can *give*.

Thank you, Dad, for the door you opened for me. I could never get enough of spending time with you and Mom, partly because

I loved the feeling of wholeness that you brought to our family. Thank you for loving Sarah, Lydia, Emily, Chloe, and me like your own children. You loved books. I wish you were here today as I type these last words in the manuscript for this book that is going to help people. You helped me in ways I can't put into words. I love you and I miss you.

Saved the best for last. To my Lord and Savior, Jesus Christ, without whom I wouldn't have life, gifts, talents, a past in which I can find peace, and a future full of hope. Thank You. Thank You. Thank You. You are my number-one "Door Opener."

> "Ask, and you will be given what you ask for. Seek, and you will find. Knock, and the door will be opened."
> —Matthew 7:7

Self-made isn't a thing. We don't do anything alone, and we can't succeed without help from others. Regardless of whether you believe in a Higher Power, let us realize that we are called to *receive and give, and be door openers.*

About the Author

"Find a niche and crawl into it."
—G. Patrick Kealey, MD

A real estate industry veteran specializing in real estate finance, Brent has made a living *practicing* what he *teaches* as it relates to the Time Value of Money. Since 2012, he has been teaching and developing curricula for college courses. Currently, Brent is an instructional track faculty member in the Department of Finance at the Tippie College of Business at The University of Iowa, where in addition to teaching undergraduate and graduate courses, he also advises students. It was at The University of Iowa as an undergraduate student that he learned the value of lifelong learning and first saw himself as a future college finance instructor.

Brent credits his education at The University of Iowa Tippie College of Business with directly or indirectly opening multiple doors of opportunity over his tenure in business. In addition to being a teacher, Brent is also an independent (indie) author and cofounder of Boxholm Press, LLC. Boxholm Press, LLC is a family-owned-and-operated publishing company providing educational content, products, and services.

Before he found teaching, as they say in the business, "The real estate industry found him." That "detour," which included an MBA degree, provided the path to the front of the classroom. Over the course of his tenure in Corporate America, Brent worked for a global real estate asset manager where he developed a niche for being a "utility player" who could originate commercial mortgage loans as well as work out sub-performing and nonperforming CMLs. He held positions on both sides of the "ball" twice: during the Great Recession and just prior to the Great Resignation, which he participated in and that was brought on by the COVID-19 pandemic.

For twenty-two years to the day—the time he worked in the real assets group of a global asset management company—Brent earned proficiency in underwriting, structuring, negotiating, and originating complex commercial mortgage loan transactions with the ultimate objective of maximizing return *on* investment and mitigating risk for institutional investor clients, all while also providing exceptional client service. He was entrusted with making new loan origination and workout recommendations for commercial mortgage loan assets with an aggregate value in excess of $1.5 billion, which does not include countless underwritten proposals for institutional financing or loan modification requests, recommendations for leasing actions and other higher-level servicing matters, and deals for which he was the number-two underwriter.

Brent got to learn the business of real estate from some of the best and brightest in the industry. Sharing company with people who are smarter than he is has always been a strategy that has paid off for him, continues to this day, and keeps him on the lookout for people to meet and books to read.

His approach to teaching is as original as a real estate deal is unique. He takes a pragmatic approach to finance and believes that most people possess what it takes to "Be smarter than the problem." Students have found success in his classroom in part because of the focus on a practical education and opportunities to teach material to peers. In his classroom, there are as many teachers as people.

Brent is constantly providing students of finance with opportunities to further refine and develop the hard and soft (marketable) skills that "pay the bills." His classroom is a special place and the intersection between specialized knowledge and skills that are in demand in industry. He genuinely cares about his students' success and has borrowed a mantra from the real estate industry having made teaching a "relationship business."

But life is about balance. When Brent is not teaching, you'll likely find him spending time with his wife, Sarah, their three daughters, Lydia, Emily, and Chloe, and two dogs. When he isn't spending time with family, writing, teaching, or practicing in the field, you might find him running on a singletrack trail and listening to a podcast or audiobook, drinking coffee and reading a book at a local coffee shop, or writing his thoughts down with a fountain pen. With no plans to retire in the traditional sense, he plans to serve others as long as time and money have value.

"Pop (Open the Back Cover) Quiz" Answers

"Work hard to develop relationships, and do what you say you are going to do."

—Jim Sellers

Below you'll find the answers to the "Pop (Open the Back Cover) Quiz":

1. $522.24

2. $1,300,000

3. $8,132.49

There is one more question for you to consider: Did you find this book on your own, or was it and the associated "Pop (Open the Back Cover) Quiz" given to you by someone else—possibly even a prospective employer or client?

Regardless of how you performed on this short "Pop (Open the Back Cover) Quiz," you're holding in your hands the best resource on the market for learning and teaching how to apply the Mathematics of Finance to analyze and evaluate real-world Time Value of Money situations.

The Time Value of Money is a hard skill, but it's not difficult to learn. The investment of time in reading this book is nominal and is far less "expensive" than a prospective client walking down the street from you to potentially form a new relationship, or a prospective employer not giving you the nod for a job.

Whether you are an aspiring or current finance professional or a prospective employer or client looking to hire one, there's more where these Q's and A's came from in the first-of-its-kind user manual for the Mathematics of Finance in the book *Would Your Boomerang Return? What Birds, Hurdlers, and Boomerangs Can Teach Us About the Time Value of Money.*

"Pop (Open the Back Cover) Quiz"

"If you work it [learning] like a job, you can't fail."

—Gary Whittington

Why would anyone hire a finance professional who doesn't fully understand the concept of the Time Value of Money? Below are three basic questions to gauge one's ability to apply the Mathematics of Finance to analyze and evaluate real-world Time Value of Money situations:

1. Twenty years from today, you expect to take the first of twenty consecutive semiannual withdrawals of $20,000. Starting next month and at the end of each month over a total of twenty years, you will make deposits into a savings account that is expected to earn a simple annual investment yield of 7.5% with quarterly compounding. What level amount would you need to deposit at the end of each month over the next twenty years to finance the future payment stream such that there will be no remaining balance in the account after the last withdrawal?

2. You want to establish an endowment that will fund higher educational opportunities through the payment of tuition for qualified individuals who share your hometown. The annual distributions from this endowment will be financed solely with the fund's annual return *on* investment. In other words, the portfolio is expected to maintain a level balance immediately following each distribution. Assume a true annual investment yield of 4.00%. What is the minimum amount needed to fully fund this endowment such that annual distributions of $50,000 can be made in perpetuity starting today?

3. You plan to deposit $2,000 today and at the end of each of the next five years into an investment account that is expected to earn a simple annual investment yield of 7% with quarterly compounding. At the end of the sixth year, you would like to take the first of seven consecutive annual withdrawals of $1,750. What do you expect for a remaining balance after the last withdrawal?